TEAM OF ONE WE BELIEVE

To Tracy Rosa,
Outstanding football Coach
and friend,
Best Wishes Always!

George M. Gilbert

George M. Gilbert
(H.O.F.)
2018

ISBN: 1502599163
ISBN 13: 9781502599162
Library of Congress Control Number: 2014917800
CreateSpace Independent Publishing Platform
North Charleston, South Carolina

DEDICATION

I dedicate this work to my family, including my wife, Judy, my two sons, Michael and Matthew, and my daughter, Elaine. My family have always been supportive through both the good and bad times associated with having a husband and father who is a head high-school football coach.

I would also like to dedicate this work to Gary Rhew, athletic director at Tri-Central High School. Mr. Rhew took a chance in offering an old football coach one last opportunity to coach.

I wish to thank my son Mike for editing this work and inspiring me to give back to the Tri-Central administration and community a memory that will last forever.

A final thank you goes out to the coaches, parents, and players of the 2013 Tri-Central High School football team. What happened at Tri-Central was a combined effort of skill, talent, and chemistry that came together to achieve what at the time seemed impossible.

TABLE OF CONTENTS

INTRODUCTION

My name is George Gilbert. On December 10, 2007, I was fired after twenty years as the head football coach at Clinton Central High School in central Indiana. At the time of the firing, I had coached for twenty-nine years at three different schools. Clinton Central School Corporation is a small rural school thirty miles north of Indianapolis in Clinton County. In football, Clinton Central is a class-A school with a high-school population of around 330 students. In 1988, I was selected to take over this program, which was at the time on a three-year run without a win. I was told on being hired that if I was unable to bring life to the program, I would be the last coach, and football would no longer be a part of the athletic department at Clinton Central.

Needless to say, over the next twenty years Clinton Central developed into a respected high-school football program, winning several conference and sectional championships. After twenty years, I was released from my coaching contract but would continue to be employed as a classroom teacher. I am a social studies teacher and teach US history, world history, and sociology. I was devastated, as the board was unanimous in their decision to release me, voting 6-0 not to renew my contract. I present this first, but it will be noted in more depth as it pertains to the direction of this story.

Being fired is part of the risk when anyone takes on the responsibility as a head coach. There are often many reasons for dismissal, from losing to poor leadership. The point that needs to be the focus now is that at age fifty-two, with over twenty-nine years of coaching experience, I no longer had a school to coach at. Football had been a part of my life every summer since I was ten years old with my first experience in flag football. I would go on and play every year; my career as a player culminated in 1977 after completing my college football career at Manchester College in North Manchester, Indiana. The following year I was hired in Ohio to coach football, and my coaching adventure continued until December 10, 2007. Over those twenty-nine years of coaching, I was fortunate enough to be a head coach in three schools for twenty-seven of those years. And now here I was without a coaching position and not getting to end my career on my terms.

By the way, on December 5, 2007, just five days before the firing, I was selected by my coaching peers to coach in the Indiana All-star game held in Indianapolis in July. This was an honor to be selected, and it would be my first appearance as an Indiana All-star coach. The dilemma I faced was whether or not I should continue with this opportunity or, due to the situation, bow out. Well, this was not a hard decision; I planned to coach in the All-star game, for I felt I had earned that right, and no one was going to take that away.

The story that I plan to tell is true. The things that I write about happened, and this is a story that I feel compelled to tell. The story will be filled with the ups and downs of developing a program and what it looks like from a high-school coach's perspective. I am currently still coaching at Tri-Central and teaching at Clinton Central. I hope my situation, and all that happens in this story, may serve to give direction to others. I believe in the hope that doing the right thing will always win the day, which perseverance will serve others as it has served me in my life. Finally, I believe in the old cliché that "when one door closes another will open" for good people who try to do what is right.

It is now time to begin this five-year journey. The journey will begin with a year off and how I became a coach again. The adventure will lead to an unbelievable chain of events that allowed an old coach one last shot at dignity.

CHAPTER 1

Dismissal

It was 10:00 p.m. on December 10, 2007, when I finally got up the nerve to find out if it was true that I had been fired as a coach. I had spent the past twenty years coaching football at Clinton Central. Could it really be over just like that? Surely the issue would be tabled to allow those who believed in all that I had done there to come forward and stand up for the coach. I had been the man who took a school that was thinking about ending the sport there and developed a respectable football program in class 1A in the state of Indiana.

I got up the nerve to call the local newspaper in Frankfort. I asked for the sports department, and a familiar voice said, "Hello, sports." The local sports editor and I did not get along well. Some of that was my fault, and some of it was his way of getting people to read his articles.

I asked, "Brian, what happened tonight at the board meeting?"

He said, "Coach, no one contacted you?"

I answered, "No!"

He said, "Tonight under miscellaneous, the board voted 6–0 not to rehire you as football coach at Clinton Central High School." He went on, "It was based on the recommendation of the principal and athletic director."

I was speechless at the news. Just like that, it was over. Some time passed before I could respond to Brian. When I did, I said, "Wow! Well, thank you for at least telling me."

Brian asked, "Do you have something you wish to say at this time?"

I said no, that I would contact him after I had time to digest all that had happened.

I sat on my bed and tried to focus on what had just transpired. We had beaten an undefeated area school in week one of the sectional, and then we lost the second round of the tournament, finishing 7–4. I had just been selected as my region's All-star coach. Now here I was. With no challenge from the community, I had been fired. I could not sleep that night at all. I finally got up around 4:00 a.m. and went to my football office and cleaned it out. By 7:00 a.m. I had completely shut down a twenty-year segment of my life as if it had only been a one-year run. How was I going to deal with the students that day? What would I say? How would they handle what was happening?

The answer for everyone around me at school was simply to ignore everything that was happening and say nothing. A lot of eyes looked at me in the weeks to come, but after a time it was like a death, and everyone moved on. Yes, there was a small group of backers who shared in my disappointment but nothing substantial enough to want to do anything about it. I was incredibly embarrassed, and I decided that I was done coaching at age fifty-two.

It is a difficult task to continually run a successful high-school football program for a few years, much less for twenty years. Through the years there will be those people in the community who will not like you for many reasons. Perhaps you did not play their son enough; you yell too much; you yell too little; you are too hard on the boys; you are not hard enough on the boys; your offense lacks what they think it should have; your defensive philosophy is not right for the community; you are arrogant; you are a pushover; you lack organizational skills; your weight-room expectations are too high; you are too demanding; you are not what they want, even though they often do not know what they want. It is so easy to judge those around us and decide their value without knowing who they really are or what they truly represent. My mother was part Native American, and she would often say, "Don't judge anyone until you have walked a moon in their moccasins." This saying annoyed me when I was young but makes perfect sense to me now.

After twenty years, the community had decided that I no longer had what it took to run the Clinton Central football program, and there was nothing at this point I could do about it. My anger grew into resentment as the school began interviewing candidates for the job. I knew we had a talented group coming back, and whoever became the next coach would inherit a couple of years of my blood, sweat, and tears. The man the board selected was an alumnus of Clinton Central, a guy who had wanted my job for years. Now everything was starting to become much clearer to me. This whole firing looked more and more like it had been orchestrated to this end. The man they hired would be friendlier to the boys than I had been, he would have high expectations on the field but demand less off the field, and apparently this was the course the school had decided to follow. The program would follow a direction that would in no way reflect the twenty years I had put into it. I continued to resent all that had happened. I decided to change directions, coach the All-star team, and have a good time for that week; it might be my last week of coaching the sport I love so much.

In July 2008, I spent a week coaching the North All-Star team as the defensive coordinator. It was a great week, and I was treated well by players and coaching peers. I was embarrassed that I did not have a school to represent me, but at this point I resolved to make the best of the situation.

During the week and after the game, the local sports editor, who was a new guy by the name of Phil, continually made the point that this was my last opportunity to coach. After the game, Phil came up and asked me, "Coach, how does it feel to coach in your final game?" I'd had enough, and my response was short and to the point: "You don't know that anymore than I do! If this is it, I can make peace with it, but I am sick of hearing about it!"

The school year began in August 2008, and for the first time since I was a little boy, I no longer was involved in football. My family sensed my pain, and my two sons, Mike and Matt, along with my daughter, Elaine, went out each Friday night to watch games. This was such a wonderful fall in 2008, as we spent a great deal of time together, and I was seeing if I could handle life without football. My family has always been behind me and my profession. Anyone who coaches seriously knows that without a loving family to support them, it would be impossible to do what needs to get done. My wife would stay at home and allow us to go out to games, and then upon my return she would talk to me about the evening. My wife is a professional therapist, and she has always been my rock when I need her and my greatest critic if I need to fix something. My wife has had to put up with so much over the years—she even gave birth to our two sons during football. My father and mother died during the season, and I had a heart attack during a game in 2006. In 2001, I lost a player during two-a-day practices, and all that surrounded the tragedy was very trying for our community as well as for my family. This will not be the venue in which I go into details of this tragedy, but without the strength of my wife and family, I don't know if I could have made it through such a difficult time.

My daughter was a freshman at Purdue in 2008 and a member of the Purdue track and field team. This also offered me a distraction from football. Judy and I traveled around America to watch our daughter compete, and that helped me adjust to my new life without football. In January 2009, I began reading about a local team having issues with their football coach. A war of words began between the football coach and the school's athletic director. The school was a member of the same conference Clinton Central was in, and a team that I had defeated twenty-two times over my tenure at Clinton Central, playing each year both during the season and several times in the playoffs. The rhetoric began to heat up more on the football forums and in the newspaper. In February, I opened up the football forum on the computer and noticed the following headline:

"Tri-Central will not renew football coach's contract." I decided to read more on what was going on, and much of it appeared similar to what I had gone through at Clinton Central. Things did not add up, though. I had known the principal and athletic director at Tri-Central for years, and what was being published about them wanting football to be gone at Tri-Central did not make sense to me.

By February 2009, I began to see more coaching jobs open up, and I still felt a little fire in my belly. The fire was small, but I thought that if the right job would open, I might apply, knowing that it would be difficult to land a position at the age of fifty-two. I did not have to wait long, as an area school opened, and it caught my eye. The football job was open at Maconaquah High School, some forty miles from where I live, and they were a class-3A school. I decided to apply, thinking, *What have I got to lose?* I updated my resume, which was a process in itself after twenty years of it lying dormant, and I stuck it in the mail. Surprisingly, I was contacted two weeks later by a school representative who asked if I would like to interview. I have had ample experience interviewing over the years, and I felt after the interview that they really might hire me. I never heard from them. As the first week went by, I realized how this process worked; I did not get the job. I thought, *Why am I putting myself through this anguish over something I don't even know if I sincerely want?*

The letter came in the mail a week and a half after the interview short and sweet, saying thank you but no thank you. For some reason, this sort of kindled that fire in my belly a little more. The day after I received the no-thank-you letter, I got on the Internet football forum and read that Tri-Central was now accepting applications for the head football coaching position and experienced candidates could now apply. I thought, *This is the worst job in Indiana football.*

I had only lost to Tri-Central five times in twenty years. Their players had always seemed undisciplined, and they lacked direction and numbers. Could this be the program for me? Tri-Central played in the same conference as Clinton Central, and the teams were somewhat rivals.

They are currently involved in a mess over at Sharpsville. Do I wish to put myself in the middle of a coaching graveyard with only five winning seasons in school history?

I sat in front of my computer at Clinton Central, not thinking or saying anything. Then the bell rang, and I had to go back to teaching US history. When classes were over that day, I continued to sit in front of the computer, wondering what to do.

CHAPTER 2

The Hire

After sitting in front of the computer for a while, I looked up and noticed it was 4:30 p.m. I decided it was time to head for home. I decided I would send Athletic Director Gary Rhew a quick query about the football job at Tri-Central on this cold February evening. I wrote, "Mr. Rhew, I would be interested in gaining more information about the Tri-Central football job. Do you feel you might be interested if I applied?" I hit enter, closed my computer up, and headed for home.

I didn't feel it was time yet to discuss this job possibility with my wife until I really was interested in applying. Tri-Central had only won twenty games over the past fourteen years; they lost 118 games. After further investigation, I found that Tri-Central had only five winning seasons since they'd started football some forty-two years before. I had beat Tri-Central most of my coaching career against them, and I was not a popular guy in Trojan country. Usually the games were quite lopsided over the twenty years. We played each other once to twice a season, depending on whether or not we drew them in the playoffs.

When I arrived at school the next morning, I turned on my computer and checked my e-mails as I do every morning. I noticed I had an e-mail from Gary Rhew, the athletic director at Tri-Central. Mr. Rhew's e-mail seemed encouraging and overly polite. He shared that he would really like for me to apply and gave me directions for application. After going through the interview process at Maconaquah High School and then not getting a call back, I really did not know if I wanted to pursue a rival school and get turned down by them. Being a head coach at the high-school level is very humbling at times. It is hard to apply then find out you are not the guy they are interested in. It is a process we all deal with in coaching, but it takes a great deal of confidence to be faced time and again with not getting a job you work so hard at trying to get. I was cautiously excited about the fact that at least the school's athletic director was interested.

That night I discussed the Tri-Central job with my wife and asked her opinion. I respect my wife's opinion greatly, as she has had to deal with the roller coaster of life with a football coach. I told Judy about my interest in the Tri-Central job and how it might be difficult, as they could not afford to hire me as a teacher and coach. I would need to continue to teach at Clinton Central and daily make the thirty-mile trip to the northern Tipton County School. I shared that they were perhaps the worst (in terms of football) of any of the schools that I had been at. This would include Clinton Central, which was on a three-year run without a win when I was hired back in 1988. Members of the board at that time told me that if I could not find a way to make football better at Clinton Central, then they would stop offering it as a sport.

Judy sat on the couch and said, "Is this something you really want to do?"

I replied, "I really don't know, but I think I will apply and go through the process to see what happens. Judy, I would really like to leave the coaching profession on my terms, and if they hire me, I might get that opportunity." I added, "I have never been lucky enough to walk into a good situation as a coach. I have always been faced with a program that was in trouble. I think maybe this has been my calling, and this will be my last opportunity to see if the passion is still a part of me."

Judy then said, "I think you should follow your heart. If this will make you happy, then go for it!"

Judy has always been supportive, and she has always been my greatest fan. We have always supported each other in everything we have done, and I am truly blessed to have such a great friend who happens to be my wife.

The next morning I prepared my resume; I also got online and filled out an application for the coaching position at Tri-Central. I sent an e-mail to Mr. Rhew, advising him that I had taken care of the necessary paper work and would look forward to hearing from him. He wrote me back and said thank you, and that was it.

A couple of weeks went by, and I heard nothing about the Tri-Central job and began to believe that I must not have made it to the interview round. I was sitting at home on a Thursday evening, and the phone began to ring around 8:00 p.m. I thought it was my daughter (who was a student at Purdue at the time), as she would usually call about that time.

I answered it, and it was Gary Rhew, the athletic director from Tri-Central. He said, "George, we would like to interview you for the head football position here at Tri-Central. We are interviewing next Monday and Tuesday. Which day you would like to interview?"

I replied, "Tuesday would work better for me."

Gary added, "We will interview at 6:00 p.m. and 7:00 p.m. Which time works better for you?"

I answered, "6:00 p.m. would work better for me."

Gary said, "OK, then I will see you Tuesday evening at 6:00 p.m." I thanked him for the call.

On Tuesday after school, I prepared for the interview. I prepared my playbook and several examples of organizational skills to try and sell myself to them. For some reason, I prepared for this interview as if it were my first. I was not nervous, though, as I might have been years ago. I still had a teaching position at Clinton Central, and if I did not get the job, then perhaps I was too old to be considered to head their football program, or it was not the right door opening.

I arrived thirty minutes early, as I have always done when interviewing. I knew a great deal about the school and its sports history, so I did not need to do my usual walk around the school. Tri-Central had been receiving a great deal of bad press concerning the non-renewal of the last coach during the spring of 2009. Tri-Central was always known as a basketball school, and it did not help that the principal and athletic director were former basketball coaches. Tri-Central had a long history of success in basketball, both boys' and girls'. The girls recently had won three state titles while the boys were state runners-up.

As I got out of my truck, there to meet me at the door was Mr. Rhew. I told him I was early and that I could wait, but he said everyone was back in the conference room already, and we might as well get started.

There were about ten people sitting around the conference table when I walked in. Everyone was cordial. We made some small talk, and then the interview began. I have gone through many interviews throughout my coaching career, and this one seemed similar, but I could feel this interviewing for a football coach had become a very big deal at Tri-Central. The program had been highly scrutinized by the former coach in the press and much of his attention was focused on school administration. I shared with them how I worked. I told them I hate drama and that I always tried to be painfully honest when faced with tough decisions. I was asked about my plan. I said we first need to get boys out for football, and then the plan would gradually come into play. I told them that many sitting in the room had witnessed my coaching philosophy over the years and that I would run a similar program for Tri- Central.

Mr. Rhew asked, "Do you feel you can get along with the other coaches and their programs?"

I replied, "I hope so. I would definitely want to get the weight program going. I will work with all the coaches."

Mr. Rhew added, "We have recently had to deal with some issues about Tri-Central not caring about anything other than basketball. This has not been good for our community, and this is something that is absolutely not true."

I interrupted, "Mr. Rhew, it is the job of the coach to take his program and build it from where it is to where he wishes it to go. I will always respect other programs, but I will not whine. If football parents, players, and coaches want respect, then it must be earned. I will not compare my program to others, and the boys will respect all other programs. The boys will keep their hair trimmed, and facial hair will not be allowed. I will build a program based on sacrifice and character. If we can get boys, coaches, and the community to gain a vested interest in fixing the problems here, we will move forward. If we are unable to fix these problems, then I will have been the wrong choice to lead the football program. This will not be an easy task, but I believe I can get the job done here. I hope I haven't overstated my position. I am passionate about what I do, and I put everything into my classroom as well as the athletic field of play."

Mr. Driggs, the principal, stated, "George, we are at the point where we might need to make some tough decisions about football here, and if we hire you, you might be our last chance to make this work here. What do you think?"

I replied, "I will not promise boys positions, and I will not promise any of you football success. I will demand discipline, character, respect, and work ethic throughout the program. If I succeed in getting people to believe, then success will follow." I added, "By the way, Mr. Driggs, in 1988 I was told the same thing you just stated by a board member at Clinton Central, and the program is still running strong today!"

At this point, Mr. Rhew asked if I had any questions for them. I did not, so he asked me to get my materials together and thanked me. On the way out Mr. Rhew told me that he would let me know one way or another by the end of the week. He stated that they planned to hire the football coach on Monday, May 9, at the next board meeting. I thought the interview went well, and I felt the board and members of the community that interviewed me were sincere and respectful throughout the interview. Now, the hard part began; I would just need to wait and see if I got a call.

I never heard anything Tuesday or Wednesday, and I began to believe that I was not their choice. Then on Thursday evening, May 5, I received the call.

Mr. Rhew said, "George, this is Gary Rhew from Tri-Central."

"Hi, Gary. I assume you made up your mind."

He stated, "Yes! We have decided you are the man we want to head our boys' football program. We would like to hire you on Monday. You will not need to be there at the meeting, but the press will probably contact you shortly afterward for comment."

I said, "Thank you, Gary. I hope I can live up to your expectations."

Gary said, "We are not worried about that. You are a proven, experienced coach, and we are excited that you would be interested in coaching here."

I replied, "Great! So when can I meet with all the boys at Tri-Central to introduce myself to them and let them know what my plans are?"

Gary said, "How about next Thursday? I am sure you will be hearing from the Kokomo sports editor, Dave Kitchell, in the next day or so."

I replied, "That will be fine!" He again congratulated me and said he would be in touch. Now the real work would begin.

CHAPTER 3

2009—I Believe

Goal: Survival

My coaching career has continued through three decades. This new job at Tri-Central would be my fourth head-coaching assignment. I have experienced the youth of generations x, y, and currently z. Teenage boys have changed in many ways over the years. Yet still they are quite similar to the boys I first coached in 1980 at a high school in Ohio. All of us are looking for trust, loyalty, confidence, discipline, a sense of belonging, and the belief that no matter what happens, our personal relationship will never be in question. The great cancer facing all of us during this "new millennium" is entitlement. If we can find a way to get people to focus their energies toward a cause, then we can build a team, a company, and yes, a family. My first objective was to get the young men at Tri-Central to believe in me. I needed to be me—as I have always tried to do over the years—and not what I thought they wanted. I have lived my life by strong moral standards with a belief in God, a belief in my family, a belief in the importance of teaching, and a belief in the importance of coaching. Great leaders possess some very basic fundamentals that are easy for others to read when in their presence. The youth of America need routine, repetition toward excellence, a sound but not punishing discipline, and the opportunity to make mistakes without the feeling of failure. Once an athlete feels his coach does not believe in him, resentment develops, and everyone loses at that point.

On Tuesday, May 10, 2009, Dave Kitchell from the Kokomo *Tribune* called me. He first congratulated me on being hired by Tri-Central and asked if he could do a brief interview with me. I agreed to the interview, which was published on May 11, 2009, in the Kokomo *Tribune*:

New Hire Changes Face of Tri-Central Football
Longtime successful coach George Gilbert will direct program
By DAVE KITCHELL
The history and tradition of the Tri-Central football program wouldn't suggest that its new football coaching hire would include a person with either vast experience or a winning track record.

Somehow, some way, TC has found a coach with both qualities.

At Monday night's Northern Community school board meeting, former Clinton Central coach George Gilbert was hired to replace the coach, whose contract wasn't renewed after last season.

Gilbert sat out the 2008 campaign, but coached Clinton Central the previous 20 seasons, winning three sectional championships while assembling a 121–94 won-lost record. Gilbert, 54, also coached two years at Pioneer and five at Wayne Trace High School in Ohio.

Tri-Central's struggles at establishing a winning football tradition is no secret and athletic director Gary Rhew is excited to have a proven winner on board.

"We've faced (Gilbert's) teams in recent years and they have always been well-schooled and ready to play," Rhew said. "I know he's confident he can change things here and he'll work hard to do that. He believes kids (at Tri-Central) are no different than at Clinton Central. It's just a matter of getting the mind-set right and kids to believe in the program."

Rhew also believes the hire will dispel rumors.

"We have never talked about getting rid of foot-ball—I don't know where those rumors come from," Rhew said. "I don't think we could have made a better hire and it should let people in our community know that football is here to stay."

Of course some of those rumors were likely fos-tered through frustration. Over the past 14 seasons, the Trojans have had four winless records, six more when they had just one win and an overall mark of 20–118.

Few incoming coaches, however, could have any better feel for Tri-Central football than Gilbert. During his stint at Clinton Central, his teams played TC 24 times, winning 20. Enrollment at the schools is nearly identical—Clinton Central 341, Tri-Central 344. And there's more. Back in the late 1980s, Clinton Central football was mired in the same muck as TC is today.

"When I took the job at Clinton Central in 1988, everyone told me that it was a coach's graveyard," Gilbert said with a laugh. "They hadn't had a winning season in 17 years, had only five in school history and they were coming off three straight 0–9 finishes.

"I remember we had nine kids show up the first day of practice and we started the season with 18. In the second game of that first season we beat Hamilton Heights and everything changed from that point. We developed a program that was pretty special."

Gilbert said he didn't want to speculate on what kinds of problems TC football has encountered in recent years, but did point to the low number of varsity players as a crucial element.

"I understand they graduated 12 seniors and had about 28 players total," Gilbert said. "From what I understand they had a good eighth-grade class, but I won't allow them as freshmen to get beat up at the varsity level. You can't build a program around freshmen. Next season I'd like to get 40 players out and keep them involved in football—that would be a victory in itself. That's a goal. If we can consistently get 40 kids committed to football, we can win some games."

Gilbert, who will continue to teach at Clinton Central, said he missed football last season and is eager to get back on the field.

"I didn't live and die with the Friday nights, but I love coaching kids during the week and I missed that," he said. "I guess Tri-Central will either rekindle that fire in me or put it out altogether. It won't be an easy task but I'm looking forward to it."

• Dave Kitchell is the *Tribune's* sports editor. He may be reached by e-mail at dave.kitchell@kokomotribune.com

The following day, Thursday, May 12, would be the first opportunity for me to meet and give the male students in grades eight through eleven information about my background and the direction that I planned for Tri-Central football. I took the day off work at Clinton Central and arrived at Tri-Central an hour before the football assembly. When I arrived, I was greeted by several teachers and administrators, congratulating me on my new appointment. Mr. Rhew saw me and came over to let me know that I would meet with the boys in the auditorium and that everything was ready. I headed over to the auditorium and watched as boys passed me, checking me out as they headed off to class. There were no signs of emotion. They had seen a great deal of coaches come and go. I was sure they were thinking, *What is this guy going to try to sell?* I was well prepared; I had started writing my speech for them the night I was hired.

When I entered the auditorium to get ready, I noticed a familiar face in the back. I then walked up to that familiar face and said, "Mr. Gene Conard, how are you doing?"

Mr. Gene Conard is a longtime journalist (for over fifty years) who wrote for several area newspapers. I had worked with him for over twenty years when I was head coach at Clinton Central, and Gene was always respectful with a fresh, unique style of writing. For the past twenty years, Gene had worked covering only Tri-Central football in the fall. He had his work cut out for him each week trying to pull something positive out of the beating Tri-Central took almost every week. Gene looked up and said, "Well, Mr. Gilbert!"

I broke in. "Mr. Conard, you don't need to be so formal, just George will do."

"OK, and Gene will work fine for me." Gene asked me if he could do an interview when I was done with my remarks to the boys. I agreed. At that point a bell sounded, and boys began to come in the auditorium.

As the boys began filling the auditorium, Mr. Driggs and Mr. Rhew were up by the podium talking to someone, so I headed up in that direction. The man they were speaking with was a member of the current coaching staff, Shane Arnold. Shane introduced himself formally and said that he would like to speak with me after the assembly, to which I agreed.

The school's principal, Mr. Dave Driggs, would introduce me. Mr. Driggs had retired as the athletic director and head boys' basketball coach some years before. Mr. Driggs was very successful at Tri-Central throughout the years, and late in his career he was able to make it to the state championship game. I have a great deal of respect for Mr. Driggs, and I really liked my new athletic director. At this time, both men were being scrutinized over the school's commitment to football. They both needed for me to succeed to help smother the fire in the community. Since Tri-Central was not very successful, when the job opened, they would be faced with candidates with no experience, assistant coaches looking to move up, or coaches who had been fired from other jobs. I had been fired, but the firing came out of mysterious reasoning. They'd seen their school teams play mine for twenty years and felt that if there was going to be a light at the end of the tunnel, then they were hoping I was carrying it.

Mr. Driggs brought the gathering to order, and the boys sat quietly as he introduced me. There was a hush as I walked up to the microphone. Below is the exact speech here that I gave that day.

2009 TRI-CENTRAL FOOTBALL MEETING
May 14, 2009
Thank you, Mr. Driggs!
To you soccer players and cross-country runners… understand I do not wish to recruit you or mess with your programs…I will be supportive of what you are doing as I will be supportive of all the athletic teams. So at this point you can chill and listen to what I am saying or go to your happy place.

This is the most important meeting I will have during my tenure as football coach at Tri-Central High School. None of you remember, but in 1991 Tri-Central had a great team. That year Clinton Central played them twice in close contests; Central lost twice. Both games were close and very exciting! Central played Tri-Central in the sectional championship and went into half time with a lead…but during the second half, Tri-Central would not be denied and won the sectional championship in front of a huge crowd at Clinton Central. What I want is what your community wants…to provide a quality football program every year…one that you are proud to be a member or fan of, and one that you will have the confidence each week that there is no team at your level in Indiana that you fear to play and that you do not have a chance to win against. I am not the taskmaster that people have often said I am. I will not ask you to do anything you are unable to accomplish. I will challenge you to be the best you can be and hopefully you will surprise yourself (story of Curt Rawlings). Each week I will design a game plan that will give you an opportunity to compete.

To compete, numbers are important in football.

-Generals cannot win wars without soldiers.

-Forty is the magic number this season…48 is ideal for class A.

-Eliminate quitting, or going through the motions.

To believe

-Have faith and see results

-No excuses…I do not make excuses or blame.

-If the team loses it is my fault, if the team wins, it is the players that make it happen. (I do not put in the paper negative criticism about players or staff… only that I did not do my job when team lost.) I am not trying to seek pity, only defer attention from players. I believe a leader must take responsibility.

-When the team wins, we will come to the sidelines and sing the school song (this has been a tradition with all my teams), then we will pray, and I will leave the team alone to enjoy victory.

-When the team loses, we will shake hands, find a place to pray, and head directly to the locker room. I do not yell at players after losses. I will go around individually and shake each player's hand and confide how much I appreciate them as a member of the Tri-Central football program. I believe you should never feel that my loyalty to you as a person or to the team is ever in doubt. Doubt destroys people's motivation to challenge and focus on success. I will always be there for you.

Coming from Clinton Central

-I will continue to work and attempt to make my classroom the very best classroom possible. I teach US history, sociology, and health. On my desk is a bust of Abraham Lincoln, our sixteenth president of the United States. Whenever I feel down and think of giving up I look over to A. Lincoln and stop feeling sorry for myself.

Lincoln failed in business, he failed as a politician early in his career, his fiancée died, he had a breakdown, and he failed again in politics. Lincoln failed in his political career twenty-one times before he won... and when he won he became president of the United States. When he won he did not win the popular support of America and when he did win, eleven states left the Union. He was faced with distractions, discontent, and unprecedented problems, but he never lost faith nor that desire to achieve. If at some point he had given up, America would not have had one of the greatest presidents in US history. He was faced with paying the ultimate price, and that was his life.

The difference between history's boldest accomplishments and its most staggering failures is often, simply, the diligent will to persevere.

I will remain loyal to my students and committed toward them achieving in my classroom.

-I will take that commitment here in the afternoon and transfer it to the Tri-Central football field and support, teach, and be loyal to each player, student, and community member close to football or any athletic sports teams.

-This is not an ideal situation; excuses could be made from you, your parents, community or even me. I will tell you this—I will not make excuses…I dealt with this type of situation when I coached in Ohio. I worked at a middle school and coached at the high school…it is not perfect but workable. I did have success in Ohio just not the through the dailyy contact that teachers have working in the same building. We can make this work… it will depend on believing and giving it a chance.

Blue-collar coach

-I don't golf or drink alcohol or attempt to be someone I am not. I will tell you what I think and move forward. I don't hold grudges, as all people make mistakes, and all mistakes should be forgivable.

-I don't like individualism on the football team. Every member is important and deserves the dignity deserving of all players, no matter if you are a starter or on the scout team. Actually, scout-team players are vital to preparation for games, and those players are very significant in my mind.

-Be a part of something special…make history. Why can't this school be successful in football? I think it can.

-It is easy to judge if you have never been on the witness stand.

-Keep an open mind.

-I don't introduce a starting lineup but rather all players on the varsity roster at home games.

-All players are important, from freshmen to seniors.

-A team is only as strong as its weakest member, and all players and coaches need to be respected.

Tri-Central needs forty-plus boys on the high-school team. A school that cannot keep the boys on the squad their junior-senior years will never experience continued success. On Friday evenings, seniors should be representing the school—and the best juniors and possibly some sophomores if needed. Sending a freshman out to battle eighteen- and nineteen-year-old men is a difficult task, and one that will encourage walking away. I want to develop a program here that allows young players to get better without the stress of Friday night and offers older players the opportunity to go out and beat up some of the schools that have been beating them up. I cannot do this without you! I need players—players to practice and players to play...Players who will be dedicated and not just put time in until it is time to pick up a basketball or start cutting weight for wrestling. I expect a total commitment during the season, and then I expect our players to have a total commitment to other coaches and other programs. WHY CAN'T ALL TEAMS BE EQUALLY IMPORTANT AND EQUALLY RESPECTED? I AM NOT A WHINER...WE WILL CREATE WHAT WE SEEK IN THE FOOTBALL PROGRAM AND NOT INFRINGE ON OTHER PROGRAMS. I WANT A PROGRAM THAT WILL EARN RESPECT THE OLD-FASHIONED WAY AND THAT DOES NOT INVOLVE MAKING EXCUSES OR RUNNING MY MOUTH ABOUT SUCCESS OF OTHERS. IF I WANT SUCCESS, THEN I NEED TO WORK TOWARD IT, NOT TRY TO DRAG OTHERS DOWN BUT HELP OTHERS TO RISE UP AND TOGETHER PROVIDE THE BEST FOR OUR SCHOOL AND COMMUNITY!

You will hear all kinds of legends about me…remember this—if I am such a mean, nasty guy, why did Central always have forty-four-plus athletes on the squad for over twenty years and the stands full each time the team played at home? Central also over the years gained state ranking during fourteen of those seasons.

-I do not believe in running lots of sprints…I figure we will run enough playing the game the way I expect it to be played.

-I will never run practice over…When I list the time we end practice that is when practice is over.

-I do not believe in standing-around time…we will go to work, and practice time will fly as long as players focus.

-I do not practice on Saturdays other than two-a-days but instead offer films for boys to come and watch in the morning with only injured players required to attend after my radio program.

-Summer practice is over by 2:00 p.m. during two-a-days.

-Weights are set up so you can either come for an hour and fifteen minutes in the morning or afternoon three times a week during the summer.

-I will start morning weights next Monday at 6:15 a.m., and it will last until 7:15 a.m. I have a packet of times and information available to hand out at the conclusion of this meeting. I truly believe in the importance of strength training. REMEMBER, IT DOES NOT MATTER WHERE YOU START, AS NO ONE IN THE WEIGHT ROOM I RUN WILL EMBARRASS ANYONE ELSE. YOU WILL GET STRONGER AND BE PROUD OF WHAT YOU DO. I KEEP RECORDS FROM ONCE YOU BEGIN IN THE

WEIGHT ROOM UNTIL YOU GRADUATE FROM HIGH SCHOOL, AND YOU WILL NOT BELIEVE YOUR PROGRESS BY THE TIME YOU LEAVE!

-During the school year I will provide student athletes the opportunity to lift from 6:15 to 7:15 a.m. on Monday, Wednesday, and Thursday mornings.

-Seven-on-seven is one night a week, and that is Monday, and we will learn the system this summer.

I will work to make you proud to be a member of the football program, but right now I need help at getting it started. It will not be easy, but it is clearly possible if boys will give football a try. I need players! I don't care if you never played before or had a bad experience, everyone will be on the same page this year, learning a new system and hopefully a new direction. I do not have empty promises for you. I will guarantee that you will be glad you were a part of the ground level of this football program. You will be the risk takers and the true leaders of Tri-Central to come out and commit to changing the direction and history of Tri-Central football. REMEMBER THAT NO MATTER WHAT YOU HAVE TRUE SUCCESS AT IN LIFE, IT REQUIRES SACRIFICE. WITHOUT SACRIFICE, VICTORY IS EMPTY AND NOT MEMORABLE, BUT WITH SACRIFICE, YOU WILL REMEMBER EVERY PART OF WHAT YOU HAD TO DO TO GET WHERE YOU ARE! There is no greater feeling than to run onto the field through a community tunnel playing high-school football.

People love drama! Recently Tri-Central has received some interesting press. I am not concerned with that. I AM NOT CONCERNED WITH WHAT I CANNOT CONTROL. I am concerned about taking this program where it needs to go and building something with your help that all of you will be proud of. I remember my first year at Clinton Central and how students were actually betting on how many points the football team was going to lose by. In no time at all, all that changed. We can't concern ourselves with the future, we must concern ourselves with now.

When I was a five-year-old, I was a very sickly child and suffered horribly from asthma. My family was extremely poor, and I was in and out of hospitals. My doctor told my parents that I needed to get active in some type of physical activity, and maybe my health would improve. My mother immediately started me taking lessons to twirl a baton. Yes, here I was, a little boy twirling a baton and going and competing in twirling contests. Well, by age seven, I was pretty good, and my health seemed to improve, but my father felt batons were for girls, so he decided that I needed to learn a manly sport. He wanted to take me to a small gym on Broadway Street in Gary, Indiana, called Tony Zale's Boxing School and teach me to box. My father had been a golden-glove boxer, and he felt this would be good for me. My mother only agreed as long as I continued to twirl the baton. I worked hard at twirling and dreaded going to the gym for my boxing lessons. I remember one Sunday afternoon when a friend of my father's brought his son in, and they decided that their sons should go a few rounds. This young African American boy had been boxing a long time, and he was two years older than I was. I remember him hitting me so hard that I fell down and started to cry. My dad, in all his consoling ways, came up to me, and I told him that boy was mean and I did not want to do this anymore. My father said that I was scared, and that was a good thing. He told me you can never learn how to box without learning first how to be a punching bag. He then got a big smile on his face and told me that I was an excellent punching bag. He then said once you learn how to get hit, the next level is learning how to hit. He was right. I still went to the gym until I was around thirteen. I learned how to box, I learned from getting hit how to hit, and I had some success, but not a great deal. At age thirteen, I stopped twirling the baton and boxing and instead started playing football. I learned how hitting was a great deal less painful than getting hit and how great it was to play this game of football. Football has done a great deal of good in my life. I would never had been able to afford college without football paying my way, and being a coach football has been very rewarding.

For many years, Tri-Central has been getting hit by other schools. Isn't it about time that the Trojan football program do some hitting for themselves? Let's move from being the punching bag in the area to being the one doing the punching. If this is to happen, it will depend on you. We need at least forty players for next fall. Why wait and plan for future years when we can fix this problem starting today and build now to succeed now?

Let's make Friday nights at Tri-Central memorable...Let's develop a tough-guy program, one with which everyone in the community is proud to be associated.

When I was finished, the boys got up and headed to their next class. I felt like I had prepared a great speech, but I did not notice what I had hoped to see. I have always taken pride in my ability to speak publicly. I usually knew when it was right and things went well.

Unfortunately, I did not feel that way when I was done. I felt some listened, but most did not believe! I would need to focus on getting the young men who committed to football to believe. This would be a great task, but I had been through this before. I just needed to find the right mix to make it work. I truly was disillusioned. I thought of a line in the movie *Fields of Dreams*: "If you build it, they will come." Obviously this was no movie, and it would take some serious work to convince the youth at Tri-Central that football could be successful.

As I stood there shuffling my papers, Mr. Rhew came up and congratulated me on an outstanding speech to the boys. Mr. Rhew, I would find, was a very respectful, hardworking man who believed in honor and respect. He told me he had some things to take care of and that he would leave me to talk with Gene (reporter) and Shane (assistant coach). I thanked him, and he was off to other duties.

Shane shared that he was impressed by my speech and welcomed me as the new head coach. Shane Arnold came across as a really nice man. Shane said that he would wait to talk with me until Gene was done with the interview. I told Shane that he should sit in on the interview with me.

He said, "Oh, no, sir! I do not want to be in the way."

I remarked, "Coach Arnold, you will never be in the way, so just sit back here, and we will talk with Mr. Conard." I added, "OK, Gene, what would you like to ask me?" Gene was a tall, gentleman in his late seventies. In the past I'd always felt comfortable around Gene. He had a laid-back approach and did not talk around the issues. His straightforward approach, marked by his understanding of the difference between "on the records" and "off the records," allowed me to relax and not be fearful that he would use the off-the-record things I said, as so many reporters do today. With that, the interview began:

> Gene: Coach Gilbert, you had a great deal of success at Clinton Central over the years. Do you think that success will be possible at a school that can hardly field a team year in and year out?

Answer: Yes, Gene, I think it is possible. I feel I must first get boys to buy into believing in what I am trying to sell. I need to gain a commitment from boys to lift weights and take a more serious approach to preparation. I need to start working right away and show the boys that through a sound work ethic and fundamental knowledge of the game, change can occur anywhere, and that includes Tri-Central.

Gene: Coach, the big kids and the skilled kids do not wish to play football here. What is your plan to get them involved?

Answer: What has happened here in the past I have no control over. What happens from today on I control. I must make good decisions. I will work hard to recruit the boys to want to play.

Gene: This is a basketball school! It has always been a basketball school. What are you going to do to change that mentality?

Answer: Nothing! It is my job to build my sport and respect all others. I will work closely with all the boys programs. The boys need to see continuity and respect from the men who lead. I will say this: the best way to change things is to win. Success will bring football out of the cellar and into the limelight.

Gene: Coach, you have always been known as a smash mouth, run-oriented offensive coach. Tri-Central has been known over the past ten years as a team that throws the ball a great deal. What are your plans offensively?

Answer: We will run the ball! We will use play-action passing, but we will learn the fundamentals of blocking and assignment football. Yes, we will run first.

Gene: George, I have known you for years, and if anyone can fix this broken thing here, it is you.

I am not trying to flatter you, I just want you to know that I believe you will be the last coach here if it doesn't work out. You have a straight-shooting approach. I don't know if that will work here. I wish you the best, and I will be in contact with you periodically, asking for updates. I know you will not give me crap to print, and I know when this thing gets better you won't have to say anything, because it will be visual. George, this is a mess. Good luck my friend. You are certainly going to need it.

I thanked Gene for his time and left with Shane to do a walk-through of the field house. Shane and I both drove our pickups back to the field house.

When we arrived, Shane got out first and opened the door. He said, "Coach, this isn't much to look at, but it is all we have." After the walk-through we went into the coaches' office and sat down to talk.

> Shane: Coach, it has been really bad here. It has been a difficult program to be a part of.
>
> George: Well, Shane, if it is so bad, how has is it you are still here?
>
> Shane: "Coach, I love football. I truly enjoy working with boys, and I really would like to see Tri-Central football improve.
>
> George: Well, that will be our task. What are some of the issues?
>
> Shane: Respect, commitment, discipline, and most of all, attendance. The boys are accustomed to getting punished a great deal. There is a great deal of yelling at practice, and during games there is a great deal of confusion. Much of that is due to attendance issues.

George: All these things you mention are fixable. Tell me about the staff.

Shane: The staff? I guess that would be up to you. In the past, the new head coach would interview everyone and then decide who would stay and who would go."

George: No, I will not work that way. If the current staff wishes to return, then I will allow them to return. I will set up a coaches' meeting, and we will discuss my philosophies. Then they will have the opportunity to decide for themselves whether to stay or go. After the first year, if I need to make some hard decisions, then...I guess that is a part of my job.

At this point, Shane and I talked candidly about our background and our families. I think I made Shane very nervous this first time we met. I have a personality that sometimes comes across stronger than it is intended to be. Shane kept calling me "sir," and finally I told him that I was not a sir. "Call me Coach or George, but not sir.

This would be a struggle not only for Shane but also for the boys, as the young men in Tipton County were expected to call authority figures sir. The Tri-Central community is one where there is a great deal of respect for teachers and coaches, which in itself is odd in this day and age. It would take me several years before I would be able to end the sir thing and get boys and coaches to call me Coach!

I met with the coaches the last week of May. I currently had three men who wished to continue on the high-school staff, one of whom was Shane. Shane had been the offensive coordinator, and I told him that I would give him more freedom in the offense as he learned it. Shane seemed to be fine with his role but obviously not happy. I was glad he was not happy, as this would force him to focus on my offense, learn the offense, and then show me he was capable. The defensive coordinator was a wonderful man who would work hard but had been pretty much burned out and stayed on to help me get adjusted this first year. The other high-school coach was a local deputy sheriff. He also had been coaching a long time and seemed like he would give a true effort.

I had a high-school position open, and I knew where I wanted to go with it. There were two local football heroes in the community who at one time or another had coached in the football program. These two men were a part of the only sectional championship team Tri-Central had produced. It was 1991 when the school won their only sectional championship, and yes, the team they defeated was my team at Clinton Central.

I remember as if it were yesterday the comeback Tri-Central put on. Clinton Central was ahead at the end of the first half. Much of the comeback was due to the efforts of these two men. First, Memo Perez had been the quarterback who orchestrated the comeback that resulted in the Tri-Central victory. Coach Perez possesses that thing you just can't identify, but you know he is confident and that he would see through anything he focused on. I met with Coach Perez and asked him if he would be interested in coaching with me, and he said that he thought he could work it out. I told him he would help coach the defense and work with the offensive receivers. He was not happy about the assignment working with receivers, but I had no one else, and if he came on board, that would be his assignment. He agreed, and he was in.

Second, Jason Tolle, who has a great job as an engineer at Chrysler. I also remembered Coach Tolle from the 1991 squad; he was a lineman on offense and linebacker on defense and played the game as it was meant to be played. Coach Tolle also possessed a great deal of heart, and I felt his personality would mesh well with the staff. It helped that he and Coach Perez were close friends. These two men were extremely focused on doing what was necessary to see the football program finally have some long-awaited success. The school had had five winning seasons in forty-two years, and they were ready to help change the longtime lack of success at Tri-Central.

This first year I would call the offense to start the season, and depending on how Coach Arnold was doing, give him some opportunities to work toward being the offensive coordinator. Coach

Rhoades would handle the defense, and Coach Perez would handle special teams. Coach Tolle would work with the line and Coach Rhoades. Coach Jeff Pike (our deputy sheriff on staff) would head up our junior varsity team and work with the defensive line directly.

The weight room was open from May on, and I truly had my work cut out for me. Few boys made the effort to come in and lift weights, and those coming in seemed to think they knew more than me. Boys would come in and only want to bench and curl. Watching them bench was very difficult. The strongest boys were lifting around 185 pounds, and everyone in the room seemed to be impressed with them. Obviously, I was not impressed. At Clinton Central, the athletes bought into the weight room, and I had great numbers from day one. The boys came into the room wanting to learn technique, and they did. And now, I had boys come in with drinks and snacks, playing instead of lifting. I began teaching the parallel squat and clean lifts. This was a horrible experience. I would go to Tri-Central (a thirty-minute drive one way) in the morning before school and five to ten boys would show up. Several of those boys would not lift consistently, and it seemed I was constantly getting new weak boys in the room. Without consistency, teaching strength training and technique is nearly impossible.

I decided to continue the good fight, but I began questioning whether I made a sound decision in taking the job. I was a stranger, coming onto their turf and telling them what to do. I decided I would continue routinely going in the morning and evening and try to develop some continuity in the weight program.

In 2009, the weight room did not improve. Strength training and commitment were two things the boys were not interested in. I attempted to run a seven-on-seven program on Monday nights during the summer, and I would be lucky if ten boys would show up. August was quickly approaching, and I still did not know if I was going to be able to put a team together.

Finally, a week before football, my numbers were now at twenty-two. This was not great, but it was a start. The major problem was that most of the high-school team was made up of incoming freshmen and new seniors. Some of the seniors had never played, but the freshmen class coming in was made up of ten boys, and most of them were athletic.

The first day finally came around, and I really wondered what I was going to have to work with. That day, twenty-seven boys showed up for practice. I would only have twenty of those twenty-seven available, because seven waited till the first week to schedule their physical appointments. In Indiana, all boys must pass a physical examination, and they have from May to August to get this done. At Tri-Central, these boys apparently waited until that week, which showed how strong their commitment was.

The first session of practice displayed how unprepared they were. Boys were vomiting and sick after the first ten minutes of practice. I could not believe what I was witnessing. We barely made it through the first session. I had a meeting scheduled between the sessions to go over how things were going to run with me in charge of the program. I had the team assembled and the information below was provided.

FOOTBALL MEETING 2009

Introduction of staff

Team first

Putting on the blinders

No individuals in program—all as one. E pluribus Unum

Playing within boundaries

Goal 1—finish with those who start. No quitters.

We will work to improve…understand being good may happen, but we will need to work very hard to achieve it.

Locker room

Each day the locker room will be cleaned by a class, starting today, with the senior class paving the way all through two-a-day practices.

When school begins, we will clean up and not have a messy locker room. Discipline is important, and if we want the custodians to clean our locker room, then we must do our part.

Flush toilets!

Wash your clothing!

Each class has a coach assigned to them for dealing with issues. Please keep that coach informed of issues that need to be addressed.

Grades

School—homework

Discipline—doing what you are not supposed to do—drinking booze, tobacco, etc.

Girlfriends

Pictures on Friday! Bring money and packet info.

Team travel gear must be ordered if not already.

Free time—use wisely.

Fluid intake and putting weight on that you lose

Saturday scrimmage

Equipment handout—Coach Arnold

Field cleanup

Learn the school song.

Cookout night before first game—invite parents and bring digitals or cameras

Expectations game day

We are only as strong as the weakest.

Do not worry about statistics, worry about our team getting better. It is never about what you have done, but rather what the team has done.

Always be positive about members of the team... never embarrass, harass, or degrade any member of the squad. Never blame any individual player for bad things that happen, we all will share that blame when we fail. I do not ever blame you publicly for our misfortune, it will always be my fault, but as you learn football from this program, and learn in life, you will realize that blaming is a rationalization or excuse to be used only by those who are weak or unsure of their own ability. I like to work with young men who understand that what happens in practice or behind closed doors in meetings needs to stay there. Let others think what they might, and gossip what they choose, as you will have the confidence to truly know the facts and truth of our mission and direction.

The order by which you live your lives is very important. Here are the guidelines I believe in:

First   God, if you believe in God, is always number one.

Second   Family—your family always comes first after your relationship with God.

Third   Academics—this is why you are in school.

Fourth   Commitments—sports, 4-H, etc.

Fifth   Miscellaneous—friends, girls, etc.

It is important for all of us to have direction and some sort of order to how we live our lives. Success does not just happen, it must be sought after, fought for, and focused on every day by how we live our lives.

The team barely made it through two-a-days. It seemed I had to constantly deal with the issues of absenteeism, lack of discipline, and boys who seemed to not really care about anyone other than themselves. Just about every day during the 2009 campaign, I was faced with some sort of discipline issue. I had seniors who never played and freshmen who thought they were better than they really were. I also had several sophomores and juniors in the mix, who added to the tension on the team. My job was simple and difficult at the same time. I had to be consistent but careful not to go overboard when fixing the many problems related to the team. I had boys worrying about how many times we gave them the ball offensively. I had boys wait till the game was numerically over while playing against other schools' younger players to display their talents. What a mess. Everything was going badly. The team was 0–3, and I was faced with removing two seniors from the team due to attendance issues. Then the incident occurred.

It was Wednesday of the fourth week of the season. Every day I was faced with excuses why boys were not practicing. For most of the 2009 season, we were unable to scrimmage for lack of numbers. It was just horrible. I felt like the program was going nowhere, and I was becoming more angry each day. I arrived at the practice facility at 3:40 in the afternoon to see ten boys in street clothes standing over by the trainer. I quizzed Coach Arnold as to what was going on. He told me that the blood drive took place that day, and ten players had given blood and could not practice due to that.

I said, "Really? These boys are not allowed to practice?"

He told me that school officials told them if they gave blood, they would not be allowed to practice, and they gave blood anyway. I was outraged, to say the least! I had never been faced with anything similar in my long coaching career. I had had it! I walked out of the field house and stood a second, observing the boys laughing and relaxed while the other fifteen boys on the squad were going through drills. Seven of the ten boys were starters on the team. Apparently they had no idea of how narcissistic their choices had been that day and probably felt, *what can the coach do? We did something good, and he won't be able to say anything.*

Well, they were wrong. I announced, "Gentlemen, I cannot believe the decision you made today and how your actions reflect the attitude I am currently fighting here. You made your choice, and now I will make mine. Get out of here, now! You will be back tomorrow. If anything happens like this again, I will throw you off the team. I have had it with your silly excuses to miss practice, your inconsideration for everyone here who would really like to see us improve. Now, leave!"

The boys went out to their cars and were hanging out instead of leaving. Now they were testing the waters.

I ran to the fence and screamed, "I said get out of here now! You have no right to be on campus grounds! Go home, and I will deal with all of you tomorrow!" At this they jumped into their cars and left. The next day I called a meeting at the start of practice and announced, "As of today, you do anything that I feel is disrespecting our program in any way, and you are gone! From this day forward, everyone will be at practice in uniform. We will either build this program into something, or we will destroy it. If you are not a part of the solution, then you must be part of the problem. I am done with problems here. I will speak no more on this subject, but mark my word, I will not tolerate any more distractions from what we are trying to accomplish. I know we are not going to win much, if at all, this year, but I guarantee each of you that your commitment working with me will change from this day forward, or you will be fired. Let's go to work!"

Practice-wise we did get better, but we continued to struggle on the field as every team beat us up. Midway through the season, we started being everybody's homecoming, as we really were not very good. We ended the season 0–10. I had one 0–10 season in Ohio, but it was nothing like this. We went 0–10 with ten seniors, ten freshmen, and seven sophomores and juniors. To make matters worse, the school I coached at for twenty years beat us 130-7 in two games. Clinton Central embarrassed us, and the boys I had coached since they were little boys made fun of our boys and my program. It was my job to remain poised and show our community that we would lose with dignity, and someday we would win with dignity.

One thing I think we did accomplish was that later in the year, the boys seemed to be upset about losing games; earlier in the season, they acted as if they won when they were soundly defeated. We had made some progress, but we had a long way to go. A couple of the better players played only for themselves, and that would need to change in 2010, or they would need to be replaced by boys willing to buy into the program, even if they possessed less talent. I didn't feel we were able to get everyone sold on this I Believe concept. I would continue to work this focus point during the off-season and hoped to add to it in 2010.

All in all, 2009 was a terrible football season at Tri-Central. I was beginning my reign 0–10. Looking back, I feel the importance of the 2009 campaign was that we reached bottom in the state of Indiana in high-school football. We ended the season ranked 310th of 318 schools playing football in Indiana. Wow! It was time to focus on 2010.

CHAPTER 4

2010—I Believe

Better

Goal 1: Defeat Rival School—Week Two

We graduated eleven seniors from the 2009 team that went 0–10. Many coaches would want to forget such a horrible season and continue to try new things to get the program going. I will never forget that season, but I felt change would add more horrible seasons. I had established the direction, and although not many of the players bought in to the "believe" philosophy yet, I was not going to veer from the path I felt the program needed to follow. In the 2010 season, we were still going to work hard on this I Believe principle, with a new emphasis on getting better. I decided to add this one word as a key to the 2010 season. We were going to be far from good, but better was not only possible, it was inevitable, considering what happened the year before.

I continued to be faced with dissension among team members. When a team does not win, it becomes extremely difficult to get players to buy in. We needed a goal to work toward and accomplish. I told the boys at the start of the season that our goal would be to defeat the school five miles to our north—our strongest rival in the area, Taylor High School. Taylor was going through their own set of issues. They had defeated us the year before, 48–12, and that was one of the few games they won that season. Tri-Central had lost to them now five straight years. In 2009 when they defeated us, I felt they were out of shape and undisciplined. I would spend the entire off-season focusing only on defeating Taylor High School. It would be a game at home and an excellent opportunity for us to start the success. I knew that I would have to push the boys hard during two-a-days to be in better shape than our rival, and I knew if I stayed consistent with my philosophy we would have better team discipline. I also knew that they would have better athletes than we did, so we would need to play conservatively and wait for our chance to win.

The fallout from the 2009 season continued, as I already stated. We graduated eleven seniors. The incoming junior class had six boys who played in 2009, and two of them quit the program. The sophomore class had four boys who played the year before, and two of them decided football was not for them. The surprise came when the freshmen class lost four of ten players entering the 2010 season. Therefore, we were going to enter the 2010 campaign with twelve boys coming back out of twenty-two who were on the team the year prior. I was not happy about this at all. Most of the boys not coming back were boys who definitely were not playing football for Tri-Central but rather for themselves. Looking back now, I see it was probably for the best. Unfortunately, I still was fighting the mentality that being a starter was the only thing that was important. Boys felt that if they were not going to start on offense or defense, then why bother? The now-sophomore class had several boys who believed, as did their parents, that they were better than the other boys. This problem was an infection facing the football program to which I had to find an answer. At this time I had no answer except to remind each boy every day that every player is important for success, and no one is better than anyone else.

I have never made a big deal about who starts and who doesn't. I don't introduce individuals before games but rather I expect the announcer to say each player's number and each player's name as we come to the field before the game. I felt that this current sophomore class had too much rivalry among themselves to truly buy in.

The incoming freshmen class really excited me. The parents all liked each other, and the boys seem to get along very well. Most of the freshmen never missed anything. They came to weights routinely, and they came to all meetings and seven-on-sevens throughout the summer. The class would produce ten players in 2010, and seven would play through their senior year. The class would pick up three other boys who would make their class better and special. The class was missing a quarterback and running backs but had young talent and seemed to buy into what the coaches were selling.

Going into the season, we would not get every player in the weight room, and we did not have a total buy-in, but we now had enough players buying into this I Believe idea to start the turnaround.

Changes in staff occurred before the 2010 season. Coach Rhodes decided to leave the program, and this gave me the opportunity to move Coach Perez up to defensive coordinator and move Coach Tolle up to our offensive line coach. I also hired Coach Jeremy Kennedy to help in both the junior-high program and at the high-school level. Coach Perez came up to me and asked if we could change direction defensively. His brother Gabe was an outstanding high-school football coach at the big-school level. Memo believed that this new defense, the 3–4, would not only help the team but make his transition to coordinator easier. Coach Perez sold me on the defense. At this point, 2009, we gave up 48.9 points a game. It did not take much convincing. Coach Perez was passionate about what he wanted to do, and I have always believed that it is important for members of the coaching staff to have a vested interest in what we do. The more people committed to success, the harder everyone works to achieve that success.

Coach Perez set up training sessions for our entire staff to go and learn this defense from his Brother Gabe's defensive staff. The sessions went well, and we were all excited that this new defense could make us a better team if we could teach it to our athletes.

Coach Arnold also wanted to make some changes in offense. Coach Arnold knew pass offense very well, and he wanted to add to what we were doing. I was a little less receptive to what Coach Arnold wanted to do.

For the past thirty years, I had run the veer offense. I truly believed in it, and I knew it. I could adjust what we wanted to do immediately on the field instead of waiting to make adjustments at half time. I did not want to make drastic changes, but I did allow him to do some additions to our offensive package. I knew that I had an outstanding staff; my job would be to direct them. I would need to allow them to add their personality to what we were doing. Coach Perez also became our quarterback coach in 2010, and he wanted us to run the true veer offense with the quarterback reading every play. I was nervous about this, because we really did not have that guy yet in the program. Coach Tolle gave me fewer issues that first year when he took over the offensive line. He worked hard to stay within my game-proven blocking assignments that first year of his leadership. That would change. As Coach Tolle worked our line schemes, he would change much of what we did to fit his athletes.

So here we were with a new defense, a more comprehensive offense, and a line coach who was extremely innovative at the skill level of his athletes. At first, I was slow to allow change with all the high-school coaches but soon realized I needed to allow these men to coach. This would probably be the best decision I made as head coach at Tri-Central High School.

When two-a-days started, we did have some new faces besides the talented and close freshmen class. We were fortunate to gain four boys who would prove to be outstanding players and team leaders in 2010. These boys would become influential to the rest of the team. One boy in particular came out as a junior, and he would have an impact on our program for the next two years. Corbin would become a team leader; he bought into the We Believe concept totally and played that way every time he stepped onto the field at practice as well as in games. We still did not have a great off-season, and it proved to be problematic, as the boys were in terrible physical condition when drills started. We got in condition, though, because we now had leadership that we did not have the season before. Then the great scare occurred on the third day of practice. My skill as a head coach would be challenged, and how I responded to the situation would affect us and perhaps my tenure at Tri-Central.

As I have already pointed out, our freshman class was very talented. Perhaps the most talented of the group was a young African American boy by the name of Darius. Darius was big, fast, and extremely athletic. Darius seemed to be doing fine, I thought, but after practice on the third day, Coach Tolle advised me that I needed to talk with him, because he didn't think Darius was going to make it. I thought, *What? This boy will start on both sides of the ball as a freshman. What could the problem be?*

As Darius was preparing to leave for the day, I could see in his eyes what Coach Tolle had noticed. I told Darius that I wanted to talk with him. Darius was very upset when we sat down to talk. He told me that he did not want to continue. I asked him why, and he said it just wasn't any fun. I told Darius that two-a-days are never any fun for anyone, including the coaches. He told me that he didn't like getting yelled at and that it took him more time to learn things. I told Darius that I didn't care if it took him four years to learn; I was willing to do what was necessary to keep him on the squad. He smiled through his tears. I told Darius that football coaches yell at players, but it is never personal. I said that it's when the coaches don't yell at him that he should be worried. I still did not feel confident that I was winning him back. I told Darius that this was his first experience at playing a high-school sport. He needed to give it some time before he made his final decision. I felt he had outstanding potential, and we needed him.

I called for Coach Tolle to come over and talk with Darius and me. Coach Tolle had that thing that all coaches want but few possess. Coach Tolle was not a coach who yelled a great deal. He prided himself on speaking quietly in such a way that boys listened. Coach Tolle told Darius that he would help him individually and that he would not let anyone yell at him. I asked Darius to give us some time, give Coach Tolle some time, and then if he felt the same way, I would accept his decision. Darius said he would give it some time.

The rest is history. Darius would become the greatest lineman that I have been privileged to have on any of my teams. I can't say he is the best lineman that I have ever coached; that would be for Coach Tolle to say. Coach Tolle, through incredible patience, won this boy over, and they became great allies. This young man became an incredible competitor and a great team leader. By the end of summer he would lead the freshmen to buy into I Believe.

Tri-Central is an interesting story in itself. The football tradition does not exist. There had only been five winning seasons in over forty-three years of trying, and still at home contests we had an outstanding crowd. The 2010 season would start on the road in Indianapolis playing the Indiana School for the Deaf. We were in need of a game. Our first game opponent was entering a conference and could no longer play us. The deaf school saw that we were a year- in–year-out struggling program like them. The athletic directors signed the deal that they would be our first game. We were able to fill twenty-six jerseys that season. The thing that I noticed was that the boys were starting to believe in what we were doing. Now we needed to win!

All during two-a-days, I talked only of our rival and the goal of defeating Taylor High School. Everything we did was in preparation for that game. When we arrived at our first opponent's field, I told the boys that we needed to win that night as a means of making the boys at Taylor nervous. We did win. It was ugly, but we were able to gain the first victory of my tenure at Tri-Central. We had a respectable crowd for a class-A program, especially one with such a poor success rate. It had become a custom for our fan base to cheer for first downs due to the fact we never scored much. In 2009 we averaged 8.9 points a game, usually while opponents were draining the sidelines late in games. I have always told every team I have coached that a win is a win, and a loss is a loss. What I mean is that a one-point win is as good as a fifty-point win, and a one-point loss is even more devastating that a fifty-point loss. We did defeat the deaf school by a large margin, and after the game, some of the boys were actually acting as if we were better than we really were. Sometimes when teams win, the mistakes are masked by the success. It is the job of the coach to unmask those mistakes, or winning will only be temporary.

We had our first happy voyage home together after a win on the road, and I did allow the boys to enjoy the moment. On Saturdays during the season, I would do a local radio show and talk about the game. After I was done, I would travel to Tri-Central and watch game film with the team members who showed up. I was surprised that we were able to get quite a few boys after this first win to come in. I went over the game with them, speaking all the time about Taylor High School as I dissected their performance. The boys listened and asked questions as the high-school coaches added their comments on the performance the night before. It was the first time I felt we were getting better.

Week two was our goal week. This was the most important week of the 2010 season. I had challenged the boys that this was a game we must win. Coach Arnold coached the girls' softball team at Taylor, and when I arrived at practice on Monday, the talk had already begun between the players. The boys of these two schools got along, but it was a rivalry, and both teams needed this win.

Taylor played in an outstanding football conference. In 2009, they won three games and beat us up pretty convincingly 48–12. When I decided that this would be our focus game, I was taking quite a chance. Why not challenge the boys with a conference win? It had been four years since that occurred. Why not challenge the boys with a sectional tournament win? It had been sixteen years since Tri-Central had won a first-round game in the I.H.S.A.A. tournament. No, I selected Taylor because it was such a rivalry for our players and the community. Taylor High School is just nine miles away from Tri-Central, and the communities were very close and competitive with each other. For me to get the players, school, and community to start believing, the team had to make a statement on this one Friday night. The entire focus during the off-season was on this single evening of high-school football. To make things worse for us, the Taylor team also won their first game of the season and were looking forward to continuing their dominance over Tri-Central.

Coaches must take calculated risks all the time. It is one thing to talk about what you plan to do, and it's another to prepare and then execute a plan to change. I arrived early that Friday evening. As soon as school was out at Clinton Central, I jumped into my old 1992 Ford pickup and started the thirty-mile ride to Tri-Central. I arrived at the school around 3:45 p.m. Coach Arnold was already there, working. He was preparing the field (sometimes I would help) as he always did, setting field markers and getting equipment ready. Coach Arnold was sort of shocked to see me so early. He said, "Coach, is everything all right?" He didn't think I would show up for a while.

I told him that this was the most important night of football for the program I had brought to Tri-Central. I told Coach Arnold that if we could not find a way to win in this game, it would be difficult to gain the confidence of the players, the student body, and the community. I truly believed this one night would define the direction of the program, and whether I would be able as head coach to get this program going in the right direction. One other sad note: this group of boys had never been a part of winning a home game since they had become high-school players.

After we finished preparing the field, we went into our office and sat down and began discussing our game plan. It was an extremely hot August evening, and I knew that would be an important issue late in the game. We needed to make sure the boys continued to be hydrated all evening. I told him that we would not wear football pads and helmets during pregame to keep players cooler; we would put the equipment on right before we went out to play.

We talked about what we wanted to do offensively. I was giving him total control to run the offense. By now it was around 4:30 p.m., and the other coaches and players were starting to arrive.

As I had dictated, the locker room was quiet. The before-game and after-game team direction was coached to the players the same as the offensive and defensive plays. This season, I wanted to make sure that from this year forward, there would be continuity, routine, focus, and unity each and every Friday evening. The boys seemed much more focused as they arrived. I told them that we were going out in T-shirts and shorts during pregame. They were a little shocked, but they accepted what their coach was asking. We took the field with our specialty players who went through a brief warm-up and began punting, kicking, and returning—all pregame fundamental work—while the quarterbacks warmed up their arms.

As we were working, the Taylor specialty players arrived on the field with their coaches and started working also. At 6:00 p.m. our linemen joined the workout, and now we were in full swing toward preparation for the game. When the Taylor linemen arrived to start their warm-up with the rest of their team, some of their players were already starting to taunt our players. I told the boys to keep their mouths shut and continue to focus on our objective. Our team did as I wished, as it was easy to see that I was in no mood for us to get involved in a war of words.

We finished our pregame and headed to the locker room. I noticed that we already were getting quite a large group of spectators coming into the stadium. Some were moving to our bleachers, but Taylor's fans were showing up in numbers, too.

In the locker room, you could hear a pin drop. The boys had never been this focused during my brief tenure. Once dressed, every boy was in a chair waiting quietly. All of my coordinators discussed last-minute directions and expectations.

I came into the locker room in front of the boys and told them, "Let us all go to one knee, touch someone, and thank God for this great opportunity to play this great game of football tonight." We prayed the Lord's Prayer together. The boys sat back down as I gave my last minute motivational remarks before we took the field.

Boys, I am very proud of you and your commitment thus far this season. We have prepared since May for this game. There is nothing in any of our lives for the next three hours more important than this game. You have been prepared, and it is up to you now to stay focused, play together, and hit Taylor. It all comes down now to you. I believe in you as I believe in our coaches and our community. What I need from you is for us to be able to coach you at half time. Don't allow this game to get out of hand so we will have a chance to win in the fourth quarter. Good luck! Play hard! Hit! Stay focused! And remember to HIT!

At this point we left the locker room, organized two lines of players, and began toward the field. As I have always done throughout my career, I led the boys to the field in the middle, talking loudly all the way. I said, "It is a beautiful night. Look at this crowd of people who have come out to watch you, it's *Friday Night Lights* at its best. This is what you have prepared for. Make sure your chin strap is snapped, your belt is tight, and your focus is strong. No stupid penalties. Play disciplined, and hold onto the stupid ball!" With this final remark, I told them to take the field.

They took the field with new confidence, and I felt they were ready to make us better. At half time, we were ahead in a close game. The game had been difficult for both teams. The heat was horrible. We had worked the boys very hard in two-a-days. I felt confident that they would be in better shape than Taylor, and it became apparent by the end of the first half. At half time, all the coaches worked hard coaching up the players.

In my second year at Tri-Central, I had turned over all facets of coordinating the game to my assistants. I talked briefly with Coach Arnold, the offensive coordinator, Coach Perez, the defensive coordinator, and Coach Tolle, the special-teams coordinator and our offensive-line coach. Each coach spoke to the team about assignments and our plan for the second half. When all the coordinators were done, we had little time left. I just got the boys up and said, "Let's go out and finish this thing we started."

The second half was close until the fourth quarter, just as I had thought. Taylor, I felt, had better athletes than us but less discipline, and they were not in very good physical condition.

The game was close, and our quarterback broke loose with five minutes left in the game, which put us up 27–13, and we won. Our crowd acted as if we had won a championship. The student body came rushing to the field, and our boys did not know what to do.

I had prepared them numerous times for after-game protocol. They were to shake hands with our opponent, followed by going in front of our home stands and singing the school song. They would ring our victory bell and finally huddle in the end zone with a final prayer together. At that point they could visit family or head to the locker room. If we lost, we would shake hands and head to the end zone for a prayer.

I don't think discussing a game right after it is over has any merit. I did not yell at boys after a loss, we just said our prayer and got to the locker room. In the locker room after a loss, I would shake hands with every boy who played. I told each of them how much I cared about them and how proud I was of them.

But tonight, we had this huge win, and the chaos was unbelievable. I kept quiet and watched as everything was transpiring around me. I watched the coaches, who were as excited as the players, I watched the parents, who were extremely proud of their boys, and I listened to a crowd of students chanting a chant that I still hear today from that win: "WE BELIEVE!"

The rest of the season did not fare as well. The 2010 team won one more game during week eight before losing in the first round of the playoffs, ending our season with a 3–7 record.

The impact of the season was clearly that we did get better. I set a goal for the team before the season, and the boys achieved it. The team played somewhat closer to opponents and played harder and longer. It was clear to me that we were heading in the right direction—or so I thought at the time. Now we needed to get more boys in the weight room routinely during the off-season, and perhaps the 2011 season could be the change in direction I was hoping to see. The good news was that one of our halfbacks, who also played linebacker, emerged as a junior as the type of leader the team needed.

Corbin became a better player each time he took the field. He had just completed his first year playing high-school football. Corbin was an outstanding athlete with outstanding leadership potential. His family was one of our large agricultural families in the community. His parents were very supportive and expected their son to be respectful and show character, and he represented himself and family well all season. Corbin was the first real leader for the program, the guy I would spotlight as the leader for the younger players to listen to, and I hoped the freshmen class would learn from him. The freshman class seemed to be the only class that truly liked one another. It was my intention to spend a great deal of time advising Corbin on how to be a team captain so a trickle-down effect might occur.

I felt that the sophomore class everybody told me when I arrived a year ago would be a great class was beginning to unravel. Several boys possessed talent in the class, but they played as individuals, and I didn't know if I'd be able to salvage the group or be faced with losing talented boys because of their unjustified personal agendas. The 2011 season would be the critical year for Tri-Central football and for me personally.

The third year at a school for any head coach is the most important year for the program they are attempting to develop. Year three is the buy-in year for the community, the parents, and the players. At this point, I was still struggling with numbers, commitment, and off-season preparation.

I am not a complicated man with incredible innovative skills when it comes to X's and O's. I believe in hard work, the untiring devotion to fundamentals, and the process of preparation. It is common for people to say the offense I teach is "old school," in that I run the Houston veer, which I have run from day one of my coaching career. Criticism of my offensive philosophy has always been that it is too basic and easy to defend. The irony of all this criticism is that my offense over the years has averaged over twenty-eight points a game. So, perhaps being old school isn't so bad. I have always been a run-first coach, and that will never change. People love to see the ball thrown around as it is more exciting to spectators. Ball control and execution have always been my focus on offense.

The 2011 season would be the year to see if the boys were going to buy into what I had been trying to sell them.

CHAPTER 5

2011—Now

Goal 2: Defeat Conference School—Week Four

It was the beginning of January 2011 when I decided it was time to begin preparation for the 2011 football season. I was anxious to open the weight room and begin workouts for the upcoming football season. It was also time to prepare calendars of practice times and expectations. I was set to begin my thirty-second year in coaching and my thirtieth year as a head coach.

It is hard to believe, but I have always looked forward to preparing for a season. I enjoy the daily challenge of fitness training. Their devotion to getting bigger, faster, and stronger in the off-season would determine how well our team would perform during the season. I knew that the 2011 season would be a pivotal year for our program, but success requires work and getting in the weight room. I would need to work with the boys to assist them in getting bigger, faster, and stronger. This will be a pivotal year, and I knew it was going to also be a difficult year.

The weight-room attendance really wasn't any better in early 2011 than it had been in past years, with the exception of the group of freshmen now considered to be sophomores in the program. That group of boys made few excuses, and for the most part they attended regularly.

Corbin, my senior leader whom I was counting on, broke his ankle and would not be able to lift most of the winter. The admirable thing about Corbin was that he still showed up to workouts. He became the consistent leader our team needed. He would talk to boys and encourage their pursuits of lifting and fitness goals, all while hobbling around, putting weights on bars and providing spots to his teammates. I saw something special in this young man and wished he had more time in the program.

The something I clearly saw was character. Corbin brought out the best in others due to his sound upbringing and his work ethic, which he developed working on his family's farm. I have always believed that young men who grow up on a farm with parents who have sound character and maintain high expectations develop the type of character athletics strives to achieve.

Thomas Jefferson once said, "Farmers are the most noble of creatures," and I truly believe it. I have coached a number of boys who have grown up on farms, and good character is often established as a result. These boys usually are the boys who are self-motivated and determined, and personify the sacrifice and will to overcome adversity that this great country has long been about.

I was approached by one of my upcoming juniors who had been a two-year starter, and he told me that he might be leaving. The boy was one of our starting running backs at six foot three and 210 pounds, and he started at defensive end. I was shocked. I asked what was going on, and he said that he was thinking about leaving Tri-Central and enrolling at Kokomo High School because of some issues at home. I tried to talk with him and convince him that I would be there for him if he needed to talk, but I said I would understand if he left. He eventually decided to transfer. With our depleted roster, it would be nearly impossible to replace such a quality athlete. It wasn't long after my running back/defensive end left that my starting offensive/defensive tackle for two years informed me that his family was moving to another state. At that point, I was starting to question my decision to take the job at Tri-Central. I am sure the boys could sense my displeasure with the way the off-season was unfolding. Before we had begun, the adversity was even greater than I had expected it would be, but we had to trust that hard work would help us overcome even the most difficult circumstances.

The good news was that the incoming freshmen were a class very similar to the sophomores. The freshman class had talent, speed, and most of all, they liked one another and worked well with the sophomores. About half of their class had committed to the weight room, so our numbers had grown from a handful to about fifteen boys lifting regularly. The numbers were not great, but they were better than they had been in previous years.

I set up a team meeting with parents in February. I was hoping to see all the boys who had signed up to play and hopefully some new boys interested in playing football. Instead, the night was a disaster. The meeting was scheduled for 6:30 p.m., and when it was time to start, most of the high-school football players from the year before were not present. There should have been twenty boys from the 2010 team at the meeting in addition to the incoming freshmen. Only eight players from the year before were seated with their parents. I counted freshmen players with their parents and came up with an additional eight players. I was outraged that only sixteen boys showed up when I was expecting over thirty. To add insult to injury, only four varsity starters from the season before were there. I could not hold back the anger. I have always been a guy to tell people what was on my mind, and sometimes that got me in trouble. I did not censor my outrage. I shared my frustration with those who were present. I discussed the issues that needed to be corrected if we were to achieve our goals of transitioning the Tri-Central football program to a culture of winning. I addressed the lack of commitment, respect, dedication, and plain human decency to the program and to me. I went on for around twenty minutes, telling them what I saw as the main problem at the school: a lack of commitment. Why do we do that? Why do we take our frustrations out on those who seem to care? I think the answer is simply that they need to know. They listened to my criticism, and they then had the option to share my concerns with those who were impairing the program's progress, or they could passively accept the current attitude with the understanding that positive change was not likely during their children's playing careers at Tri-Central. I handed out the calendars and shared what needed to be done if they were sincere about their aim to enact lasting positive change in our struggling program. After I finished, I thanked the parents and the athletes for coming. I did not apologize. They needed to understand the sacrifices that their coaches had made to make the minor improvements they had enjoyed thus far.

They also needed to understand that lasting positive change requires substantial commitment and discipline. Everyone wants to win. Few are willing to exert the effort necessary to actualize that desire.

As I looked around that room at all of the empty seats, I thought about how I had been driving thirty miles twice a day to the weight room, only to be greeted by a handful of boys who were willing to make the same sacrifice to achieve our team goals.

A team goal requires a team effort. Individuals must be willing to sacrifice their own desires and comfort in an effort to work for the welfare of the group. The team goal must be a priority. Athletes must understand that improvement starts with the individual but doesn't end there. To achieve any group goal, individuals must work to improve themselves as a means to improve the group. The collective improvement can only be accomplished if individuals are accountable for their own behaviors and the behaviors of those who share their goal. Weakness and excuses must be eliminated if we were to improve individuals with the end goal of improving the team. The stress of the lack of commitment and the "Oh, well" attitude was really angering me to a point where I obsessed about it the rest of the night. Winners accept responsibility, because acceptance of responsibility nullifies excuses. I had to get my athletes to understand that by accepting responsibility, each athlete could then understand his proficiencies and deficiencies as well as appreciate the progress that the program had made, while understanding that considerable work was necessary in order to transition Tri-Central to a truly successful program.

The following week I began confronting my players and asking why they were not at the meeting. I only talked to a few before I tired of their excuses. The excuses included "I didn't know"; "I forgot"; "I had already made other plans"; "I had homework to do"; and "I didn't have a way there." Despite all of their excuses, not one of them told me in advance that they would miss the meeting. The use of excuses to rationalize their lack of commitment had become so commonplace that the boys expected me to accept them as justifiable. The athletes knew I needed them to play and thought that allowed them to dictate their attendance. Most of them showed that they lacked the understanding of what constitutes a team and how a team becomes successful.

What could I do? The question echoed in my mind. Some of the boys had challenged me and the pursuit of the team goals. I have always refused to tolerate excuses, and there was no way that I was going to relax my expectations just because a few boys wanted to take the path of least resistance. Right before the start of seven-on-seven, I told the team that I no longer was interested in any excuses for missing workouts or meetings. From that point forward, their responsibility was to call before a schedule conflict to advise me that they were going to be absent. If not, they would experience a punishment so severe that they would not forget the value of accepting personal responsibility for their presence and punctuality. If I handled each situation independently, and they did not know the possible outcome, then the unknown punishment might give me the advantage to fix the problem that initially appeared unfixable. I also handed all discipline issues privately between the athlete and me. I would meet with them behind closed doors in my office, or if we were on the field, I would take them behind the field house where no one knew what was happening. The unknown can be a great tool. I would meet privately with them, if punishment was due, and punish their behavior. Then I would tell them that I was going back to practice; they should follow after I had made my way back to the team. I also advised them that they were not to talk about our meeting to anyone. If I found out that they discussed our private meeting with anyone, then they would be off the team immediately. This was done to keep the rest of the team unaware of what happened in a private meeting with their head coach. It also served to build a level of loyalty that we had not developed up to that point.

The need to hold private meetings with athletes who tried to defy me and disregard the team goals ended when the athletes fully understood that excuses would not be tolerated from anyone. Every member of the team would be accountable to himself and the team, and there would be no exceptions. Assistant coaches and athletes were unaware of what was said during my discipline meetings with individual players. The boys were beginning to realize that if Coach Gilbert started yelling, there was a good reason, and something needed to be fixed immediately. I tried not to orchestrate my outbursts with what was happening at practice. I think the boys realized my sincere passion for the game and my extreme commitment to fundamentals.

It is easy to work all the time in practice on schemes to win while slacking on fundamentals. I have never agreed with this approach. If we needed to run a play thirty times to get it right, then we ran the play thirty times. Any time there was an error with fundamentals, we corrected it, and the boys were beginning to realize that they must stay focused in practice as well as in games and do what they had been taught to do. That way, if something did not work schematically, they could rely on their fundamentals to avoid a potential disaster.

A coach can easily modify schemes during a game to counter the opponent's plan, but it is impossible to teach fundamentals quickly. Fundamentals require muscle memory, and that must be rehearsed through daily repetition.

The 2011 summer became problematic. We struggled to get athletes to seven-on-seven workouts, and the boys were still not totally committed to the weight room. We definitely had some outstand-ing young players, but not many. By the end of the summer, I was becoming more and more worried about our numbers.

On the Wednesday morning before the season was to begin, I met with Mr. Driggs, our principal, and Gary Rhew, our athletic direc-tor. I told them that we would have enough players to start the sea-son, but if we sustained many injuries, we would not be able to finish the season. In the past two seasons we'd had more injuries than I had experienced the last ten years at my last job. We had been forced to continually play young boys, we had been unsuccessful, our players did not work hard in the weight room during the off-season—all of that contributed to injuries.

It is more likely that coaches have players go down in games they are losing than in games they are winning. I told both of the administrators that I had had it. Obviously, none of the young men were willing to completely buy into what I was selling. Maybe that was an unfair statement. Perhaps some boys were buying in, but not enough. I told the administrators that I was frustrated and stressed out, and maybe it was time the school pursue another direction with-out me.

Mr. Driggs added, "George, if you are unable to make this work, then maybe it is time for us to make those tough decisions."

Mr. Rhew stated, "George, it's not you. This is a laid-back com-munity, and football has never received much attention. People will come to the games. We always have great gate receipts, even though we don't win. You have made a difference. The whole attitude of the football boys is different. We all see incredible things happening with the football program, and we all support you and the discipline you have brought to the program. Let's get started with the season, and if we need to cancel some games later in the season, then we will do it. One last thing—you are doing a great job, and we appreciate having you here."

I thanked both of them. Both men had been incredibly support-ive of everything I was doing in the football program. I really did not want to leave my profession after getting fired at Clinton Central and then coaching two years at Tri-Central with a 3–17 record. I have never given up, and I really did not want to give up at this point, but I was totally frustrated with the traditions that had found their home at Tri-Central. I had to come up with something quickly. Practice started in five days.

I decided it was time for a final plea to the boys. I called for a meeting of all lettermen. I asked the boys to meet me at the stadium bleachers. We met for the meeting on a Friday night. Sixteen boys showed up. I told the boys how pleased I was that they showed up, but we really needed to talk. I told them that I felt we could have a better season, it was realistically possible that we could achieve our goal of beating Clinton Prairie and possibly having the first winning season at Tri-Central in years. But we would not be able to get the job done if we didn't find a way to get more boys to play. I shared that I was at my wit's end. It was time for the true players of the program to step up and do their part. "You need to talk to your friends, boys in the community, and anyone who will listen to get more boys to come out and play at the start of practice on Monday. I will not accept boys after Monday, so you need to make it clear that they cannot wait and come out after most of the two-a-days are over and expect me to take them on the squad. They need to begin with you on Monday or not at all."

I made the meeting brief, and I made it clear that I was losing patience very quickly. I told them that they should talk about what I said among themselves. When I left, the boys were still sitting in the bleachers, talking. The problem of finding additional players was now in the hands of the team. The boys had been asked to develop a vested interest in the program.

On Monday, I arrived at practice early, as I had always done. It was important for me to get to school, get all equipment ready outside, and fix coffee for the coaches. I would then sit in a lawn chair and welcome players as they arrived. I had not heard from any of the boys since our meeting on Friday. I felt that nothing would change. We would have seventeen boys show up to start practice. As the boys began to arrive, something happened that gave me new hope and gave the boys a new sense of togetherness. As practice time drew close, we had twenty-seven boys ready to practice. Of the ten new players, all of them except two would stay in the program and become impact players over the next two seasons.

Practice went well during two-a-days for the first time in my three-year tenure. The boys seemed to have confidence and direction as they got in shape and learned what their coaches' expectations were. A senior boy, Corbin, brought everything together with his leadership. All the boys either liked Corbin or were afraid of him, so his presence drew attention. Corbin was never arrogant or nasty to any of the boys. He expected them to do no less than he did and stay focused all the time. It was easy to see that if the team could find success with Corbin as the team's leader, great things would lie ahead. If, as a team, we could continue to get better under Corbin's leadership, then the juniors would become better leaders, and the great class of sophomores would have a tradition of leadership to improve on. It seemed hard to believe, but I was starting to get excited again, and that excitement became visible to players and coaches alike. We seemed to be heading in a new, uncharted direction.

As the season quickly approached, it was evident that we would still be playing many young players. Our senior class had three varsity returners and two new players who would not be able to get on the field. The junior class had four boys, and three of them would be playing varsity. Therefore, we would have six seniors and juniors who could play on Fridays, leaving the rest of the varsity positions to younger players. We were going through what a lot of teams are faced with when interest levels and successful productivity on the field are low. Boys will play and lose interest so the team is consistently young, and when fourteen- to sixteen-year-old boys are expected to compete with seventeen- to nineteen-year-old boys, it creates an adverse effect, resulting in losses and injuries. This year would be a critical year. Success was paramount if I had any hope of keeping the younger players in the program all four years.

Tri-Central had been on a seven-year losing streak since the 2004 season, when the team went 6–4. Tri-Central had become over the years every school's dream homecoming. Mr. Rhew, the athletic director, again scheduled the Indiana School for the Deaf for our first game. We had an opening in our schedule, and as one might come to realize, everybody wanted to schedule Tri-Central for their first game. The Indiana School for the Deaf even thought this would be a great opportunity for them, as Tri-Central had the kind of track record that they felt they might be able to compete against. In 2010, the school was one of Tri-Central's three wins, but it was earned—not a blowout, by any means. This year was a blowout, and we were able to win rather easily, as our program seemed to have improved more than our opponents', who were still struggling.

The following week we played our closest rival, Taylor. Taylor had been our target game a year before. This year I made Clinton Prairie our target game; they were a higher-level opponent than Taylor. Our boys played outstandingly, and we were fortunate enough to shut them out, defeating the Taylor Titans 26–0. After competing two weeks into the season, our defense had yet to be scored on by our opponents' offense. The following week we played our first conference game and defeated Carroll in a closely contested game. Our defense played well in the victory. We were now 3–0, and people were starting to notice us for the first time.

This was the second season that Coach Perez had employed the 3–4 defense, and the results were starting to be impressive. Coach Perez is a quiet, confident man whom the boys really like to play for. Coach Perez was working with me to get the staff more knowledgeable on how to coach positions in the 3–4. We were not quite where we, the staff, needed to be. I could tell it was frustrating Coach Perez that the mistakes occurring during the games were directly due to individual position technique. I assured him that we would continue to grow. The coaches would get better as long as we didn't make things complicated and continued to address the fundamental adjustments that needed to be made. Coach Perez seemed to understand, and the progress in defense continued, even though our offensive progress outpaced the defense in 2011. When Coach Perez put in his 3–4 defensive, Mr. Rhew approved the order of a new seven-man sled. I told him the most important coaching aid necessary for us to become a more fundamental tackling and blocking team was the LEV sled. The sled cost $10,000, and I told Mr. Rhew that the football team would raise money to pay for it. I wanted the boys to gain ownership in the program. We would help pay about half of the cost before Mr. Rhew told me not to worry about the rest. I am not a coach who asks my athletic director for a great deal, and Mr. Rhew never turned me down on anything that I told him I needed to make the team better.

The sled became our greatest tool of instruction for both offense and defense. It was very apparent that defense was where the use of the sled led to the most noticeable progress. Our tackling drills on the sled emphasized hitting in the proper position, and our fundamental tackling skill at all levels of football was continually getting better.

The team was now 3–0, and it was Clinton Prairie week. Clinton Prairie, at the time, was a solid team, one that we had not beaten since 2004. The first year I coached at Tri-Central, Clinton Prairie scored on the first six times they touched the ball. It is important to know that those six touchdowns did not come from drives. They were first plays of drives. The night was embarrassing. Now we were going over to their field again, and this time they were our target team for 2011. They had scored ninety-seven points on us the last two meetings. Everything was riding on this game. By making Clinton Prairie our goal game for 2011, I was sending a message to our players that we needed to take our team to the next level of play. I knew there would be teams on the schedule that we were realistically not going to be able to defeat this season. I also knew that for us to have a winning season, we had to defeat Clinton Prairie.

All of the two-a-days up to week four had been focused on the game with Prairie. By game time, I felt very confident that we would at least have a chance to win. Offensively, we struggled some moving the ball, but we had two outstanding junior running backs who did what they had to do behind a sophomore line to score points. We won the game, thanks to an outstanding performance by our defense. Coach Perez had his defense ready for anything Prairie wanted to do, and Coach Tolle assisted him and motivated the offensive line to lead us to victory. When the clock ran down to zero, Tri-Central was now 4–0, defeating Prairie 21–12. The team had won their goal game for the second consecutive season, and the boys were gaining confidence in themselves and their coaches. People in the Tri-Central community were cautiously optimistic about the football team. The key was whether or not we would find two more victories to achieve that winning season and change our course forever. Our catchword for the season was NOW, and it was the most fitting catchword possible for the team to recognize that we did not have many tomorrows if we did not take care of business NOW! There was a new sense of preparation since the team was 4–0. Boys were coming to practice regularly all season, but the intensity was increasing. The coaching staff had been intact for two seasons, and the staff worked diligently in preparation. I don't know if we would have been able to be where we were without Coach Tolle. Coach Tolle is a mechanical engineer at Chrysler and coaches our offensive line, special teams and helps Coach Perez as the second most knowledgeable coach on staff as far as the 3-4 defense. Coach Tolle has the preparation along with the work ethic of a head coach and he constantly is looking for ways to help the team win. The competitive spirit of the coaching staff clearly had a positive influence with the chemistry of the team as they prepared to improve each week. Coach Tolle and Coach Perez were local heroes in the Tri-Central football program. These two men were key players when Tri-Central won its only sectional title in 1991. The men are best friends and have an exceptional knowledge of the game, but most important, they possess the ability to translate that knowledge so the players can use it. Week five was upon us, and we would be playing a new opponent at their school. It was their homecoming.

We beat Monroe Central and were 5–0 for the first time in school history. The following week was an exciting week with all the positive press from the newspapers. Everyone was truly thinking that we were on a roll to do something special. I knew that reality was about to settle in, as three of our last four games were against state-ranked teams with a history of success. Our next opponent would be Clinton Central, the school I coached at for twenty years. We lost our first game against Clinton Central and then went on to lose two more games heading into sectional. There was one bright spot during the second half of the 2011 season, and it occurred on October 8 when we defeated Wes Del High School to go 6–3 on the season. That win guaranteed us a winning season. A winning season was the ultimate goal all along, and the boys achieved it by working hard and becoming more of a family, a team, a unit. We lost to Clinton Central and to Sheridan by substantial margins—tough losses. The other loss was to Shenandoah, a ranked 2A team.

We entered the sectional thinking that we might have a chance to win our first sectional game in seventeen years. In Indiana, all schools are automatically in the tournament series, and each sectional is an open draw. We drew Lapel High School, who had finished their regular season with only one win. I told the boys that even though they had won only one game, they were a pretty good team and that their conference was extremely difficult. The game was incredibly physical, and we lost that night 25–14, effectively ending our season. However, our team had made monumental progress on their way to accomplishing many goals. We finished 6–4, we won our goal game, we produced the first winning season since 2004, but most of all, we became a team. Corbin, my senior linebacker/running back, led the team in a way that the younger players were willing to follow. The answer to player leadership was the most important thing that came out of the season for me. I knew at this point that we would have the possibility of doing some great things with the returning players in 2012. I felt if we could get them to take care of business during the off-season, get the boys into the weight room, and get them to attend all of our seven-on-seven workouts, perhaps 2012 could become a memorable year. I also knew that we could not afford to lose lettermen from the team as we had done in years past. The boys had to come back if we were going to get noticed. Everything would ride on the sophomore and freshmen classes. We would only have three seniors coming back in 2012, so it would depend on the leadership of the upcoming juniors to give the new team direction.

CHAPTER 6

2012—We Believe

Goal 3: Defeat Clinton Central—Week Six

The 2011 season was a success beyond the fact the team recorded the school's first winning season in seven years. A new level of intensity developed as the boys realized success for the first time in their high-school football experience. We had fewer attendance problems during the week, more team camaraderie, more focused play, and fewer injuries. We graduated three starters who did a great job leading and allowed our younger players to mature and understand the importance of leadership. The program was making strides forward, but we now needed to focus on the state-level teams and how we could raise our level to compete with them. The first two goals we met were games that we could win with discipline and fundamentals. We now needed to set as our goal was a team that had dominated us year in and year out for over twenty-five years: Clinton Central.

The Clinton Central program was one that I knew very well. During my long tenure as head coach at Clinton Central, Tri-Central was only able to score five wins. When I first arrived at Clinton Central, the program was in a state similar to that of Tri-Central. In 1988 when I met with the board of Clinton Central, one member told me that if I did not find a way to jumpstart the program, I would be the last football coach at Clinton Central. The fix there was similar, but not identical.

Starting out in 1988, I had a talented sophomore group of athletes, a group of motivated parents, and a community wanting to see their football program improve. At Clinton Central, the weight room became the first focus, and the boys and their parents responded. At Clinton Central, winning came fast. The first year we went 5–6 and never looked back. The weight room was always packed, and the team won weight-lifting tournament after tournament.

The first year (2009) that I coached at Tri-Central was my second year away from the Clinton Central program. Tri-Central ended up playing Clinton Central twice that year—once in a conference game, and the second time during the first round of the tournament series. They beat us twice by a combined score of 130–7. They embarrassed my new program, and they definitely embarrassed me. The puzzling part of all of it was that I had coached the Clinton Central boys since they were little boys. Their arrogance and trash-talking during the games was hurtful. Clinton Central went on that year to win the school's first regional title but lost in the semi-state game. The interesting fact is that when I left, the boys' discipline and direction changed. I think that was part of why the school felt there needed to be a change. I believe my expectations had grown tiresome to the parents, and I imagine to the athletes as well. The weight room at Clinton Central changed drastically. The school invested in new equipment and a new weight program for the boys. Interestingly enough, though, the boys stopped being committed to lifting weights, and there wasn't a demanding coach driving the boys to lift. That would give Tri-Central a window of opportunity. The other key factor was that the coach who replaced me moved on, and Clinton Central would have a new head coach starting the 2012 season.

Clinton Central was returning a junior class of outstanding football athletes. The boys had been successful at all levels of football up to that point. The team was coming off a solid 8–3 record and looked to be in position for another great season.

The two key factors that I was hoping would give us an advantage were their lack of off-season preparation and a new coach. I felt we were returning a great group of young men with a strong junior class of leaders and a sophomore class that worked well with the juniors. The incoming freshman class was also excellent. There were four good freshmen who would work into the lineup at some point and help us be successful. The senior class had only three boys left. This was the class that everyone in the community felt would change the course of Tri-Central football. Of the three boys playing as seniors, all of them would contribute and do a terrific job in 2012. Two of the boys were running backs and extremely gifted, but they did not totally commit to the We Believe motto we had set for 2012. The other senior boy did commit to the motto and would present a strong presence on the field but had a quiet personality. The boys really cared a great deal for A.J., and although A.J. never spoke up much, he played hard in practice and games. A.J. earned the respect of the entire team and was well liked. The other two seniors did a great job on Friday night and wanted to lead but lacked that little something to get everybody to buy into their leadership.

The true leaders of the team surfaced—the juniors. The juniors would listen to the seniors and keep the team going in the direction it needed to go.

I had decided to turn the weight room over to my special-teams coach in the early spring. I set up a series of meetings with Coach Hatcher and went over the program that we were using, and he was very receptive. Coach Hatcher also coached basketball, and the head basketball coach also became committed to the weight program we were teaching. Tri-Central now had the football and basketball programs using the same weight program, and that would be incredibly important. Coach Hatcher and Coach Zahn (the basketball coach) were young coaches in their early thirties. They both were extremely motivated and driven. It was very difficult for me to step back and allow someone else to run the weight room—I had been doing it for over thirty years—but it would come to be one of my best decisions as head football coach. The two coaches who took over had my demanding personality, but because they were younger, they were able to better motivate the guys to show up and complete workouts.

Coach Hatcher was the only member of the football staff who actually worked at Tri-Central. To have both of these outstanding men as members of the teaching staff, interacting with the boys every day and demonstrating great character, provided the necessary leadership to motivate the boys to get into the room and lift. I would still make my appearances, but I would be careful not to undermine their authority and leadership in the weight room.

For the first time, Tri-Central had most of the boys lifting weights and getting stronger. The weight room was where the boys got bigger, faster, and stronger while working together. The camaraderie, the routine, the discipline, and the commitment toward getting better together gave the athletes a vested interest in success that would accentuate our 2012 theme, We Believe.

I met with the coaching staff in late January 2012 to discuss our upcoming season, review our playbook, and listen to off-season concerns from the coaches. As a staff, we got along very well. I have always believed it is better to get to work and get done so we all can spend time with our families. I have always tried to have an agenda when meeting with coaches so the meeting flowed, and nothing that needed to be discussed was omitted.

The first thing on my agenda was to let the coaches know that Coach Hatcher had taken over my duties in the weight room. I explained my reasoning and shared that he was doing a great job. My next course of business was defense and the defensive playbook changes. I asked Coach Perez to take over and discuss his concerns and what changes he felt needed to be added to the playbook. Coach Perez was always well prepared, and it was clear that he had spent a great deal of time reviewing game tapes. Coach Perez talked primarily to staff members about how we needed to improve our teaching techniques and the expectations for our position coaches. He pointed out problems in practice organization as well as individual player technique. I told Coach Perez that I would be more than willing to adjust our teaching times accordingly to meet his expectations. The coaches asked questions. Coach Perez wanted more time for pursuit drills. He believed that if we made pursuit drills a priority, our defense, which was already pretty fast, would become faster. He told me that he was considering incorporating some different pass coverages in the playbook. I told him all changes must be completed by the end of March, and he just smiled and said he would have them to me if he decided to add them to his defensive playbook. Coach Perez also said that I needed to get our inside linebackers to read their keys better and get to their assigned holes according to the slant faster. I never felt threatened, and I was in complete agreement with him.

This is an example of a great staff. When coaches don't feel threatened, talked down to, or belittled, everything flows well. Our coaching staff was very loyal to one another, and the respect we all had for each other was evident to players, parents, fans, and anyone else who came in contact with us. This was an ideal environment, because the coaches could worry about the important things, like helping young men become the best they can be.

Next on the agenda was offense, and I knew there was going to be some lively discussion about proposed changes to the offense that I had been running for thirty-four years. The offensive coaches were ready to challenge me about possible changes. The two coaches who led the way were Coach Arnold, our offensive coordinator, and Coach Tolle, our offensive line coach. First, they wanted to add a midline series to our offense. After some discussion, I felt that would be a good addition and OK'd it. Then Coach Tolle wanted me to revamp the blocking schemes on all plays to be consistent with teaching terminology. This would be a major redo of our playbook, but he told me that he would help me. After some discussion, I agreed to the changes; it was probably time for my playbook to get out of the twentieth century and into the new millennium. As I was trying to digest all the change they were requesting, I saw them look at each other, and there was a hesitation right before Coach Arnold began to speak.

He said, "Coach, I would like to implement a new way to name offensive pass plays and adjust our passing tree to go along with the new terminology."

I said, "What? Are you serious?"

He said that he was, and then Coach Tolle spoke up and agreed that the way we currently titled pass plays was confusing for his offensive linemen. I said that I did not know if I wanted to make such a monumental change to a game-tested system that I recognized and felt comfortable with. The discussion continued for twenty to thirty minutes. I finally saw that I was losing the battle. I told them that we would need to compromise. I said I would enter their new system but leave my system available to make the transition for me a little slower. They agreed and told me that they would help me prepare the changes for the playbook. This was another very important move on my part. If I was going to continue to expect my coaches to have a vested interest in the program, the playbook needed to no longer be mine, but ours. They worked with me to create the changes they wanted, and it was difficult for the boys for a while. Change is always difficult. Everyone enjoys feeling comfortable, but sometimes being comfortable is a way to become complacent, and there was no way I wanted that to happen. The last thing we talked about was player personnel. I said that I would have a meeting in March and I hoped that athletes and parents would attend. I did not want another off-season meeting like we had had the year before. Everyone left the meeting in good spirits and knowing what they had to do to get ready for spring and seven-on-seven competition.

I was extremely stressed out about our March preseason meeting. The day of the meeting I was worried about how I would handle a lackluster gathering, and whether or not I would be able to keep my composure, which is something I did not do the year before. When I arrived at school for the meeting, I did not realize there was a junior high basketball makeup game going on. I thought to myself, *Well, I won't have any eighth graders at the meeting. Isn't that great!*

I went to the cafeteria and set up my paper work to hand out to the boys and parents. It was thirty minutes before the meeting, and I was there by myself. The parents and athletes at Tri-Central seem to be a late crowd at everything, and it was hard for me to get used to that. At Clinton Central, I usually had an early crowd to all meetings.

The meeting was to start at 6:30 p.m., and it was now 6:20 p.m. The mother of one of my athletes came running in and said, "Coach, the doors are all locked and everybody is waiting outside." She went over to the outside door by the cafeteria and opened it. I could not believe how many people were waiting outside. Parents and athletes came pouring into the cafeteria (well, pouring in for us). Parents of the eighth-grade boys who were still playing basketball came, and their sons arrived after their game was finished. I was truly excited.

We had a great meeting, and everyone was excited about the upcoming season. I had forgotten how meetings should be, since this was my first real positive meeting experience at Tri-Central. We were finally starting to resemble a quality football program, and it was exciting. Boys were lifting weights, people were talking about football, participation was up, and those who played in 2011 were coming back. We had a great team meeting. There was a moms' club meeting to find ways to add to their sons' season, and it looked like people in the community were buying into We Believe.

At the beginning of April, I had finished my playbook updates, got them approved by staff, and had the 2012 Tri-Central playbooks ready to hand out. The only real changes the coaches were planning to implement were offensive. The new pass-numbering system was going to be difficult for me; I had used the same pass-numbering system my whole career. A pass-numbering system is a way of calling in plays using a passing tree with specific receiver routes defined by a number. The major change was that we were going to have the opportunity to change a route—or all routes—on any of our plays. We now would be able to adjust a route instantaneously instead of having to take time to instruct on the sidelines during a game. It truly was a great idea but one I really was struggling with.

In late April, we had our first seven-on-seven workout. When I started at Tri-Central, I designated Mondays as the night I would like to work with the athletes whom I share with other coaches. That way it simplifies the organizational time for everyone. The problem was that spring sports were going on, and athletes in track and base-ball had games on Monday evenings. It became somewhat of an unavoidable inconvenience. Our numbers were still good, and when the track and baseball boys could make it, they did. The first seven-on-seven practice was spent on learning the new passing system. It was important for Coach Arnold to feel comfortable coordinating the offense. Some of the boys were receptive, but others started making little comments under their breath about the new pass-route system.

It was very important that I set the standard on the new system immediately and not tell the boys how I really felt about the change. I backed the new system and told them I did not want to hear negative comments. "This is a done deal," I told them, "and you will need to learn your responsibilities and numbering system for us to continue to get better as a team." I told them that this would allow a great deal more freedom for coaches to adjust quickly between plays in an effort to orchestrate a game-changing pass route during a game. The boys listened to me and immediately began to focus. Nothing more was said. I would continue to feel uncomfortable with our route-numbering system, not because I didn't understand it, but rather because I was comfortable with my original system.

I think this is one of the difficult tasks facing head coaches. Making fundamental changes must be well-thought-out, and those changes, when implemented, must remain consistent, or a message is being sent to athletes that coaches are indecisive. I still struggled with the change offensively, although the decision to alter our pass-route structure was one of the best decisions I made at Tri-Central for our players, coaches, and program.

The seven-on-seven season for us began at the start of June. The boys were lifting weights, and we would meet on our designated night to scrimmage. We set up scrimmages with Marion High School and Maconaquah High School, both of which are larger schools than Tri-Central. Each Monday our coaches and athletes showed up to play. The coaches wanted to also implement an eleven-on-eleven thud scrimmage. I was apprehensive about doing that but ultimately agreed as an opportunity to involve our linemen. I really grew to enjoy the eleven-on-eleven scrimmages.

They allowed us to put a full team on the field. I felt the greatest impact of the eleven-on-eleven scrimmages was defensive. Coach Perez was able to work all summer on pursuit, and the boys continued to work hard at pursuing faster. We had a great turnout all summer long and became very competitive with the larger schools.

During the course of the summer, our quarterback, Cody, started to understand football and his role as the quarterback of the team. Cody would have two outstanding senior running backs in 2012 and a big fast offensive line. It was clear that we were going to be a run-first team, and he needed to work hard at running the offense and being able to exercise the play-action pass.

Cody was a true student of the game. He had an outstanding GPA, and he was highly competitive. Cody wanted to win in all the sports he participated in, and he was eager to learn what he needed to learn in order to become better. The problem facing the team was that we were one lineman short. We had boys, but I needed for someone to step up, or I would have to move an athlete from a skill position to right tackle.

I was told by my juniors that one of the boys in their class who played as a freshman wanted to come back out. They wanted to know if I would allow him to play. I told them that he should come out and meet with me; from that discussion I would make up my mind. They were all fine with that, since I was going to at least meet with him.

The boy met with me in July. His name was Josh. Josh had played in the backfield and also played some receiver. Josh was five foot six and weighed 150 pounds. Josh walked into my office, and I asked him to sit down. Josh apologized for not playing his sophomore year. He told me that he really wanted to be back on the squad.

I always try to be candid with my athletes and not build any false hope. I think one of the true injustices in athletics is when coaches tell a boy one thing and then do something different. Josh was a hard-nosed, tough young man, and I did have a plan for him if he would buy into it. I told Josh that I was glad he wanted to come back and that I did have a position for him if he was interested.

Josh said, "Coach, I will play anywhere. I just want back on the team."

I told Josh that I needed an offensive tackle. In my offensive system, tackles need to first be able to run, and second to not be afraid of contact. The guards needed to be big, but not the tackles. I told him one of the best tackles that I had coached was similar to him in size. I said that he would have to give us a total commitment and work incredibly hard, but our team would be good, and if he was able to fill the right tackle position and do well, the team might be one of the best teams in the school's history.

Josh told me if that was what it would take for him to get on the field, then he would give me all he had. I was confident after our meeting that Josh would live up to his commitment. I have always had that special ability to recognize when a boy is being genuine with me, and I truly felt at that moment this boy would be the missing piece of the offensive puzzle.

Practice officially began on Monday, July 30, 2012. We had the largest team turnout during my tenure, with thirty-one boys present and ready to prepare for the season. I changed the format of practice in 2012, because most of the staff work outside of the school. Only one other coach besides me was employed as a teacher. Although we had similar schedules, I didn't teach at Tri-Central. We went with an afternoon schedule that basically ran from 3:30 p.m. until 9:30 p.m. each evening. Our numbers were not great, but they were better. The major difference was the quality of athletes we had to work with. We would have three strong athletic classes filled with boys who possessed great character. Our senior class that so many in the community thought would be the largest and most outstanding group to come through only had three boys left. The three boys in the senior class were outstanding athletes. It was just unfortunate that we had lost ten members along the way to either quitting or moving away.

One of the seniors would become the stable member of the class and do an outstanding job all season keeping the team on track. One of the seniors became self-absorbed, and he continued to try my patience all season long as a reminder of the type of athlete I had first worked with when I arrived. He was an outstanding player and a really neat boy at times, but other times he would be extremely narcissistic and question decisions that were intended to improve the team, not just individuals. The third boy had incredible athletic talent. His greatest drawback was motivation. The boys liked and respected him. The problem would develop when the two outstanding running backs would bicker over little things and then pout. It would eventually come down to the juniors taking the leadership role of the team. The one quiet boy led and worked well with the juniors, and the juniors gradually assumed ownership of the team.

As the team continued to practice through two-a-days, there was a growing feeling among the players and coaches that our team might be special. As practice continued into the second week, we continued to discuss our goal for the season. Tri-Central had had very little success against Clinton Central over the years. Clinton Central had outscored us in three years by a score of 223–40 in four games. We were unable to compete with them at all. The last meeting in 2011, where we went 6–4 during the season and were undefeated going into the Clinton Central game, they defeated us 40–13. For over thirty years, Clinton Central football was at a higher level than Tri-Central. This season they had a strong, athletic team coming back, but with a new coach. If our football team could compete with Clinton Central, much less beat them, it would provide us the knowledge that we could compete at the state level in the Indiana class-A division. We also would need to contend with being Clinton Central's homecoming and play on their field. The homecoming issue was not as great a problem; being as bad as Tri-Central football had been for so long, we were everybody's homecoming.

Practice was extremely focused during two-a-days, and attendance was outstanding. We were able to keep injuries to a minimum, and no injury was serious. Each day we were better than the day before. Coach Perez was now in complete control of the defense. None of the boys would look at me anymore when he said something. He controlled every aspect of our defensive system from organizing practice to yelling at players if that needed to happen. Coach

Perez's personality is such that he never has been much of a yeller, but when he becomes angry, he has the complete attention from everyone.

During two-a-days, we devoted a great deal of practice time to team pursuit drills. I mandated from the time we put our sled together that we would have team sled time every practice to work on the fundamentals of hitting, and now that commitment had been extended, on the request of Coach Perez, to include pursuit drills. When the ball was snapped, our players looked as if they had been shot out of a cannon. Coach Perez emphasized the concept of eleven men on the ball. It became clear during two-a-days that the boys were beginning to believe that they could be outstanding defensively.

Offensively, Coach Arnold is also in complete control at the start of the 2012 season. Coach Arnold is more of a yeller than Coach Perez, but his yelling is always purposeful and precipitated by a lack of focus or our athletes not working toward their potential. Coach Arnold is an extremely polite man to the boys, parents, and the other coaches. He has a quiet reassuring demeanor, as long as the boys are learning and working hard. He will give them many opportunities to fix problems, but when all else fails, Coach Arnold has no problem getting the boys attention, and usually the level of offensive practice goes up immediately. The reason I mention this is because often coaches rant and rave all the time, and boys struggle to differentiate what is real from what is being orchestrated. It has always been very clear that when our coaching staff is upset, it is real, and things need to get fixed immediately. Coach Arnold also gained the right of full control as a coordinator. He has a passion for the game that has become contagious to our players. He is an outstanding coordinator because he not only has all the boys very focused, but he listens very closely to Coach Tolle, our line coach.

As the line coach, Coach Tolle has the most difficult task of all the coaches. Jason Tolle is from the area and played at Tri-Central. Coach Tolle continued his playing career at college and earned a degree in mechanical engineering. He currently works at Chrysler Corporation in Kokomo. Four years ago, Coach Tolle had just seven boys to work with during the 2010 season, and in 2012 he had enough boys to have a first and second team, along with a partial third team. He not only works wonders for our offensive line, he is also close friends with Coach Perez, and he contributes greatly toward our defensive successes. Coach Arnold and Coach Tolle have a special relationship and work well together. I think they sometimes conspire together when they wish to change or adjust something in our offense before presenting their ideas to me. The neat thing is they do bring their wishes to me, and they are always prepared, because they know I often am conservative and do not wish to change game-tested strategies.

During the 2012 season, our offense underwent major reconstruction, and perhaps the changes were long overdue. The best decision that I made in 2012 was to allow these men to make the necessary changes to maximize the potential of our current athletes.

The last phase of the game that I still controlled was our special teams. In 2012, I decided to move the newest member of our coaching staff to special-teams coordinator. Coach Hatcher had already taken over my leadership role in the weight room and was doing a great job. I decided to give him more ownership as our special-teams leader.

Coach Hatcher is young, and it is refreshing to see a young coach so diligent at his job. He spends a great deal of time scheming and watching film to put our players in the best possible position on special teams. Special teams often do not get the time needed to prepare, but big games are won or lost by the effectiveness of special-teams play.

Coach Hatcher also approached me with ideas that he wanted to try, but I was less receptive in 2012. I based my reluctance to alter the special-team schemes on my decades of experience. I wanted him to start with what I had established on special teams. I was hopeful that he would systematically and with sound reasoning approach me with his ideas of change. I assigned Coach Kennedy to assist him because special-team preparation is time-consuming, and coaches often do not get the amount of time during practice to work out any issues with drills or fundamental work. This means that they need to be prepared at practice to be able to get done what needs to be rehearsed. Coach Kennedy and Coach Hatcher handle our technology needs as well as our receivers on offense and our defensive backs on defense. Coach Kennedy does a little of everything for the program and performs every duty with the passion necessary to ensure success.

As we prepared for the 2012 season, the question was what role I would fulfill. I had given up the defense to Coach Perez and Coach Hunter, our defensive line coach. I had given up the offense to Coach Arnold and Coach Tolle. And I had given up special teams to Coaches Hatcher and Kennedy. My role would be to organize practice daily in such a way that my coordinators remained content with the amount of time and attention their position specialty received. I would be responsible for keeping practice moving and making sure we did not deviate from the predetermined schedule. I would be responsible for talking to parents when necessary. I would talk to all media. It was my responsibility to make difficult game decisions pertaining to schemes or strategy. And finally, I would make sure that every coach and player had enough responsibility and pride in fulfilling their responsibility so that every single person involved with the program understood that their vested interest began with their contribution for the betterment of the entire team. If we encountered failure, it was my duty to accept it, since I was ultimately the one responsible for the direction of the program.

I have always believed that true leadership needs to be available when it is needed, not arrogantly displayed. I never talk negatively about our boys when we lose a game. I take full responsibility. The boys play a game that they love. The last thing they need when things go badly is a coach placing blame. There is a time to be critical. Right after a loss is the wrong time, as far as I am concerned. The critical analysis usually will take place during Saturday morning film sessions. That critical analysis is centered on playing the game and never to project blame or disrespect.

I feel a team loses for several reasons. The first possible reason is that they are outmanned. There is not much a coach can do about this during the season; this issue must be dealt with during the off-season in the weight room and speed training. The second potential reason deals with fundamentals. That reason should always be blamed on the coach. It is the responsibility of the coach to ensure necessary repetitions during practice to develop muscle memory and mental reps so that during the game, the athletes can anticipate what will happen during the course of a play and respond accordingly. The third potential reason is mental. This is the most difficult to fix. We had been working on this phase of the game at Tri-Central, but it was a work in progress. As the season approached, it became clear that our mental game was the best it had ever been, and our boys were faster, stronger, and more fundamentally sound, and they truly believed in one another and our focus. Our primary focus was the Clinton Central game, which was week six of the season. The hope was that by then, we would be at our very best.

As the season unfolded, we came out strong and fast. We had duplicated the 2011 season through five games by winning all of them. Those five victories were decisive this season, though. Our offense was averaging over forty points a game, and our defense was giving up fewer than two touchdowns per game. Our quarterback entered the season with a year and a half of experience, and due to some changes in fundamental technique, he was getting more confidence and skill each week. Cody could throw the ball very well, even though we were a run-oriented team.

Coach Perez (our defensive coordinator) was also our quarterback coach, and he had wanted for two years to change our quarterback pitch technique. I had continued to fight him on that aspect of our offense, but that season I decided to allow the change. I told Coach Perez that if we had fumbles or bad pitch incidents, I would hold him directly responsible, and he agreed. Again, the change would be a critical adjustment toward our team having more success.

Cody responded well to Coach Perez's instruction. Cody was running our split-back veer offense very well, and we were scoring frequently. On a side note, I remember when I first came to Tri-Central, our fans would get excited when we were able to get a first down.

Now that we were scoring, it had changed a loyal fan base to an excited fan base.

Defensively, our team was playing extremely well. The boys were practicing with a new level of intensity and playing together. We were not a great team yet, but if the players continued to work hard and stay focused, our defense would put us in a position to have a memorable season.

One of the criticisms leveled against our success from people involved in social media was that our schedule was relatively weak. People forgot too easily that we had been considered a weak program. I had strong feelings about the criticism of strength of schedule.

First, I think it is unfair to label any program as weak. It is difficult enough to practice day in and day out only to go out and lose a game. It takes a great deal of character to keep fighting the good fight and working on changing the direction of a program. Most schools do not have the luxury of selecting different opponents because schedules are locked in according to conference contracts and travel time. Football is a sport that becomes a nightmare for athletic directors because teams only play once a week, and each has a limited number of games. I don't understand why people cannot just be excited when teams are doing well and cheer the efforts of those who are striving to improve. Tri-Central had defeated former focus opponents two years in a row, and now those teams that had made it their job to beat up Tri-Central were considered weak by our critics.

Clinton Central came into our game with a record of 3–2, losing to two top-ranked teams in Indiana. To add to the drama, Clinton Central had made the Tri-Central game their homecoming. The talk all week was how Clinton Central was going to flex and show that Tri-Central was not worthy of being considered a good football program. Clinton Central had several outstanding performers on their squad, and it became even more personal when they played against their old coach. There had never been any taunting or needless rhetoric. The Clinton Central boys had been very respectful the last couple of years, although I would never forget the first year. We played them twice, and the boys were nasty.

Their coaches allowed them to run up a score in two games of 130–7. I wanted Tri-Central to defeat Clinton Central after all that had transpired, but it would be unfair to pull boys from Clinton Central and Tri-Central into unnecessary drama. Sometimes getting even has a bittersweet effect, and I wanted the boys to focus only on the game and the importance of going out and playing to the best of their abilities. I have always separated the classroom from the athletic field. I have always taken my responsibility as an educator seriously, and I continued to give Clinton Central students my very best daily. I do believe the athletic field is an extension of the classroom but must be kept separate, and the boys at Clinton Central respected my separation. Students at Clinton Central would simply not talk about football during week six when we played each other.

The week seemed to go fast while preparing for Clinton Central, and the boys were as focused as I had seen them during my tenure. Everything seemed to be in place, and now it was time for the boys to go out and execute the plan we had prepared for them.

It was finally Friday, the day that we had prepared for all season. In 2010, our focus game was week two, and in 2011 our focus game was week four. We had two more weeks of preparation for our game with Clinton Central, and we were fortunate to get through the first five weeks undefeated. The game's importance became magnified because Clinton Central was a well-established program, and winning the game might quiet some of those who felt our team did not deserve much of the positive press we had been receiving.

The boys arrived at the field house at 4:00 p.m. We planned to have a brief meeting to go over our objectives before we left at 4:30 p.m. All the coaches arrived by 4:15. There would be another obstacle other than Clinton Central facing us this evening—the weather. Coach Tolle had the Weather Channel popped up on his cell phone, and it looked as if a storm was headed straight through Clinton County, with a possible arrival time of around 6:30 p.m. We had our meeting, and the boys were extremely focused and ready for the journey ahead of them. Clinton Central is located about thirty minutes due west of Tri-Central, and as we headed toward the school, it became apparent that the weather could become an issue. Rain is one thing, but lightning is another, and the Weather Channel display looked like the storms moving in were littered with lightning. It was a hot September evening with ominous clouds overhead. The boys' determination didn't waver as we pulled into the parking lot. They were prepared. All they had to do was execute and finish.

The boys got dressed, and we headed to the field for pregame activity. Our pregame process is rather generic. We take the special-teams specialty players, quarterbacks, and receivers out at an hour and twenty minutes before game time. Boys warmed up. We were finishing up the first segment of pregame drills, and our linemen were walking to the field when the first flares of lightning became visible to the north. The linemen joined the team, and we circled up for warm-ups. Just then, the sky opened up with crashing lightning. We immediately sent the boys to the locker room with the coaches to see what was going to happen. We planned to play if at all possible. I went to find Mr. Rhew, our athletic director, so we could meet with Clinton Central officials to put together a plan. The rain came and left and came back, but the lightning did not seem to stop. Finally, after a long wait, we all decided it was best to play the game on the following day. I went in and told the team, and they were visibly upset because everyone was ready to play. Now we would wait one more day to find out where our program was and where we might be headed.

The game was scheduled for 6:00 p.m. the following evening. It truly was an outstanding early fall afternoon, and the weather was expected to cooperative. We arrived at Clinton Central around 4:30 p.m., did our normal pregame, and then headed back to the locker room to relax briefly before the game.

In the locker room, Coach Hatcher usually meets with the team first to go over special-team assignments. He is followed by Coach Perez who gives the boys his last minute instructions. Coach Arnold follows Coach Perez and discusses offensive strategies and always gives the boys a small but deliberate pep talk. I usually allow some dead time before I approach the team. I have coaches who control all facets of the game for us. My primary function is to motivate before a competition and make sure the boys are in the proper mind-set when they leave the locker room. My pregame motivational messages differ greatly, depending on variables presented upon arrival at the opposing school (opponent taunting, distractions, crowd, etc.) and the mental state of the team. I have been a coach for over thirty years, so it is easy for me to see when I need to have an adrenaline-rush speech to focus them or make it short, simple, and to the point. I try to stay out of sight while coaches are speaking to the team so as not distract coaches or players. When it is time, I move quickly to the team and present myself in front of them. I might have them go back to their seats or ask them to stand, depending on how long I have and how I need to motivate them.

That evening I asked them to stand. I looked around the room and started to talk several times but then stopped. I made eye contact with each and every boy then led the team in a slow-to-fast hand clap until they were ready to explode, and we headed to the field.

On the way to the field I have a specific script that I have followed ever since I was a young coach. Boys form two lines outside the locker room with seniors and lettermen in the front. All the coaches walk in the middle of the two lines, with me walking between the two boys leading the team. I repeat key things all the way to the field: "It is show time. Make sure your chin strap is buckled, and make sure your belt is a little tighter. This field is now our field. No stupid penalties. Hold on to the ball, play together, keep your mouth shut, and stay focused. Field position, three yards, and a cloud of dust. Discipline, fundamentals, block, tackle, fundamentals, hit, hit, hit." At the corner of the field, I release the boys to take the field, and it is go time. There is no looking back at this point, only moving forward.

For the next two and one-half hours, the boys play without fear and regret, and with perseverance and focused determination. It is game time!

The captains of both squads met at the center of the field for the coin toss right before the game. Usually this is done at the conclusion of pregame warm-up, then a mock coin toss is done right before the game so coaches can set their final plans with their teams.

Due to the circumstances of playing on Saturday and the officials getting to the game late, it was decided to do it right before the game. We won the toss, and the boys were instructed that we would like to receive the ball. Our offense had been on fire all season long, and I felt we needed to make a statement. The boys knew that if we won the choice, our offense would be first on the field. Our defense up to that point had been equally outstanding, and I had full confidence in them. I usually want to go on defense first, but I knew Clinton Central had some explosive players, and if we made a mistake early, I did not know how our team would respond. We had heard all week through the different avenues of media that our schedule was weak and that this game would be a repeat of what happened in 2011 when we were undefeated and Clinton Central was having a difficult season but still beat us by a large margin.

Everyone on the sideline was focused as the coaches made their rounds wishing one another and each player good luck. I felt confident as I checked out the eyes and focus of coaches and players alike.

Clinton Central kicked off, and our returner had a short gain before our offense took the field. We had the ball on the twenty-yard line. Coach Arnold, our offensive coordinator, put together one of the most systematic, controlled drives that I have seen over my long career. The drive would go fifteen plays and eat up most of the first quarter before our running back dived across the goal line. Twice during the series, we were faced with fourth-down situations and converted. The point after was good, and we were ahead of Clinton Central for the first time in years. The players were extremely excited, and the focus now seemed to be driven by the thought that we could play with them. It would now be up to our defense to hold them and get the ball back. We would be facing three of the best backs that we would see all year when they went to offense.

We kicked off deep and they had a short return, with the ball being placed on the twenty-five-yard line. We quickly stopped them on first and second down. On the second down, after the ball was dead, one of their players lost control and cost Clinton Central fifteen yards when he said something to the official. It was now third down and twenty on their fifteen, and Coach Perez's defense did not give them a yard on the down. Clinton Central had one of the top punters in class A, and he dropped back to punt on fourth down when the ball was hiked over his head. He ran after the ball as it went into the end zone, and he just kicked it out of the end zone to keep us from an easy score. The officials signaled safety, and just like that we were up 9–0. At that point, our team knew they could not only compete with Clinton Central, they actually had a chance to win.

Tri-Central dominated the game in all facets and made a clear statement that we now could play with anyone in the state. The final score was 55–12. This was the greatest win to date in the three years the program had been in place. People were now becoming interested in learning more about this young, athletic, determined group of boys from northern Tipton County. The team was now 6–0 on the season and undefeated in the Hoosier Heartland Conference, with one remaining game against Sheridan. The conference championship would have to wait, because our game with Sheridan was three weeks away. Until then, the players would have to work hard and continue to make progress each week. The coaches and players on the Tri-Central team did a great job of not looking beyond the game at hand.

I truly believe that as success begins to unfold, the ability to focus on the present while preparing for the future becomes the true trademark of success. The formula that defines our program is based on the three Ps: preparation, presentation, and passion. The transformation taking place at Tri-Central was something that does not come along very often in life and when it does, the legacy is priceless.

Tri-Central had made substantial progress, but there was still considerable improvement necessary for us to become a championship program. Despite the odds, we had achieved every team goal that we had established. The progress was palpable, and so was the excitement. We had to channel the energy into motivation and belief that our potential was still unfulfilled.

The following Wednesday when I arrived at practice, I was met by Gary Rhew, our athletic director, stating he needed to talk with me privately. Mr. Rhew stands about six foot eight, and it is easy to tell that he was an outstanding basketball player when he was younger. Gary coached basketball for years, and when Dave Driggs moved up from athletic director to principal, Gary got the job. These two men worked extremely well together, and both are more than kind to me and the needs that I present to them are always followed up on. Dave Driggs had been the boys' basketball head coach for years, and Gary was his top assistant. When I arrived, both of them were being questioned as to why the football team was constantly ignored while the basketball program got all the press and whatever they wanted. It seemed to me, coming into the school four years ago, that it was nothing more than sour grapes. It appears that football had been bad for so long that the community has run out of people to blame, so they now focus their negativity on Dave and Gary. I never did buy into the drama. I told both of them that I did not expect anything for the program that wasn't earned by the boys, and that is exactly how things have run to date. When I need help with sleds, dummies, shoulder pads, helmets, uniforms and anything else I feel the football program needs, I hear absolutely no debate. Mr. Rhew takes care of everything, and quickly.

My philosophy is built on developing a team based on sound principles, and if those principles are practiced, success will follow. I don't want people to just come to games because they feel sorry for the boys in northern Tipton County. I want people to come to games because they can't wait to see the boys in action. I want them to witness the result of disciplined practice, assignment preparation, team-oriented performance, and most of all, passionate pursuit of achievement. America is a country built on unity, hard work, and diligent pursuit of personal goals leading to collective success. Our team now had people coming in and believing that we could win, and win or lose, the attitude of the community was going through a positive transition.

As we walked into the football office, Gary and I sat down. I really had no clue as to what he wanted to discuss.

Gary has a personality similar to mine, and as we sat down, he told me that he needed to ask me a question.

I said, "What is it?"

Gary replied, "Would you be interested in playing the conference championship against Sheridan at Lucas Oil Stadium?"

I said, "Are you serious?"

Gary went on, "Yes, I was contacted today. Three games will be played on that Saturday, and all three are for conference championships. They are calling it Championship Saturday. We would play in the second game on that Saturday."

I asked, "What does Sheridan think?"

Gary said, "Coach Wright is fine with it, and it's our home game, so it's up to us where we want to play it."

I added, "Yes, yes, this is a great opportunity for our athletes and our community to play at the best football venue in the state and to have the opportunity to go center stage. This will be a great deal of extra work for you, and we will probably not make as much revenue due to expenses that we might not incur if the game was here. Gary, if you are fine with us playing there, then I would love to see our athletes get this opportunity."

Gary replied, "That will be fine. When do you want to tell the team?"

My answer was, "Me? Oh no, this kind of news needs to be presented to the team by their athletic director! You have done so much to help us turn this program around, and you have had to deal with so much crap over football. You need to be the one to present this wonderful news to the team."

Gary added, "Let me contact Lucas Oil management and finalize the deal, and then we can announce our plans as early as tomorrow at the end of practice."

I wanted to tell the coaches, players, and everyone I knew about the wonderful news, but I knew I'd better hold off. It would be devastating to tell them something like that only to have to come back later and say things just did not work out. I went out to practice and acted as if it was any other Wednesday afternoon as we prepared the defense to play Monroe Central on Friday.

The following day I received the confirmation e-mail from Mr. Rhew about the game being moved from Tri-Central to Lucas Oil Stadium, and he said he would be out at practice when I arrived to talk with the boys. I look back at this development and truly believe that Gary had an idea that we might continually get better and that the Lucas Oil Stadium game might help us down the road. I arrived after my thirty-minute drive from Clinton Central, and again I was greeted by Mr. Rhew. He wanted to know how I wanted to handle it. I blew my whistle and told the coaches and boys that we needed to have a meeting in the field house right now. I wanted them to get in there quick so Mr. Rhew could share this wonderful news and then get them back out on the field to go through our Thursday preparation for our week-eight opponent, Monroe Central. The boys at Tri-Central always hustled for me, and they took off on the sprint, but my coaches were looking at each other, confused. I usually do not like to alter practice routine unless something very important needs to be addressed, and they all knew that. As we headed to the locker room, Coach Arnold asked if everything was all right. I told him that Mr. Rhew had some important information to share with the team. When the coaches made it to the main team area of the field house, the boys were already assembled in front of the whiteboard in chairs. Seniors were across the front, and the rest of the team sat in ascending class order. Everyone was waiting quietly.

I approached the front of the team and announced that Mr. Rhew had some information to share with them, and with that I turned over the meeting to Mr. Rhew.

Mr. Rhew kidded the boys a little to break the seriousness of the moment, and then he shared with them that we were considering moving our conference championship game against Sheridan to Lucas Oil Stadium on Saturday, October 13, with our game time set at 4:00 p.m. At first the boys seemed stunned and a little in shock. Then the eyes started to move toward one another, and smiles came to their faces. Next, there was a quiet excitement that came over the room and you could, figuratively speaking, cut the air with a knife. Mr. Rhew told the boys how proud he was of them and how this opportunity was well-deserved. The coaches also seemed shocked by the news, and then gradually a humming began to take place in the room. At that point, I redirected their excitement to the task at hand and told them to get back out to the field and continue the preparation to beat Monroe Central. When the team emerged from the locker room onto the practice field, the boys could no longer hold in their excitement, and they started giving each other high fives and hugs. The coaches returned to the field also and embraced the moment with the boys. As Gary and I stood at the door, we enjoyed a sight long overdue at Tri-Central. Of all the conference championships to be played during the last week of the season, it seemed as if fate had opened a door for our football team to have such a wonderful opportunity.

In the next two weeks, we easily extended our undefeated season to a historic 8–0 record. The team now had made school history, and the next game would be for a conference championship. Sheridan High School has long been the best class-A football program in the state of Indiana. The Blackhawk coach (Bud Wright) is the most successful coach in Indiana history and was currently in his forty-eighth season as a head coach. Coach Wright had long been my greatest rival. There is not a coach in class-A football who has lost more games against Sheridan than I have over the past twenty-four years. During my long tenure at Clinton Central, Sheridan only would play one class-A school during the regular schedule, and that school was Clinton Central, a school north of Sheridan about twenty miles. Not only did I get to play the most dominant school in the state during the regular season, I would also usually have Sheridan in the same sectional as Clinton Central. There was a span of over eight years while I was at Clinton Central when Sheridan either won or was runner-up in the state, and Clinton Central lost to them regularly. During those years, many of my teams were outstanding, but we couldn't find a way to beat Sheridan. Coach Wright and I have always shared an intense rivalry on game night, but we have always been good friends off the field. One of the greatest criticisms about me over the years is that Coach Wright is a much better coach than I am, and I agree.

During the week, we prepared as if we were playing our last game. The boys were extremely focused, and the coaches were confident that our plan would give us a chance. The problem that we would be faced with was that this was the first time since 1991 that we would be in a championship game, and I knew that nerves might be an issue, along with playing at Lucas Oil, which is the home of the Indianapolis Colts.

The talk during the week was typical. Sheridan people were puffing their chests, stating that Tri-Central would not stand a chance since our schedule was so weak, and they would be led by Coach Gilbert. Sheridan is a community with intense local pride, and the focal point for the past forty-eight years has been Sheridan football. The community has high expectations every year and seldom loses to class-A programs.

My direction to the coaching staff was very direct and open-ended. I told the coaches that this was a game that we must work to play close, and if the opportunity arose late, then we might surprise Sheridan in the fourth quarter. I emphasized to the coaches the importance of playing close and directed this to our team. I did not want them to go out and play tight or play not to lose. We were huge underdogs, even though we were undefeated. I felt it was much more important for us to play with them and not allow them to do what they had traditionally done to us by physically beating us up. When you stopped playing hard, Sheridan had a history of being relentless and destroying all confidence that had been worked for so diligently. Our boys did not want to play in a spotlight game and get embarrassed. I thought they could handle not winning the game, but not being embarrassed. All the time for talking was over as we finished our final preparations on Friday evening.

Our community was excited about the game being played at Lucas Oil Stadium. Where we were playing overshadowed what we were playing for. It truly was exciting to see how the community was beginning to come together and support the football program. The parents raised money and scheduled a charter bus to transport our team to the venue. The parents were working very hard to make this a special day to remember for their sons, and the charter bus was just one of the many things they did. The parents also made up T-shirts to sell so they would all stand out at Lucas Oil. It was great to see such a transformation taking place, but what would happen to the Tri-Central football program if we lost?

The boys arrived on schedule, loaded the charter bus, and met with coaches one last time before we got on the bus and headed to the National Football League's number one sports stadium. It was truly a storybook ride thus far, and it would be interesting to see how the story line would unfold. The brief meeting went well, and we were off to Indianapolis to play a very good team in a league championship on the State's greatest stage.

We arrived about two hours before our game so the boys could hopefully get rid of the jitters while watching the championship game before us. The boys were very quiet as they entered the locker room and set their gear in the locker space provided. We had to share a locker room with Linton High School, and they were finishing up in the locker room when we arrived. Our players were wide-eyed while checking everything out. The boys never were given a walk-through, so they were sort of shocked to see the television outlets and the quality of the dressing room. They walked out into the stadium and took seats in the bleachers to watch the game before our own. The lights in the stadium were impressive, and it was easy to see how excited the boys were.

We hadn't been there long when Sheridan arrived and sat in the bleachers close to our team. Sheridan has played and won nine state titles in Indiana. Playing at Lucas Oil was not a big deal for them. They also played a high-level team just about every week during the season, so rigorous preparation was pretty much automatic, especially since they have such an outstanding coaching staff led by a living legend. Coach Wright's sons are also highly successful football coaches.

The third quarter had just started, and it was time for our boys to head to the locker room to suit up and get ready to play.

It was very quiet in the locker room as the boys put their gear on. Coaches were quietly going over the game plan among themselves, trying to treat this as any other game, but it was clear that this was not just another game. I was walking around talking to boys and trying to defuse some of the jitters when a member of the Lucas Oil staff came in and asked that I step out into the hall with him. When we got to the hallway, he went over our schedule again advising me that we would have thirty minutes before the game to take the field; at ten minutes before game time we needed to clear the field and then be back in the chute five minutes later for team introductions. He reminded me again that I needed to have the team on time. I said I would and headed back to tell the boys that it was time we went to a room designed for stretching purposes. In the room, the boys went through their pregame ritual of stretching. We attempted to maintain routine, but obviously that was not possible. As the boys finished, the staff member was back to let me know it was time for us to line up to take the field for pregame. As we stood in the tunnel waiting for the signal, the boys were extremely excited. Then we were given the cue to take the field. We had an outstanding crowd already cheering as we came out for pregame. Pregame was hurried, and we tried to get things done, but the hype of being on the turf in Lucas Oil Stadium for the first time was extremely powerful. I had an opportunity to have a team at Clinton Central play in the Hoosier Dome, which was the Colts' first stadium, but Lucas Oil Stadium was entirely different and better. It was a true privilege for us to have this opportunity, especially when you thought of our long lack of success at Tri-Central.

We finished our pregame and headed back to the locker room for our prayer and my final message to the team. Game time was minutes away, and I wondered how the boys would react to playing one of the best teams in class-A football in an NFL stadium.

I went into the locker room and asked the boys (as I always would) to take a knee and touch someone as we prayed together. We thanked God for the opportunity to play the game of football and for the special opportunity to play it in the Colts' stadium. The boys prayed and then stood up for my final message. I told them that we needed to play our game and support each other every step of the way. After speaking, I became quiet and started a slow clap. The boys joined in, and we gradually clapped faster until I yelled, "Let's go!"

The boys played hard the entire game, and they were in position several times to win the game. The score late in the fourth quarter was 22–14, with Sheridan ahead. We were on offense, though, and we were able to march the ball down the field. We had a first down on the twelve-yard line with a minute left in the game. On first down, we attempted to throw to one of our receivers and ended up getting a holding penalty, taking us back to the twenty-two-yard line. It came down to a fourth down with less than thirty seconds to go. Our sophomore quarterback, Cody, threw the ball to our senior running back, Austin. Austin caught the ball, and we ended up less than a yard from a first down at the two-yard line, effectively ending our undefeated season. Sheridan would win and become the conference champions again, and we would end the regular season 8–1 and conference runner-ups. Our fans were outstanding all evening long, and when we finally lost the game, they were appreciative of our team's effort and gave the boys an outstanding ovation. We congratulated Sheridan, and Coach Wright told me how we surprised them with our skill and speed. He commented that our program had come a long way in a short time and how impressed he was with our game plan and performance.

I thanked Coach Wright and told Bud that he always seemed to have my number as a coach. I said, "Bud, I have only beaten your team three times in twenty-four years, and I will keep fighting the good fight."

Bud just laughed and said he would see me in three weeks. Yes, in three weeks—if we could not only win our first sectional game in years but win two sectional games— we would face Sheridan again for a sectional crown. Well, after the game, the only thing on my mind was getting to the boys, taking the Lucas Oil Stadium picture for the parents as we had agreed to do, and preparing to go home.

When I got to the team they were visibly upset, but I told them that I was proud of them and that we needed to take the picture for their parents. I will admit, seeing the picture later, it truly was a poor representation of our team's attitude that year, because it is apparent in the photograph how much the boys were hurting. We then headed to the locker room. I went around and acknowledged each boy who played. After a loss is always a difficult time, and sometimes I needed to tell them to look up and look me in the eye because when bad things happen, we lose together just like we win together. As painful it was for us to get our first loss of the season, it was clear our program had made some tremendous strides in the right direction.

When I first came to Tri-Central, the boys seemed unaffected after a loss. Over time, as the boys gained more of a vested interest in success, losing a game became painful. Our performance on that particular evening had flaws, but we were playing an outstanding program and played hard throughout the game. The game came down to the closing moments when we were unable to seal the victory. I truly was proud of our boys, our community that backed us even in defeat, our coaches who put together a great game plan that almost worked, and the direction we were clearly now headed in.

The following week, we opened sectional play. Again, we had not won a sectional game since 1994, and we were playing a team that we felt we should beat; we had already defeated the same team in week eight of the season. It was a horrible night with rain, wind, and extreme cold. The boys came out with the attitude that they wanted to get back on track, win the game, and keep working so they would have another shot at Sheridan in the sectional championship. The boys won rather easily, 54–6, and with that victory, they ended our eighteen-year curse of losing the first game of the sectional. The following week they followed up and won against Lapel High School, who stopped us the year prior. The team was now 10–1, and our storied season would come down to a rematch against the Sheridan Blackhawks, who had defeated us for the conference championship. The boys were excited for the opportunity, and only time would tell if they would play well enough to win a sectional championship.

For the first time since 1991, the Tri-Central Trojans were playing in a sectional championship. The team had a great week of practice, even though Mother Nature was not cooperating. Sheridan plays an incredible schedule to prepare for the playoffs, and even though their record was not as win dominant as our record, they were very good. It seemed that we were ready to play, but often a coach doesn't truly know until the game starts.

That evening, we did not come out and play well early. In championship play, a team cannot start slow when they are the underdogs. By half time we were down fourteen points to Sheridan. We had made many mistakes in the first half offensively, and I was thankful that Coach Perez and the defense were able to keep us in the game. As I approached the locker room, I heard a commotion in the locker room. One of our seniors was verbally chastising the team. I entered the locker room and told him that was enough, we would win together or lose together, but we would maintain our philosophy of unity.

Then the athlete, in front of his peers, said something else, and I exploded on him and his "all about me" attitude. I told him (a starting player and one of the best players on the team) that if he could not stop with his current attitude, then he would not play at all in the second half. I would never allow one player to put himself above the rest of the team. It would not matter how it would affect the end result if he could not show respect to his fellow players and coaches.

He apologized, and we attempted to reorganize for the second half, but the focus was displaced, and that was enough. We again lost to Sheridan during the closing moments of the game. Our season was now over. Our final record was 10–2. We ended as second in two championships.

There were many questions that would need to be answered, but at that moment the only thing I had to do was thank my players for their great effort all season long. The players displayed extraordinary perseverance and determination, allowing Tri-Central to rise up in four years to earn state recognition, despite being considered one of the state's worst football programs for the better part of fifty years.

Sheridan would go on and win the regional and lose the semistate to Lafayette Central Catholic in a close contest. Lafayette Central Catholic would win the class-A Indiana state championship for a fourth consecutive year. We would graduate three players from our squad, and each of them was talented enough that it would be difficult to replace them.

We met on Monday after our loss to hand in equipment and collect all outside equipment and put it up for the winter months. After all the equipment was put up, we had a short meeting to discuss the award banquet, weight training, seven-on-seven, and the plans for the 2013 football campaign. It was a difficult evening as we finished our meeting, realizing our season was over. We had a great deal to be proud of after putting together the most winning season in our school's history. We also had now completed our second winning season in a row, but there was this odd emptiness, as if we were being forced to end something that had not been completed yet.

After the boys left, the staff sat around making small talk. It was clear that losing to Sheridan in the sectional championship was difficult for the staff to deal with. The general consensus among the coaches was that our focus for 2013 would clearly be toward one team, and that one team would be Sheridan. Over four years, we started out struggling against struggling teams, and now we were competing against the very best teams at our level in the state. It was our goal to risk everything and prepare the 2013 team to beat the class-1A icon, the legendary Sheridan Blackhawks.

CHAPTER 7

2013—Off-Season Preparation

After losing to Sheridan in the sectional championship, the coaching staff and many of the boys (on their own) went to watch Sheridan compete, first in the regional championship and then in the semi-state game. I never made a big deal about coaches and players attending these games, but it seemed there was this sense of purpose as if it was expected. A group of coaches went with me to the regional game, where Sheridan played an outstanding North Miami High School team.

When we arrived, it was a cold Indiana night. We found a spot along the fence to watch the teams play. It wasn't long before the entire staff and most of the varsity players were standing with us as we prepared to watch the regional contest. This was the first time in the four years that I had been the head coach at Tri-Central that I felt compelled to go to a game in the tournament series after we had been eliminated. It is easy to understand my surprise that so many members of the Tri-Central football team were there with me. Looking back now, it has become clear to me that this was a different group of boys who would head into the 2013 season. Also, I had assembled a group of coaches who were already focused on 2013 one week after we were eliminated. An adventure had now turned into a quest.

The boys would gradually separate from the coaches as the game began. The game was close throughout the first half, but Sheridan pulled away in the second half. There was an outstanding crowd on hand for the contest, and North Miami played well, but they were unable to compete with the legendary Coach Wright's Blackhawks. Sheridan advanced to the semi-state.

The most interesting point was made by our young quarterback, Cody, who said, "Coach, these guys won a sectional, and Sheridan beat them worse than they beat us!"

I agreed with Cody. I told Cody and his father that it was clear we were no longer a program that would wish for our success or rely on luck. We had developed into a program that could compete with any school comparable to our size.

Many positive things came out of the players and coaches attending this game. First, everyone had to pay their way, so it was important to each player and coach in attendance. Second, that unifying force that at one time I was so desperate to develop at Tri-Central was now visible. And third, the boys now truly believed that they were capable of winning. Before success can truly become routine, there must be that transition from wanting/hoping to have success to honestly knowing you can earn success with your talents and work ethic.

The following week, we all went to Sheridan to watch the semi-state game between Sheridan and the visiting Lafayette Central Catholic Knights. Lafayette Central Catholic was the defending state champion, and if they could go all the way in 2012, they would be the class-1A state champion for four consecutive years. The Knights were coached by another future Hall of Fame coach by the name of Kevin O'Shea. Lafayette Central Catholic had only lost one game over a four-year span, and we were ready for a showdown between two great small-school programs.

Everything was as expected. The coaches all met at Sheridan, and gradually most of the varsity players showed up to watch the contest with us. It was an outstanding venue. Sheridan has one of the best high-school fields in the state and a fan base that can only be described as incredible. Lafayette Central Catholic traveled well to

Sheridan, and their stands were also overflowing with loyal fans. The stage was set for this semi-state championship game.

The game was a low-scoring defense-oriented game. Both schools had prepared well defensively for this game. The game was close, with Lafayette Central Catholic winning the game in the fourth quarter. They would go on and win their fourth consecutive state championship. Sheridan played well, and barring a few mistakes, they might have represented the North at the state championships. The importance of the game for us was how the Tri-Central boys felt about what they saw. They all realized just how good we were in 2012 by watching the postseason run by Sheridan. The boys now knew what they needed to do.

Over the winter months, the boys made an effort for the first time to get into the weight room and work hard. We were not successful in getting everyone in the weight room, but the guys whom we would count on in 2013 were in the room and were working hard. Coach Hatcher was now in control of all facets of strength training, and I had decided to stay clear and let him run the program. This was a very difficult decision for me, as I have run the weight room at every school that I had coached at, and now I was turning over the strength-training program to a young man with a strong passion for his convictions. I truly believe this was another of the quality decisions that I made. I now had turned over the weight room and special teams to Coach Hatcher, the offense to Coach Arnold, and the defense to Coach Perez. I needed to step back and allow these men to work and not micromanage them. It was difficult, but the change allowed me to see things that I never could have seen if I hadn't relinquished some of my responsibilities. I could now focus my attention on the entire program and provide suggestions when necessary.

As spring came around, it was time for our call-out meeting. I had bad memories of what happened in 2010, and as I prepared for the meeting with players and parents, I was quite uneasy about whether anyone would show up.

The meeting took place on a sunny Sunday in March, and we had a great turnout. Everyone was excited about the 2013 season, and we were returning most of the team after the success that we had enjoyed in 2012. The team and the parents were all there. The meeting went well, and the parents seemed focused on making 2013 special for their sons. Motivated parents are vital to the success of any program. Our parents were excited and eager to get involved. They believed that the 2013 season might be a special year for football at Tri-Central. I cannot recall working with a group of parents more focused and ready to do what they needed to do to help the program in any way.

At the conclusion of the meeting, I talked with the coaching staff and asked if they would be in favor of having a meeting on the upcoming Saturday to discuss personnel, offensive and defensive formation changes, and any other issues prior to the seven-on-seven Monday night workouts starting in May. All of the coaches said they were willing, and we set the meeting for 2:00 p.m. and planned to be done by 4:00 p.m. I have never been a head coach to waste time in meetings or make meetings more of a social time together. The staff knows that when we have a meeting, it will usually be at the field house, and I will have an agenda that needs to be accomplished. Most of the staff members have several young children, and I do not want to steal their dads away from them during the off-season any longer than necessary. Our meetings are organized, but not rigid. We needed to discuss what we were going to do in the offensive backfield since we graduated both of our thousand-yard rushers. We needed to address as a group some personnel position changes that Coach Perez was considering and formation additions that Coach Arnold wanted me to think about. Coach Hatcher needed to update me with his thoughts about our special teams, and I knew Coach Tolle would have some ideas for me to consider involving our offensive-line blocking.

I asked Coach Hatcher about his plans involving our special-team play. Coach Hatcher requested more practice time. At the high-school level, most programs give less time to special teams. Then on Friday night, special teams will not be noticed if everything goes well. But if there are mistakes, those mistakes can cost a team field position and even a victory. When there are mistakes on special teams, those mistakes are very visible, and the community will quickly notice a lack of preparation. I agreed with Coach Hatcher. Our program had developed to the point that if we wished to compete with the very best schools in our class, then field position would be paramount. I told Coach Hatcher that we would spend no less than twenty minutes an evening working on special teams. I also asked him to cut back on play options so there would be less learning time and more repetition. He agreed and said that he would prepare each team and submit the formations and expectations before the season for me to consider. Coach Hatcher works extremely hard in our program to stay up with the older members of the staff, and he has accomplished that task very well. He is innovative and possesses qualities a head coach always looks for in a special team's coordination: pure spirit and determination.

The next order of business was our technology needs. Coaches Kennedy, Blades, and Hatcher were asked if there was anything that needed to be discussed. Coach Hatcher advised that we still needed to pay for next season's use of hudl.com. I said that I had already been advised that a local company would again donate money toward us maintaining our use of huddle. When I started coaching some thirty-four years ago, I remember using super 8 film. In 1978, I was a young junior-high coach, and my job was to scout the next week's opponent on Friday night and write up a scouting report overnight to hand to the head coach at breakfast. A part of my game-night experience also involved getting our game tape. I would meet a courier to have the film developed overnight, and then after giving the scouting report to the head coach, go and retrieve the developed game film to take back for the coaching staff to evaluate. Technology has changed so much over my three and a half decades of coaching. I started out with super 8 film, then went to 16 mm film, and from there went to beta videos (using monstrous machines). Then it was VHS, next was DVDs, and now we have huddle. There is no need to meet coaches and exchange film today. All coaches have to do is simply send game video via the Internet using huddle. The process has really changed how we do business, because we have less travel and less downtime over the weekend. The problem is that we have lost that personal element of the meet and greet. I think technology is great, but with all good things comes a downside, and the downside is clearly less coach-to-coach interaction.

Next on the list for discussion was offense. Coach Arnold and Coach Tolle wanted to add an unbalanced attack with one back in the backfield. I asked why, and they were ready. After listening to them, I agreed that we would try it, but I wanted them to under-stand I might not wish to pursue additional formations for the boys to remember. They were happy that I was willing to consider the for-mation and were excited that the addition might become significant as the season progressed.

I then opened up the can of worms that we needed to discuss: who was going to play the most important back position in our offense, the two-back position, or right halfback. The right-halfback position as part of the veer offense is vital to the success of running the football. The young man who had played there for two seasons had just graduated; he had done an outstanding job. We would be returning two outstanding sophomores and an untested senior to lead the way at running back. As a group we discussed our options, and I admitted that I had two major concerns. Our sophomores were starters on defense, and I did not want to get them beaten up and injured by playing both ways. The most difficult task at a small school is always personnel. We don't have the numbers that larger schools have, and many boys have to stay on the field and play every play. I knew these two young men were special, but I really believed we need to platoon them at the three-back position, or left halfback, during the upcoming season. The dilemma was who would play right halfback. Garrett really wanted to play right halfback, and during the 2012 season he was upset late in games when I would not let him run the ball. But the game had been won. Why would I want to risk injuring our starting middle linebacker doing late mop-up duty at running back? I told the staff that I wanted us to watch his progress over the summer and see if he was capable of playing at a high level on offense and defense throughout an entire game. Garrett is a talented high-school wrestler who has had a great deal of success on the mat, but he is about five foot ten and weighs around 160 pounds. Besides his size, he had very little experience in the back-field since his eighth-grade year. We then discussed possibly using him on offense to give the two outstanding sophomores (Dillon and Cody) rest. We would have to wait and see.

We also thought maybe a move-in might happen, or one of the other young guys would step up. Everybody had a chuckle about a possible move-in, as we have never been blessed in that fashion. Our line was not much of a concern. Four of our linemen had been together for three years and meshed very well. The newest member was Josh, who became a starter during the 2012 season. Josh is five foot eight and weighs 150 pounds. He had done a great job at our right-tackle position the previous season. We also had depth at the offensive line, which we had never had in the past. Offensively, we seemed in good shape, depending on what happened at right halfback.

We then discussed defense. Coach Perez stated that he planned to use a few more coverages in 2013, but he did not feel we needed to add anything to the playbook defensively. Coach Perez's great-est concern was moving personnel to positions where they might be more effective. He talked about moving our outstanding sopho-mores to key positions, since we had lost three top-notch seniors. The hardest of the three seniors to replace defensively was Austin at strong safety. Austin was an incredible defensive player who could tackle well in the open field and also cover the pass when necessary. "If it isn't broke, don't fix it," we thought, but Coach Perez really wanted to look at several boys in different roles during the seven-on-seven season. I agreed that if we were considering changing boys' positions, the best way to determine whether the changes would work or not was during seven-on-seven scrimmages during the sum-mer. We all felt confident that we would be able to gain needed answers throughout the summer to make the decision clear when the boys arrived for the start of two-a-day practice.

Practice for seven-on-seven started the first week of May. We asked the boys to give us one night a week (Monday) for two-hour sessions that would run through July. The May sessions were open to all boys, and they were not directed by coaches. Workouts were completely voluntary, and any boy could come and play during the open field workouts. Turnout was OK, but it wasn't great. Spring sports were in full swing, and I did not expect spring athletes to come and work out with the format we provided.

Official Monday night workouts began in June, and I was impressed that all the varsity boys were in attendance. It would be the last Monday of June that would become significant for the Tri-Central program. We had three other schools at Tri-Central scrimmaging, first with seven-on-seven, and then with what is called eleven-on-eleven thud. The eleven-on-eleven thud is live contact in a controlled scrimmage with no to-the-ground tackling. That evening, our question pertaining to who would play the right-halfback position was answered.

The team had just finished seven-on-seven workouts against one of the best class-3A programs in the entire area, and it was time for us to begin the eleven-on-eleven thud. I was quite nervous, because the Western team was bigger than our team and year in and year out one of class-3A's top-ten teams. We started on defense, and I was truly surprised by our ability to play with Western. Our boys hit and ran extremely well and were able to neutralize Western's offense.

Then it was our turn to go on offense. We moved the ball well because Garrett, the senior right halfback, was playing very well. We moved the ball down the field and were in a fourth down, with a yard to go to score. Coach Arnold called twenty-four veer, which is a play that involves the right halfback, who is expected to dive through the line off the hip of the guard. Garrett hit the hole hard and fast and was met by Western's big middle linebacker. Garrett ran over the middle linebacker to score. The play happened right in front of me as I was standing deep in the end zone, facing the action coming to me. As the contact happened and Garrett scored, my eyes went directly to Coach Arnold's eyes standing back where the offense had huddled. When our eyes met, we both smiled. Without us saying a word, our decision about the right-halfback position was made. Garrett was our answer. Defensively our boys played well, but Coach Perez and I still had some questions about personnel that were yet unanswered. We talked and hoped those questions would be answered during two-a-days.

We finished our seven-on-seven workouts, and we all were very excited about our team coming into camp. The boys showed up for our preseason running session a week before camp. During the week, we handed out gear and put the boys through four nights of tough running workouts. The first night I was excited, because it was the first time the entire team had shown up for preseason workout together. I could tell by the attitude during the workout that the boys might have something that perhaps had never been present at Tri-Central in the school's forty-two-year history.

On the second day coming into practice, I received some alarming news. Boys were arriving, but one senior was not there yet. I asked the boys where Josh (our offensive right tackle) was, but they did not need to answer. He arrived, and I could not believe what I was seeing. Josh was in a walking cast. Josh told me that he was playing in a baseball game, slid into second base, and broke his ankle. Wow! He would be out for four to five weeks. His injury would definitely make things more complicated. The good news was that we had a wonderful young man move into the school district who played offensive tackle, but he was a sophomore. Wyatt is a tall, athletic young man whom we now would need to rely on until Josh recovered from his injury. At this point, I was hoping we would not have any other surprises. The rest of the week went well. The boys worked hard and really started to bond, because we had such a great group of seniors to lead the team.

On Thursday evening when we finished, I asked the boys to sit in the bleachers so we could go over a few last-minute things. And our team mom wanted to talk with them. I reminded them how important it was to be at practice every day and to take their commitment to one another very seriously. I introduced the motto Team of One. I told them that we were not going to promote any one boy above the team; all of them were vital for us to have success. I shared that our target game was week nine against Sheridan. I was impressed to look around as I spoke to see their heads nodding in agreement. I then invited Julie, our team mom, to talk with them.

Julie told them some of the things that were coming up, including our fund-raisers. Then Julie gave the boys a pep talk. Wow! I really wanted to find a way to get Julie to stop, but she is such a wonderful woman and had done such a great job meeting the needs of the program that I did not want to disrespect her. She told the boys that she was excited and the community was excited about the upcoming season. She said that the parents and fans were looking forward to making the trip to Lucas Oil Stadium on our way to winning the class-A state championship! When she had finished, I realized there was nothing more that needed to be said, and I dismissed the boys.

CHAPTER 8

2013—Cast of Characters

The 2013 football season would be my thirty-second season as a head coach of a high-school football program. In 1980, my journey began in Ohio, where I spent five seasons as a head coach. In 1985, Judy and I moved our two small sons to Cass County, Indiana, because I took a head-coaching position at Pioneer High School that lasted two seasons. I sat out of coaching during the 1987 football season before I was offered a position in Clinton County, Indiana, at Clinton Central High School, where I remained as head coach for twenty years. After being dismissed from Clinton Central, I again sat out a year before landing the Tri-Central High School head-coaching position in 2009.

My journeyman's career has been quite an adventure filled with peaks and valleys. The one constant has always been that each year brought a new team with its own unique talents and challenges. Even when many of the boys returned from the year before, each team has always been a new adventure with new leadership and the need to develop a new chemistry.

As two-a-days approached, the players would comprise one of the most incredible group of young men I have coached. They developed a bond that I had never seen established before with any group I have had the opportunity to coach.

I feel the necessity to set the stage, so to speak, and give a brief summary of just how special this group of boys was and how it would come about that they would create a legacy that will last in the small Tipton community for generations to come. I will give insight on the boys who were the players who would make local history and complete a storybook season filled with everything high-school sports are supposed to be about. This is truly a rags to riches story that doesn't happen often, but it does happen. Hope is offered to those who face similar challenges. In this great country, dreams can be realized when work ethic and passion lead the way.

I will start with the coaching staff. I have talked about several of these men already, but this is where I feel it becomes expedient to identify them properly so the 2013 season and the successes earned can be understood fully.

The Coaches

Coach Shane Arnold is a twenty-plus-year seasoned veteran. Coach Arnold's main contribution to the program is that he is our team's offensive coordinator and runs our scout offense on defense nights. Coach Arnold is a man of average size. Usually he exhibits a quiet demeanor off the field but can turn his pleasant Dr. Jekyll personality into Mr. Hyde when agitated on the field. Coach Arnold shows a great deal of respect to the players as well as the other coaches. Coach Arnold has a serious back problem but is always the first to jump in and get things done on and off the field. Coach Arnold often tries to defuse situations before they get to me.

He had coached at Tri-Central before I arrived, but he never really was given the opportunity to lead. Coach Arnold was the first Tri-Central coach I met when I arrived. He was the one to clue me in about how bad things truly were, and he aided me in figuring out how I wanted to approach the problems that I walked into. I recognized during my first season at the school that this man had talent and vision. The problem was clear: the cure would take some time. Coach Arnold had been an assistant coach for a long time, and that process in itself can take the fire out of a man. I could see a fire in him that needed to become a blaze. I needed for him to gain more of a vested interest in the direction I wanted to head, but I knew there would be a cost; I would give up power offensively as he would gain more. Head coaches often fear giving up power. I have always believed that if a man is deserving, then I must allow him the opportunity to gain that edge necessary to be a great leader, to allow that man to feel empowered. If done right, this spreading out of power will ultimately lead to a highly successful organization. Coach Arnold took that power progressively toward gaining complete control of our offense in 2012. As we approached the 2013 season, Coach Arnold was a head coach in charge of all facets of offense.

Coach Memo Perez is also a veteran coach of many years. Coach Perez joined the program at the start of my first season at Tri-Central as a junior varsity coach, helping out with the defense and coaching quarterbacks that first year. By the end of the season, I knew I needed to make some changes, and I offered the defensive coordinator job to Coach Perez. Coach Perez is a local hero, as he was the quarterback to lead Tri-Central to the school's first sectional championship in 1991. The decision to offer the defensive job to him was an easy one. He has demonstrated incredible passion toward fixing the problems at Tri-Central in the football program. His goal has always been simple—it is all about respect. Year in and year out, Tri-Central was considered one of the state's worst football programs, and he wanted to be instrumental in the change of direction at the school. Coach Perez wanted us to change our defense to a thirty-four defense, and again, it was that power thing, and I agreed.

Each year, Coach Perez, has gained confidence as he has gained power. During the 2012 campaign, he took complete control of our defense and ended the season with one of the top statistical defensive teams in the state. When he first took control of the defense, he would often get angry and loud. He has since learned that he can be just as effective without being loud. There are times when all coaches need to raise their voice, and no single man on our staff can get the boys to focus quicker than Coach Perez. He is a strong man, and he is a compassionate man, and the boys work diligently to please him.

A little fear might be fine, but it is really special when it is not fear but respect that fuels the direction of young men playing a game. Coach Perez is respected by everyone in the program and his contributions are immeasurable.

Our offensive line is led by Coach Jason Tolle. Coach Tolle is a close friend of Coach Perez, and they came into the program together. Like Coach Perez, Coach Tolle also played at Tri-Central and was a member of the '91 team that won a sectional. Coach Tolle was selected his senior year in high school as a member of the Indiana all-state team and went on to play college football. Coach Tolle, a seasoned veteran coach, works very hard at all that he does. He works as a mechanical engineer by day and then comes to practice and uses his intellect to create the best possible blocking schemes for our players. Coach Tolle is quiet and patient with our athletes, and the boys love and respect him. He never raises his voice much, and like Coach Perez, when he does, all the boys focus on what he has to say. It was the second season during my tenure that he became our line coach, and each year our line has become better. He is the guy on staff who, no matter what I say, is ready to ask a question. He has changed a great deal of my game-tested blocking schemes. At first I was somewhat defensive, but his results have been remarkable.

Each of these men I discuss have influenced not only the direction of the boys, but also the direction of the program. Coach Tolle has that great personality that can often break up the intensity in a positive way. On defense he coaches the outside linebackers and works closely with Coach Perez. Coach Tolle is always plotting and planning during a game, which makes it difficult for our opponent coaches to get a grasp on what he is doing.

Coach Hatcher is one of our younger coaches. He has become our special-team coordinator. Coach Hatcher has brought to the program incredible passion. Coach Hatcher possesses passion in all that he does, and that passion becomes contagious. Coach Hatcher does a great job, like the other coaches, in preparation. Our special teams have improved by his leadership, and his excitement, both in practice and during games, has a positive influence on the team. Coach Hatcher also does a great deal behind the scenes with our technology. Technology has changed the game, and as coaches, we must continue to grow with the availability of the technology if we wish to continue to be successful. Coach Hatcher, along with Coaches Kennedy and Blades, has done a great job with all of our technology needs.

Coach Kennedy works in all facets of our program and really has become our guy on staff who does whatever needs to be done without any questions. Coach Kennedy coaches our tight ends on offense and spends a great deal of time with our kickers. Coach Kennedy is also a technology guy, and he possesses expertise that has been important in giving our program the edge we need in preparation. Coach Kennedy has a quiet laid-back attitude that allows the boys to feel comfortable around him, although when he is given a reason to fix something, there is no hesitation, and the boys listen attentively.

The staff does not yell and scream all the time, so when one of the coaches gets upset about something not going right, the boys listen and fix things quickly. This being said, my philosophy with my staff is simple: they have a right to yell at an athlete if something needs to be fixed, but I require the coach talk with him so that before that boy leaves to go home, he understands it was something about performance that needed to be addressed, not something personal. We never want a boy to leave practice thinking one of the coaches is mad at him. If something needs to be addressed on a personal level, then that would be my job.

Coach Joshua Hunter has now been with us for three years and primarily coaches our defensive line and helps with our scout defense. Coach Hunter is another of the coaches who is relatively quiet by nature. The defensive linemen love to play for him, and he is constantly working on technique with the linemen. When he first arrived, he was a little shy to get involved, but it did not take long before our defensive line understood that he was their leader, and they needed to listen to him if they wanted to get better. Coach Hunter has been able to develop a relationship with his core group like Coaches Arnold, Tolle, Perez, Hatcher, and Kennedy have done: complete ownership in each of their phases they teach, with high expectations presented in a respectful way.

Coach Keller works with us primarily on Friday evenings on the headphones with Coach Hunter, answering questions for Coach Perez. Coach Keller has a job situation that does not allow him to come each day, but I feel that his defensive intellect helps us on Friday nights, and a coach needs to exercise every option toward success. Coach Keller had been with me at Clinton Central, and the boys love to be around him. He possesses the qualities that all these men possess—personalities that draw the players to them instead of pushing them away.

Our junior-high coaches are also top-notch men who work on Friday nights as well. Coach Tony Blades helps me with my position-coaching responsibilities; then on Friday evening he is on the phones with Coach Tolle advising Coach Arnold on our offense. Coach Blades is another longtime coach who does a great deal for the program, including helping with technology. Coach Johnson coaches with our line coaches, and on Friday nights he becomes one of our men on the phones, aiding the coaches on the field with what he sees from above. Coach Johnson has a great work ethic and has been a Tri-Central coach for a long time. He is also an alumnus from Tri-Central, playing back in the seventies.

This staff has now been together in the current roles presented for four years. Every man takes his responsibilities to heart and diligently prepares each and every week to give our young men the best possible instruction for success on Friday nights. The staff does not meet like most staffs over the weekend, as we all know what we need to do and come to practice on Monday prepared to develop our game plan. It is vital that each man has a true vested interest in the preparation and direction of the game plan. Every coach on staff knows that when we win on Friday night, it was their input and dedication that made it possible. These men have gradually changed the structure of our program and brought a little of their own philosophy into our program. They have gained a feeling of ownership, having taken a problematic program and made it special.

The most important thing that happens each day of practice—and has been a part of what I have always believed to be vital in high-school athletics—is a focus on fundamentals. Each coach teaches and reviews fundamental blocking, tackling, throwing, and catching every day. The players know that if they do something fundamentally wrong, it will be addressed immediately. Sometimes when something is done fundamentally wrong and success still happens, coaches allow the situation to happen. At Tri-Central that would never happen. If success occurs while doing something fundamentally wrong, the situation is addressed. The boys know that in the long run, our diligence in doing things correctly will allow us the opportunity at some point to be special and win something important. The hard part is being patient until that special time presents itself.

The 2013 Tri-Central varsity football team had thirty-nine boys on the roster, of whom twenty-one would play varsity football. The first time I met Tri-Central boys, I stated our goal each year would be to field forty players. In class-A football, a coach who can field forty players a season will probably be able to develop a successful program.

The first year, we finished the season with twenty-one boys on the field, and we went 0–10. Here we are five years later, and for the first time, we are very close to our target team. That is exciting. It will be important not to lose boys during two-a-days and keep all thirty-nine as we head into the season. The numbers become very important, as now we will, for the first time, be able to field a junior-varsity team.

The players who make up the varsity team will include ten seniors, six juniors, and five sophomores. Each boy will add to the chemistry that will make this team unique and special. The other eighteen players on the squad will have a less-than-glamorous role but very important as scout team members. This group of boys will not have any "superstars." They will rely completely on each other and look to their coaches for direction. The boys will be introduced here by first name only to preserve their family privacy, although people close to the program will know each of these boys and the legacy they have established locally. Offensive players will be characterized first, followed by defense, and finally special-team players.

The Players

The Tri-Central offense is based on a split-back double-tight-end veer offense introduced by Coach Bill Yeoman at Houston University; thus, it has become known as the Houston veer. I have run the veer offense my entire coaching career and it has been successful. I have seen football evolve from Power T, Pro I, Broken T, Wishbone, Single Wing, and Run and Shoot to the current trend of "Basketball on Grass." I have always felt comfortable with the veer offense because it involved an option attack that focuses on a straight-ahead attack commonly referred to in football circles as "smash mouth" football. The veer attack also allows for an outstanding play-action passing game that makes it hard to defend both the run and the pass. As teams in the new millennium continue to spread out and go to shotgun, the offense I wish to employ becomes difficult to defend, as not many teams do what we do. The following players are the guys who make this offense work.

> *Quarterback.* Cody is a six foot one, 170-pound junior who has been a starter since his freshman year. He has become an outstanding offensive leader, reading defenses against the run, and he has developed a strong accurate arm.
>
> *Right Halfback.* Garrett is a six-foot, 165-pound senior who has lettered three years, but this will be his first season as a starting running back. Garrett plays hard all the time and leads the team well.

Left Halfback. Two sophomore boys will share this position throughout the season. First, Cody C., who is five foot ten and weighs 165 pounds. Cody is a smart young player with good speed and a great deal of natural athleticism. Second, Dillon, who is five foot ten and weighs 170 pounds. Dillon is also a natural athlete with good speed. He plays hard all the time.

Flanker. Two boys will play at the flanker (off line of scrimmage receiver) position. First, Seth is six foot two and weighs 180 pounds. Seth is a senior, a four-year letterman, and our team's emotional leader on and off the field. Second, Colten is a five-foot-ten, 165-pound sophomore who will become an outstanding player during the 2013 season.

End. Three boys will fill the two positions on the field. First, Jade, a senior who is six foot three and weighs 170 pounds. Jade will be a major contributor throughout the 2013 season. Jade's impact as a player will be important. Second, Bryce is a six-foot-three, 175-pound junior who has started the past three seasons at tight end. Bryce is an outstanding blocker and possesses good foot speed. Third, Cale is a six-foot-one, 150-pound junior. Cale will get his first opportunity this season to start at tight end and will become a solid performer.

Offensive Line. At tackle three boys will rotate in the lineup. First, Darius is six foot one and weighs 245 pounds. Darius is a four-year starter, and as a senior, a true leader on the team. Darius is an outstanding athlete who also possesses excellent character. Second, Josh is five foot eight and weighs 150 pounds—yes, I did say 150 pounds at right tackle. Josh is a three-year letterman as a senior and has developed into one of the finest small linemen that I have ever coached. Third, Wyatt is six foot three and weighs 215 pounds. Wyatt is a sophomore, and this will be his first varsity season. Wyatt will become instrumental as injuries occur. At the guard position three boys will rotate in. First, Brandan is six foot two and weighs 270 pounds. Brandan is a senior who has started at right guard for the past three seasons and enters 2013 as the starting right guard. Brandan is a big guy who offers the line stability and experience. Second, Tanner is six foot three and weighs 255 pounds. Tanner is a sophomore who will need to rotate as boys need breaks or injuries occur. Tanner enters 2013 as a letterman, but this will be his first season as a rotating starter. Third, Ryan is five foot eight and weighs 180 pounds. Ryan also has started at left guard for the past three seasons and will start in 2013 at left guard. Ryan is an outstanding athlete who is also very fast and strong.

Center. Our center for the past two seasons has been Nick. Nick is six feet tall and weighs 220 pounds. Nick has been a solid performer in the past and has worked extremely hard losing weight and becoming one of our team leaders.

Over the years I have been less consistent in my defensive philosophy. I have run many different defenses, depending on the innovations and current offenses we have faced over the years. I have already discussed how Coach Perez changed the Tri-Central defensive philosophy after my first year at the school. Coach Perez introduced the 3-4 defense then, and I do not believe that for the rest of my career I will run anything other than the 3-4. The 3-4 defense has the capability to stop all types of offense successfully. Our coaching staff and players have bought into the effectiveness of the 3-4. The players have become fundamentally strong, and they have become skilled in the duties necessary for the 3-4 defense to neutralize modern offenses. The defensive players heading into 2013 are as follows:

Outside LB. At left outside linebacker plays a sophomore who is a two-way starter: Dillon. The other outside linebacker is also a two-way starter, a junior, Bryce.

Tackle. Three boys will rotate at defensive tackle. First, Darius, a senior, is a two-way starter also. Second, Ryan, a senior, is also a two-way starter. He is very talented defensive player. Third, Riley is five foot eleven and weighs 195 pounds. Riley is a junior and returned to the squad in 2013. Riley will have a key role in the success the Trojan football team will be in search of during the 2013 campaign.

Nose tackle. Lake is a five-foot-eight, 190-pound junior who has lettered the past two seasons. Lake played very well as a sophomore and could be one of the best defensive linemen in class A during the 2013 season.

Inside LB. Garrett, a two-way performer, will play one inside linebacker position and be our defensive captain. Garrett will call our defensive alignment and play as our quarterback on defense. The other inside linebacker will be Cody, a two-way starter as a sophomore. Cody will split time on offense with Dillon at one halfback position, and on defense will play full time at inside linebacker.

Cornerback. Cody (our quarterback) will play one of the cornerback positions defensively. Cody is as outstanding on defense as he is on offense. The other cornerback will be Davee, a five-foot-ten, 180-pound senior. Davee lettered as a junior and is an excellent defensive tackler.

Safety. Seth, a senior two-way performer, plays our strong safety position. Seth has outstanding skill and will be relied on to handle all the defensive secondary calls. The free safety will be a sophomore, Colten. Colten is also a two-way performer, sharing time at flanker on offense with Seth. Colten is the guy who will need to learn quickly, as the defensive success will be measured by his ability to make quick decisions on both the pass and the run.

It is essential at a small school that boys get into great physical condition—the expectations are high, since so many boys are asked to play both ways. As the 2013 season approaches, Tri-Central will have eight boys expected to play both offense and defense. There will be four boys who will be able to give the team depth, rest starters when necessary, or pick up responsibilities when a player gets hurt. Health is very important at a small school, because the team numbers are smaller, and there are fewer skilled players. Much of the success of class-A (small school) teams rests on being able to keep the top players healthy and on the field.

Special teams really do not get noticed except when something goes wrong. I have given Coach Hatcher more time than in the past two seasons to prepare our special teams for games, and it has paid off most of the time. In closely contested games, field position (where you start offensively or defensively after a special team's exchange of the ball) can mean the difference between winning and losing a game. A kickoff return, a blocked punt, a missed extra point, or a fumbled return can turn the tide. Early in the season when the weather is still muggy and hot, I like to play our eager young players at times to give the two-way starters a rest. As the season progresses, I believe it is important to put our top boys on the field for special teams. There are eight boys who will usually not come off the field while the game is yet to be decided. This team will have several boys who will become important on special teams.

Kicker. Our kicker this season for PAT (point after touchdown) will be a junior, Caleb. Caleb is five foot nine and weighs 155 pounds. Caleb is a two-year varsity letterman.

Punter. Our punter will be Dillon this season. Dillon starts at halfback and defensive outside linebacker and will be called on to punt when it is necessary. Since this is a run-oriented team, I do not like to punt, but when necessary it will be important for Dillon to be ready.

Returner. The team will have several boys back to return punts and kicks, but we do have a boy who specializes in returning. Keith is a five-foot-eight, 145-pound senior. Keith has great quickness and skill. He has the experience to always hold onto the ball and help put us in a good position to start offense every time he touches the ball.

This team will not have any superstars and will not have anyone spotlighted as the go-to guy. I have had teams with a few boys who are way ahead of the other boys, but this often allows opponents to focus in on who to stop. This team will be difficult to stop offensively and move the ball defensively, since there are no truly spotlighted boys. Our opponents will be faced with stopping the twenty-one boys we plan to play each Friday evening during the season. In playing twenty-one boys, we have an edge when playing teams our own size. Over my long career, I usually play fifteen to sixteen boys on Friday night. This season we will have enough depth to play twenty-one, and that will give us an edge as the season progresses.

Practice begins on Monday, August 5, throughout the state of Indiana. The season is now upon us, and we have thirty-nine boys signed up to play football at Tri-Central. My goal has always been the 1A level: forty. We will begin one short of that goal, but this will be the largest group to enter two-a-day camp during my tenure. Most of the boys coming in are talented athletes, and for the first time we will actually have competition for several of the positions. The success of the 2013 season will rest on the preparation and team unity developed during this first two weeks. The coaches will offer a direction, a plan, routine, and discipline, and the players must develop the desire to work together, accepting their roles as they learn in preparation for the season.

CHAPTER 9

2013—Practice Begins

Monday, August 5, 2013, was shaping up to be a nice day as I headed to Tri-Central, some thirty minutes from my home, around noon. This was the first practice day allowed by the Indiana High School Athletic Association for football. The IHSAA mandates restrictions for the first two days, with the intent of acclimating the players to the weather and to football. After the first two days, restrictions are lifted, and coaches can run practice within their own guidelines. This process is about to change in Indiana, though. This will be the last year when the entire two-a-day structure (after the first two days) will allow coaches the opportunity to practice when they want and do what they want. Starting in 2014, football will have tighter restrictions on practice times and contact in Indiana high-school football.

I arrived at the field house around 12:30 p.m. and started organizing the little things for when the boys would arrive. I opened the field house up so it could breathe and started up our fans to circulate the air. Our facility is rather rustic in appearance but serves the purpose and needs of our football program. I had lined the practice field last week and started moving our practice equipment out. Our practice structure is very predictable and routine. I like routine and repetition, and it appears our coaching staff does also. I set up the field and went back in to relax a little and go over the game plan for the day.

Today, as well as tomorrow, we are allow two ninety-minute practices separated by two hours. The focus the first two days is, obviously, conditioning and organization. The IHSAA does not allow contact, and players are only allowed to wear shoulder pads and helmets the first two days. On the third day they are allowed to dress in full gear and hit. I have never allowed hitting on day three, but I do have the boys dress out in full gear. We would begin contact in a controlled sense on day four.

There is no right or wrong way to design practice. Practice schedules need to meet the needs of the athletes and serve the coaches in a way that they can teach. I believe practice needs to be fast-paced and busy. I do not allow standing around and believe long drills do nothing but bore the athletes and allow them to get lazy fundamentally. Our staff knows the importance of keeping the boys moving in a direction where they can teach the mechanics important for them to play at a high level.

I will get extremely animated about two things: first, if a boy makes a mistake and puts his head down; second, if a boy continually makes the same fundamental mistakes. When these things happen, I challenge the young men to focus and always keep their head up. We do not want our opponents to see us lose composure and determination. When the team is not jelling and is losing focus, I send the entire team off the field. This brief break allows them to refocus. Leaders to begin to step up, and that team element begins to grow. I do not send the boys off the field often, maybe once or twice a season if necessary, but the effect has always been positive. Coaches do not want to become predictable in dealing with adversity. Every situation usually is unique and needs to be addressed in a unique manner.

All facets of team growth are directly influenced by the head coach, and the head coach must make thoughtful good decisions. I truly believe that success is determined not on Friday nights during games, but rather in practice away from the lights and glimmer where coaches and players only have one another, their sweat, their discipline, and their loyalty. It is at practice where the boys of America become men through hard work, dedication, and perseverance. Friday nights are special and important, as they represent the performance that has been developed and worked toward.

Everybody arrived at practice on time and ready. All boys were present, and the coaches were eager to get started. The boys know that attendance to practice is my greatest expectation and that I do not handle players missing practice well for any reason. We started practice at 4:00 p.m. and everybody was upbeat and focused during our first form-running session. We immediately circled up after the running session for stretch, and everybody was joking around but focused. When the team was done stretching, we went into conditioning drills. Each of my assistant coaches has a drill, so we divided up the team in a circuit-training session. When the circuit was done, and we sent the boys to water, I was in shock. It has usually not gone well the first couple of practices at Tri-Central, because our boys are usually in horrible condition. What I had just seen was a first during my tenure at the school. The boys all completed each drill. Our coaches gathered while the boys had a break, and we were all impressed. The boys had made it clear at the beginning of this first practice that this team was going to be different, and we coaches could see they were very serious about it. The rest of practice went well, and the boys worked hard as we drilled fundamentals. We started practice with one varsity starter injured from a summer baseball injury. It would be important for us to keep the rest of the team healthy if we planned to match the 2012 season or do better. Our right tackle, Josh, would be out about four weeks, and that would be difficult, but Coach Tolle already had a plan to deal with the adversity until Josh was ready to return.

Everything was going well in practice. Attendance was perfect, and our skill levels were already shining. The edge we would have against other schools would be with our offensive and defensive linemen— they are all veterans, and they are fast.

Friday night under the lights we scrimmaged for the first time. Everything went well until our starting left guard and a starting defensive tackle, hurt their knees. Ryan went down, and everything stopped for a brief time. Ryan collected himself and seemed fine, and we all took a deep breath as we finished practice. At the conclusion of practice our center, Nick, had a problem with his knee. He told the trainer of a recurring problem where the knee locked up on him. The trainer was able to get the knee unlocked, but Nick was in a great deal of pain. Nick told me that he would be fine and that he would not miss anything. Nick was right. He never had another issue all season with his knee, and we were all very thankful.

On Saturday morning, we again had a scrimmage scheduled, and I received the news that Ryan's knee was more serious than previously thought. We would lose Ryan for most of the season, as he would need surgery. Ryan told me that he would be back late in the season and that he really wanted to play.

Here we are, one week into practice and two of our outstanding offensive-line players and one of our top defensive-line players were out. Coach Tolle was now pressed to fill two offensive-line positions with untested boys on a line that had been intact for two years. Coach Tolle challenged the younger players to step up their game, and they would. Both younger boys knew that when those seniors were cleared to get back into the lineup, they would step in. Both boys, Tanner and Wyatt, embraced their roles and did outstanding jobs. The character that they demonstrated would become an example as well as the team's defining element throughout the season.

Other than the injury to Ryan, we had an excellent week of practice. The team was responding to everything the coaching staff was asking of them. I constantly reminded the boys in meetings and on the field that our goal this season was a hefty one. Our target game would take place during week nine of the season against Indiana's legendary class-1A powerhouse, Sheridan. Sheridan was the only team to beat us during the 2012 season. They beat us to win the Hoosier Heartland Conference, and they beat us to win the sectional. They went on to win the regional before falling to the eventual state champions, Lafayette Central Catholic.

Sheridan's loss to Central Catholic was by ten points in a game that could have gone either way. I believed if the boys could continue to raise their level of play, we might have a shot at beating them. Could we beat them twice? No program, as long as Coach Larry "Bud" Wright had been at Sheridan, had ever beaten them twice in a season.

The Sheridan community has not been so kind as far as how they feel about me is concerned. Sheridan is a community that lives and breathes football, and football is a year-round discussion. For some reason, even though Coach Wright has dominated teams I have coached, the community has always considered any team I coach a rival. This persistent attitude has endured over the past twenty-five years of my coaching career.

For us to challenge Sheridan, it would be our focus as a team to not only compete with them but to beat them, and this would be quite an undertaking. Sheridan was coming into 2013 ranked at the very top of class 1A and bringing back an excellent team to make another championship run.

I started giving the boys a focus team prior to my second year at Tri-Central. Each year I raised the bar some but tried not to be unreasonable when setting our target game. If my expectations were beyond the reality of being met, I could possibly lose the boys mentally. The direction in 2013 had sound basis, since we'd competed with Sheridan in 2012 and lost two close games.

I truly believe that a coach's major task is centered on taking young men who lack skill, talent, and confidence and making them better. Once a player becomes better, then work to help that player become good. The boy who become good then has a chance to become a great player. It is important throughout the process for the boy to realize he is getting better so that he is able to see his potential. For all this to happen, all boys need to see this transformation happening around them. When the team begins to realize what is happening—not only to them individually, but to the entire team— a new sense of team confidence begins to blossom and success is within their grasp.

During week two of two-a-day practices, the boys were truly believing in this Team of One philosophy. A troubling event would occur during the second week that would change the team. Much depended on how I handled a problem that could have easily destroyed everything before we ever were able to get on the field and play a game.

Two boys on the team, both seniors, had money come up missing. This wasn't a little bit of money—they each had forty dollars missing. One of the boys was one of our top players and leaders of our team, a young man with outstanding character and our moral team leader. He was outraged to think that one of his teammates had stolen from him.

News got to me quickly about this incident. The boys do not lock up their lockers and have never felt threatened by teammates stealing or messing with anyone's belongings, much less their wallets. This was the first incident like this in my five-year tenure at Tri-Central. This has happened at other schools where I have coached, and it's not impossible at any school.

Everything we were doing was built on team unity and loyalty to each other, and now the very core of what the boys believed was under attack. The boys started pointing fingers and threatening each other. Utter chaos was developing as accusations went from player to player with each thinking he had the answer. I told all of them to go home. This situation would be handled the following day; they were to speak no more about it until practice. Several of our seniors came in and talked with me about who they thought might have taken the money. I told them it would be difficult to find out who did it. I would talk with the team the following day. This was our defining moment as a team. None of the coaches had an idea what to do, so I would think about it. Normally I do not like to send the boys home without all issues resolved, but I knew how complicated this situation was. I could not make a mistake in how I handled it if we wanted to move forward. If we could not trust each other off the field, how would we be able to trust each other in a pivotal situation in a game? I have always believed football is one of our last opportunities to teach young men what life in the real world is all about: the ups and downs of success and failure, the false hopes of success dashed by a momentary mistake that costs you everything. Football gives young men the opportunity to play a game of life before it is truly serious, and their life depends on their decisions. We want our young men to leave the football field believing that team effort is much more important than individual effort, that unity is the basis of success in all our lives, as has been the case throughout American history.

Every time our great country has been critically challenged either by dictators or terrorists, we as a country have put aside our personal agendas and focused on doing what we need to do to win. World War II and the terror that we all faced with 9/11 brought out the very best of our country. The United States is like a big family of sorts. We fight with each other, but when we are challenged by an outside challenge we come together. I would have less than twenty-four hours to figure out how I planned to resolve the situation at hand, and I had to come up with a solution so we could continue to move forward.

I struggled to sleep that night and could not think about practice, x's and o's, or anything other than the theft and the possibility we had a thief on our team. I tried rationalizing that anybody could have come in during practice when we were on the field and taken the money. It was about 3:00 a.m. when everything became very clear to me. I knew there would be no way to prove who took the money unless they felt guilty. At this point it had become such a big deal that that wasn't going to happen. I kept wondering how we could put this behind us, move forward, and guarantee that something like this did not happen again. I would need to make a clear statement and show passion in whatever I delivered to the boys. I would need to assert my position as leader.

The following day I arrived at school early so I could inform our athletic director of the situation. He asked if I needed him to come out and say something. Mr. Rhew is an outstanding man with a great heart, and he is dedicated to helping our young people at Tri-Central understand what is morally right and morally wrong. I told him that this was a situation that I must handle, and I thanked him for being so kind. He just smiled at me.

There are times when administrators need to be involved, and there are times a coach must take the weight of the situation and do what needs to be done. I needed to inform him of the problem, about which I am sure he already knew as we are a small school, but I needed to deal with it in my own way. It now was 2:30 p.m., and I needed to get out to the field house. When I arrived, several coaches and a few players were already there. Coach Arnold asked me what I was going to do. I told him that I had a plan for how I was going to deal with this situation, but I felt it best that I share my decision with the whole team and staff together. I told him it would be important for the staff to witness the players' reaction when I gave my talk and then report back to me when we would meet after practice how they felt the boys reacted. Coach Arnold told me that he would get the boys to get the chairs out for a team meeting and share with each assistant coach what I was asking. Coach Arnold has a special sense to know what I want him to do, and he carries out his role professionally each and every time.

At 3:30 p.m. the boys, extremely quiet, were assembled in the main meeting area of the field house waiting for me to meet with them. It was also very quiet in the coaches' office, as the coaches surely could sense that I was stressed out by this situation. I decided to let the boys sit for a brief time before I made an entrance. I knew this moment would be my first game-time speech of the season, and the ramifications for failure of delivery would probably warrant a change of direction for the team that none of us wanted to see happen. It was now 3:35 p.m. and go time.

I approached the front of our team and the coaching staff sat on the locker benches behind the players. I started by looking around the room. Every eye was focused on me.

I stood quietly for a minute, and then I began. "Boys, it has come to my attention, as you well know, that some money came up missing last evening at practice. Two members of this team have been violated by having their lockers gone through and money taken from them. This is a very serious matter, one I consider a threat not only to each of you but to the very fabric with which this program has been built. Right now we should be heading to practice, as we are three days from our scrimmage with Madison Grant High School and ten days from the opening game of the season. We are here trying to deal with the possibility that someone on this team is a thief. I take this very personally. I have given this much thought, and my plan of action is built on the essence of the direction we have been working toward since I became the head coach here at Tri-Central. If we are going to continue to believe in this program—and more important, each other—this issue must be resolved now, today, and not spoken of further from the end of this meeting forward. This situation is a personal insult to me! With that being said, both of you boys who have lost money please come forward"—I reached into my pocket and gave each of the boys forty dollars in cash—"Since this is a direct reflection of this program, and not knowing if a football player or someone local stole these two boys' money, I feel it is my obligation to make this thing right."

One of the boys said, "Coach, I can't take your money."

I replied that this was a done deal. I reminded the boys how important all of them were to me, the coaching staff, and one another. "We are now, and will always be, about us, and this is the only way I can make this right, so it is a done deal. I have preached from day one that we are only strong when we are together, and I will be damned to allow the actions of someone mess with something as special as this. I do not want to hear about this meeting in the community. This is between us, and now it is over! We are a Team of One, and none of us have the right to judge fellow members of the squad. I am proud of you young men. I believe something special is going to happen this year, and I don't want us ever to show weakness when faced with adversity. Now, this is over. Let's head out and continue to raise the bar of Tri-Central football so when week nine comes around, we will be ready for the Sheridan Blackhawks! I am done with this!"

I immediately left the boys and headed outside where I was joined by the coaching staff. The coaches did not say much, but I had a good feeling about what had just happened. As we were waiting outside, the boys did not immediately follow, and that made me feel proud. If the boys had just got up and headed out, then I would have questioned our senior leadership. By staying in and having a meeting, it showed that perhaps the issue would be resolved.

The boys came out of the locker room about ten minutes later, ready and focused as if they were heading out to the game field to play. That night we had one of the best practices I had ever seen a high-school football team have. There would never be any more discussion over the missing money, and I never heard anything in the community about it. It was clear that this was family business, and it was handled. This singular negative event would allow us to finalize the family element that I was waiting to see develop at Tri-Central. The respect and dignity all the boys would project toward the staff and each other created an atmosphere in which no matter what the adversity, we would be able to face it together.

The rest of two-a-day practices went well, and it was during our final two-a-day practice that it became clear we were going to have a special season. No matter what happened in terms of wins and losses, they were committed to working hard and enduring our practices of nonstop running, to our focus on fundamentals, and to our pursuit of playing a technically correct game.

We played Madison Grant in a scrimmage game that Friday evening at their school. We did not want to show our first opponent, Eastern Hancock, a great deal, so we planned to be very generic all evening long. We could have done some things to perform better, but our coaching plan was followed, and the boys understood going in that this was a practice game and not one that we had to win to get better. Madison Grant beat us, if someone actually kept score, but we played everybody and showed very little of what we planned to do both offensively and defensively.

It was time to start the season. We were entering week one of the season, and now everything became very important. Our game plan would need to be prepared to challenge our first opponent. We were able to get through two-a-days with two boys sidelined with injuries. Josh would be out for a month, and we would lose him at offensive tackle. Ryan would be out for two months, and he was a two-way starter at offensive guard and defensive tackle. Wyatt and Tanner were ready to fill those positions, and the team was ready to get the season underway.

CHAPTER 10

2013—Season Five

The opening week of the season finally arrived. We had been able to stay somewhat injury free, except for our two seniors previously discussed. Our coaching staff made adjustments, and the boys seemed eager to finally get to play in a game that means something.

The Indiana football polls came out on Monday, and I truly believed that we would be a top-ten team entering the season, after finishing 10–2 last season. It was not meant to be, although we were honorably mentioned at fifteen going into week one of the season. Number one in the rankings was Sheridan. Our target team, the team that I set as a goal for the boys this season, was ranked in the top spot for class 1A. There were four teams that we would play during the course of the 2013 season ranked ahead of us. We still had not won the respect of those around the state who are a part of the voting process. I was angry at first, but after thinking about it, I understood. Tri-Central has only won one sectional title, and that was in 1991. Our school had only accomplished seven winning seasons in forty-two years, with two of those winning season in the past two years. Respect for our football program would need to be handled by the boys on the field, and this ranking would add to the growing incentives the boys have to make history at Tri-Central, a little rural school in northern Tipton County. It was interesting to read online what area football enthusiasts were saying about our program.

There has been a great deal written at all levels concerning strength of schedule. People seem to continually decide the value of a team according to whom they play, how many points they win by, and how many superstars they have on the roster.

The critics were not wrong when talking about our strength of schedule by any means. Tri-Central did win ten games in 2012 with most of the players returning, but the schedule was one of the weaker schedules in class 1A. Coaches do not have the luxury of selecting whom they play. Games are locked in, according to the conference a team is in, and driving distance becomes important for nonconference games. I have never believed it to be fair to disrespect teams on my schedule or anybody else's. I have always respected every team we play, and I work hard to prepare and defeat each team during the season. People in the area do not realize that the supposed weak schedule that we play has not really changed much over the years, and those schools were all beating Tri-Central every year. Now that we're having some success, it is because we have a weak schedule. This strength of schedule would hurt us in the polls all season long, but I told the boys that we needed to take care of business on the field and control what we can control. Respect is a funny thing in today's world. People seem to believe that if you demand respect, then you will receive it. I teach our young men that respect is earned each day on the practice field and in the classroom, and by how each young man lives his life. If we continue to strive to demonstrate great character, then the respect will quietly come through hard work, dedication, and a profound belief in one another.

Our season schedule consisted of nine games, after which every team in the state entered the state tournament. We began in week one against one of the best teams in class 1A, Eastern Hancock. Eastern Hancock was coming off a 6-6 season, with most of their players also returning. This could be the best team that we would see all season until we play Sheridan (a conference opponent) in week nine. All the hype of preseason was now over and we were going to focus only on preparing for Eastern Hancock.

Our coaching staff prepares perhaps much differently at Tri-Central than coaches do at other schools. We meet at Saturday morning films with the boys and go through the contest from the evening before. As we watch film, we discuss plays, fundamentals, mistakes, etc., which is pretty normal in most programs. When films are over, the coaches discuss privately what needs to be fixed immediately and how that will happen. I allow all coaches the opportunity to discuss what needs to improve and what our focus needs to be during the next week. If an outsider walked into our coaches' meeting, it would be a struggle to figure out who the head coach is, as all coaches listen to one another, and all coaches are a part of all solutions. This meeting is usually informal and does not last long.

After the meeting, the true preparation takes place for the next opponent. Most members of the staff have several children and are active in our youth programs at Tri-Central. Everyone will do their preparation over the weekend, and then on Monday evening, the plan will be introduced. I usually help our defensive coordinator break down opponent offense, as this is the most tedious job in coaching. I will then watch film looking at defense so I can give my insight on Monday to our offensive coordinator. I will spend some time looking at special teams, but my special team's coordinator does an outstanding job in preparation, and often I need to back him off some come Monday evening. Our offensive and defensive coordinators could be head coaches anywhere, and they do an outstanding job of preparation. The major task I must be sure of is our practice schedule for the week. I listen to our staff and adjust it according to time needed for position coaches. I am quite OCD when it comes to time management, and the staff knows that once the schedule is finalized, I will expect everyone to stick to it.

It was now Monday, time to introduce the plan and go to work. After all of the coaches arrived, we discussed our plan and headed to practice. We conditioned our players first and then went over special-team plans, followed by offense and finally defense. At this point, we went into the field house to watch our opponent together and discuss keys. Eastern Hancock looked outstanding on film. Their offense was fast and very athletic; there were two boys in the backfield who were perhaps the best we would see all season. Defensively they played fast and were very fundamental in tackling technique. This would be a one-time contract between the schools, and we were lucky enough to play the game at our field. The boys were upbeat all week and prepared well. On Thursday evening we invited our parents out to meet our 2013 team. I discussed our upcoming season and said that many of our opponents were very good. We then invited the parents to come to the field and take as many pictures as they wanted of players in uniform and coaches. The evening was a total success. As the last players and parents left the field, it was finally time to play.

As soon as I finished my last class on Friday afternoon at Clinton Central, I head to Tri-Central. The situation of teaching at one school and being a head coach at another school is far from ideal, but the current Clinton Central administration has been very kind during the fall, and Tri-Central has also helped make the situation work.

I got in my old 1992 Ford truck and headed to Tri-Central. When I arrived it was 3:45 p.m., and I went right to work. One of the major ways that I have dealt with stress over the years is work. I pulled my truck up to the field house and loaded up the field markers to place on the field. Coach Arnold and Coach Johnson showed up shortly after I started, and they both helped me set field markers. I asked Coach Arnold if he was ready, and he laughed and said he was.

Slowly the boys began to arrive around 4:30 p.m. They seemed very confident and focused as they began to gather and prepare their equipment for the game. By 5:00 p.m., everyone was taped and putting on their uniforms for our 5:20 meeting. At 5:20, I had each of the coordinators talk briefly to the boys about assignments. When they were done, I discussed the keys to victory. I went over the importance of playing fundamentally, staying focused, and avoiding penalties, and the importance of field position in big games. Once more I said that this team might be the best team we'd see all season, and it would be great to make a statement tonight.

As we were concluding our meeting, Eastern Hancock arrived. It seemed as if they'd brought two teams instead of one; they dressed fifty-five boys to represent their school. Usually in class 1A, team size is around twenty-five to thirty, so it was rather unusual to see such a high number. We would dress thirty-seven players, which was unbelievable in itself. Our program had averaged twenty-two players for the past eight years.

During pregame, both teams went through their respective routines. It is during this time that I get to watch our opponent in person and evaluate them firsthand. Every high-school team has outstanding players in the backfield, so I do not watch them as much as I do linemen. Eastern Hancock's linemen were disciplined, big, and fast. After watching them warm up, it was clear that we were in for a ball game.

The game was a hard-hitting, high-scoring game, with both teams making plenty of first-game mistakes. We took the lead early only to lose it and went into half time down just a point, 16–15, in a first half that we played far from perfectly. Defensively we had practiced all summer moving boys into different positions, thinking those changes might help us be better. It was clear during the first half that the changes we made did not make us better, but there was no way of telling until we were actually in a game situation. At this point there was not much we could do in terms of personnel other than coach the boys up at half time. Eastern Hancock also surprised us by not huddling and calling their plays from the line of scrimmage. There was little time to get ready to play and no time to make adjustments. Their offense was outstanding! They spread their players out, and they had speed all across their offense. One boy on their team stood out from the rest. Their running back was big, fast, and very skilled; it was clear that we were not going to be able to stop him. It became important for the second half that we find a way to slow him down.

Offensively we moved the ball well against their outstanding defense. We just made too many penalty and miscue mistakes when we were in scoring position. I felt confident that our offense would score in the second half, and I told Coach Arnold that whoever had the ball last would probably win the game. Coach Arnold and Coach

Perez were focused and did not panic. Each coach presented the issues that needed to be presented for us to have an opportunity to win. The boys remained poised and listened attentively.

It has always been my way to talk to the boys last before the game and before we left the locker room at half time. Coach Kennedy (whose job is to keep me informed on time remaining before we must return to the field) came up and told me we had three minutes left. I went in front of the team and told them that we had to play smarter in the second half, especially when we entered Easter Hancock's red zone, and we must take care of the ball. Defensively we could not give up the big play and must force them to drive the field. I wished the boys good luck. The boys did not seem tired or down but just the opposite. They knew they were playing a very good team and were focused on the challenge.

The third quarter is an important quarter in a game. On this night, it seemed as if the officials' calls and the bounce of the ball went Eastern Hancock's way. They could not stop us, and we could not stop them. At the end of the third quarter, we were down 32–23. At the start of the fourth quarter, we had the ball. Our running back seemed stopped by contact, but there was no whistle. An Eastern Hancock defender took the ball away, and the officials let the play stand. A few plays later we were down 40–23 in a game that looked like it was going to be a blowout.

At this point, with ten minutes left in the game something happened that would change our program for the rest of the year. It clearly appeared that Eastern Hancock had complete control of the game. In the past, our team at Tri-Central and our fans might have given up when faced with this type of adversity. Ironically it seemed as if everything we had been teaching had all come together now. Our fans began to cheer harder and louder, and our boys clearly had not lost their focus and were not going to quit.

The boys took the ball and marched down the field and scored. Now we were down 40–29. We onside kicked on the ensuing kickoff and won the ball. With around five minutes left in the game, we marched down and scored, making the score 40–35. At this point we had about three minutes left in the game, and I had planned to use our time-outs systematically to get one more chance on offense. We used two time-outs and had one left as Eastern Hancock continued to move the ball. There was a minute and a half left, and Eastern Hancock was facing a third down and twelve around our forty-yard line. I told the official that if they ran the ball and we stopped them, I would be using our last time-out. Everything had come down to this single play. They ran a play-action pass and completed it for a first down around our twenty-yard line. We no longer had a chance to win. On the following play they scored, and the final score read Eastern Hancock 47 and Tri-Central 35.

We had lost our opening game to an outstanding team in a game that we could have given up in. It was a spectacular win for Eastern Hancock and a crushing defeat for us. All I could think about as we were shaking hands is that this would not happen again!

By the time I got to the locker room the boys were very quiet taking off their gear while the coaches were quietly discussing the game in the coach's office connected to the locker room. I was frustrated and angry about the loss. I knew the boys gave everything they had to get back into the game, just to lose it in the end. I have a routine after game procedure that I have followed most of my long coaching career, which I have described. Tonight was different. I passed the coaches in the office and headed into the main locker room area. I admonished the boys to stop what they were doing and listen to me. Every boy immediately stopped what they were doing, and all eyes were locked on me.

I said, "This was a game we should not have lost. We did not play fundamentally for four quarters against a very good team. This is the best team we will see all season, but now our backs are against the wall, and we need to prepare even harder than we have been preparing. Everyone in this program has worked hard, and everyone deserves better. It is clear that we need to make some adjustments with personnel, and you must trust in your coaches to fix this thing before it really becomes broke. Next week we play our closest rival just five miles down the road, and we need to be ready to make a statement. Next week will be the most important week of the season. Each of you will be challenged both physically and mentally to become better as we continue our quest as a Team of One!"

I then walked outside for a minute to clear my head. The boys were motionless during my animated speech, and by the time I returned to the locker room they had again continued to take showers and get dressed to leave. I now approached each boy, and shook his hand, and told him how much I believed and cared about him. The response from all of my seniors when I shook their hand was the same: "We will be all right, Coach!"

When I got to the coaches' office, the staff was already discussing personnel changes, and Coach Perez was leading the discussion. Coach Perez told me that he wanted to move all the boys back to where they were last season. He would move Seth back to strong safety, Dillon to outside linebacker, and Cody back to inside linebacker. He wanted to know how long we were going to leave Colton (a sophomore) at free safety before we looked to move someone else in. I told him and the staff that I agreed with all the defensive changes, but I was not ready to count Colton out at free safety. This was his first game, and it would take some time for him to become acclimated to this position. Colton was an outstanding sophomore athlete and had the potential to becoming one of the best free safeties in class-1A football. I told Coach Perez it was his job to coach him up and help him improve. Coach Perez agreed, and before we left for home, we all agreed on what needed to happen for us to fix our defense so we were not faced with giving up this many points again. Eastern Hancock scored more points on us in this single game than had been scored against us in over a year. Our offense was fine, but for us to be in position to compete with state-level teams, our defense must improve.

Coach Perez is an outstanding defensive coach, and I knew if it was possible for us to get fixed quickly, he would know how to do it. Our fundamentals were fine, our team speed was fine. We just needed to fix our defensive team continuity, and I was hopeful that would happen.

Offensively, Coach Arnold does an incredible job preparing our boys but we needed to take better care of the ball, especially in the red zone, and I knew as he left that night that he would also take care of the offensive issues. Week one was over, and now it was time to move on.

Coaching high-school football is unlike coaching other sports; you only play once a week, and whether you win or lose, the wait is the same for redemption or continued success. In our case, losing the first game had quieted people from talking about Tri-Central football. This would be an important week for us to fix the problems we had and get our first win. Usually we do not meet as a staff over the weekend due to reasons mentioned earlier, but we met on Sunday afternoon to go over notes about our upcoming opponent, Taylor, and to finalize our changes concerning our defensive personnel. Usually when we meet there is some quiet small talk as we wait for everyone to arrive. On this Sunday there was no small talk. As soon as coaches arrived, it seemed everyone was focused and on a mission. We discussed our personnel changes first, with everyone agreeing on the change of direction we felt needed to take place. The decisions we made to move the three boys back to where they played in 2012 and work to make the fourth better would change our course for the rest of the season.

We then discussed Taylor High School and went over our scouting reports on them and our plan of attack. Taylor football had been going through a rough time for the past few years. Their coach was working diligently to move them in the right direction and surely felt that this was a perfect time to play us. Taylor is located just five miles north of our school, and this fact creates a natural rivalry. We knew their boys would be excited to play us and ready to get back at us for beating them the last three years. We went over our plan of attack, and I asked Coach Arnold, Coach Perez, and Coach Hatcher what they needed in terms of time. I suggested that we needed to focus on fundamentals throughout the week. I told them that we did not need to punish them but prepare them.

Coach Arnold spoke up. "Coach, you don't believe in punishing anyway!"

We all laughed, and I told them that I would put together the daily plan of action and hand it out tomorrow (Monday). All the coaches said that they would continue to watch film and that they felt confident we would be ready by Friday. Coach Arnold watches primarily offense, Coach Perez watches defense, Coach Hatcher watches special teams, Coach Hunter concentrates on offensive-line play from a defensive perspective, and Coach Tolle focuses on line play from an offensive perspective. All of these guys could be head coaches, as all of them have a serious commitment to prepare boys to perform at their best.

It was about 9:00 p.m. when my phone rang. Coach Arnold was ready to talk football. We talked about the Taylor defense for about thirty minutes.

When I arrived at practice, Coach Arnold had the boys running. Monday is our conditioning day to get the weekend out of their system. Most of the staff arrives around 3:40 p.m. Coach Arnold is usually at the field house to greet the boys each day when they arrive.

By the time I reached the field house, the boys were done with their conditioning and headed to the locker room for a water break and to get dressed in half pads for our Monday evening practice. The boys were quiet around me as they got ready, and I told them that we would have a brief meeting before we went out. As the boys were getting chairs out for us to meet, I went into the coaches' office. The staff was ready for practice. I told them that I was going to say a few things to the team, and then we'd go to work. It was clear from the demeanor of the staff that Friday was not going to come soon enough. I walked out into the main locker room and told the boys it was time to go to work. My expectations for this week were for the team to focus on details and to concentrate every night on what their coaches were asking of them. I told them that I was proud of them.

As we headed to the field, the boys seemed eager to get started. Our special-teams practice was focused on what Coach Hatcher wants to achieve. Our offensive practice went well, and the boys worked hard.

Then it was time for defense. Coach Perez called them together. Coach Perez blamed himself for some of the miscues on Friday evening and again shared with the boys the changes that we were going to incorporate that week. I was really impressed as I listened to Coach Perez give direction. Each boy listened attentively, and not one boy questioned or looked upset with his plan. Coach Perez went over the keys to Taylor's offense and then asked position coaches to take athletes and work individually on fundamentals and skills. We all worked with our defensive-coaching discipline for twenty minutes, and then Coach Perez called the defense together for pursuit drill. We had looked fast up to now when we did pursuit drill, as Coach Perez believes this is one of the most important drills we do besides hit the sled to work on tackling. Tonight, we not only looked fast, but there was an air of determination that I had not seen up to this moment during my tenure at Tri-Central.

When the coaches gathered in the office after practice, I shared my thoughts about the pursuit drill. Every coach also noticed the same thing. I told the coaches losing to Eastern Hancock in week one might be the final piece to putting this team in a direction with a purpose.

Our weekly practice plan is routine. Usually when I arrive, the boys are finishing up special teams and getting drills ready for the coaching staff. After the first year that I implemented this program at Tri-Central, the boys realized that practice would follow a general routine that would never change. They then began taking more ownership by helping the coaches prepare our work stations on the practice field. I have never seen this at any other school where I have worked, and I relished the thought of how badly these boys wanted to win and change the course of Tri-Central football.

I believe routine and repetition are essential in high-school coaching. Every day of practice we work on fundamentals, not only during drills but throughout the practice. As a staff, we never let any fundamental mistake go without correction, even if the player does something extremely athletic. He needs to play the game correctly at all times if we are going to beat not the average teams but the best teams the state has to offer in our class.

It was finally game night, and everyone was excited and ready to play the game. There were storms in the area, and the concern was lightning as we approached game time. Our team came out fast and took control from the very start, jumping out to a 7–0 lead. The weather quickly became a factor, and lightning flashed, stopping the game and sending both teams to the locker room. The IHSAA has a rule that games cannot start back up until thirty minutes after the last lightning strike. We had a long wait, but finally the officials gave the all clear, and we headed back to where the game had left off. When we came back out to play, we were flat, and Taylor scored, making the score 7–6. Our boys quickly regrouped, and we went on to get our first win of the young season, 39–13. Taylor had been winless, but rivalry games often can be unpredictable. Our offense played very well, as did our special teams. My greatest concern was our productivity defensively, and the boys performed outstandingly for Coach Perez. Coach Perez was extremely proud of the boys, which he shared with them. The only remaining concern for our defense was the continued improvement of our free safety, Colton. Colton played better, but he still would need to continue working on playing better downhill and hitting. The good news was that Coach Perez gained some confidence in him, and it was clear to me that by the end of the season, this young man might be special.

The true strength of the team was on the line of scrimmage on both sides of the ball. The linebackers and defensive backs were very talented. They just needed experience working together in their current positions to gain the continuity to become very good. After we lost to Eastern Hancock, the staff decided that once we moved the boys back, there would be no more changes, and it would be our responsibility to make sure they all became good together. We were now 1-1 and ready to begin conference play during week three against Carroll High School.

We would play at home against our first conference opponent, Carroll High School. Carroll had received a great deal of respect coming into the season, with perhaps the largest offensive and defensive lines in class 1A. One of the top receivers also had come back in their program. We had another great week of preparation, but the coaches were very concerned with the size of Carroll coming into the game. We had stayed honorably mentioned in the rankings but were behind Carroll, and the general consensus around the area was that this was Carroll's year.

It was a beautiful Friday evening, and a large crowd was on hand to witness this game. The Tri-Central community has always represented well at home games (even during the rough times), and this night would not be any different; our stands were full. Carroll also had a large following. It was clear this game was important for both programs—the winner would be in position to challenge Sheridan for the conference title. It was game time. I stood on the sidelines to witness the size of the Carroll boys, which was very impressive.

The first quarter ended with us in position to score, but the first quarter ended scoreless. We scored at the beginning of the second quarter and seemingly took control of the game. We went up fifteen points with our defense playing very well. Right before half time Carroll scored, and the game at half time was 15–6. The first half we played very well both offensively and defensively. Carroll did not have an answer for Garrett, our running back, which in part was due to the outstanding performance of Coach Tolle's offensive line. On defense, Riley, Darius, and Lake, our defensive linemen, put on quite a performance. Riley was having a breakout game, and Carroll linemen had no answer for this outstanding junior. Everyone we play knew about Lake and Darius, as both of these boys have been regulars for two seasons on our defensive front, but on this night, Riley put on such a display of talent that future opponents would be faced with an entire defensive front that was fast, athletic, and very determined.

At the start of the third quarter, our team came out and looked tired. Carroll seized the momentum and scored, making the score 15–14 going into the fourth quarter. It seemed to be a wakeup call for the boys, and we scored enough in the fourth quarter to win the game 29–22. Garrett continued to have an outstanding second half, as did Cody, who threw the ball to Seth, who caught a key touchdown pass to seal the victory. The most important development in the second half was the play of Colton, our free safety. Colton had several key open-field tackles and ended the evening with eleven tackles and breaking up several passes. Colton had figured it out, and Coach Perez could not talk enough about how proud he was of Colton and Riley on their roles in our victory. We were still not getting a great deal of respect in the football polls or on the football discussion websites. None of us, including the boys, really cared much. We were only concerned with the game at hand, not looking ahead or seeking anything that we could not control. Our focus presently would be Clinton Prairie High School and our second conference game, which would be played at Clinton Prairie, a small rural school in western Clinton County.

It was now week four, and we would be facing the Clinton Prairie Gophers at their school come Friday night. We were able to stay injury-free other than the two seniors who were still unable to play. Josh, our senior offensive tackle, rejoined the team this week. Wyatt had been playing right tackle and doing a solid job. Josh would need to get all his practices in, so Wyatt would get the nod for one more week before Josh would be ready to rejoin the lineup. During week four, our practices were very systematic in preparation. The boys were becoming closer and more focused, and we now had a record of 2–1. Clinton Prairie was a solid team but lacked numbers. This is often a problem in class 1A, one that I have had to deal with on occasion.

Their coach is an outstanding person and a skilled coach. I had played against his teams at both Clinton Central and Tri-Central, and I knew his team would be fundamentally sound and under his leadership play hard. The game started with us scoring quickly. Early in the first quarter, Clinton Prairie's top player, a 250-pound fullback on offense and an end on defense, had what appeared to be a possibly serious injury. When Clinton Prairie lost their top player, the game got out of hand quickly, and we were able to win 54–0. As it turned out, the boy was all right, and we all were glad of that. Clinton Prairie was struggling, Carroll lost again—this time to Sheridan big—Taylor continued to lose, and the only team having success that we had played, Easter Hancock, was still on a roll and undefeated.

We were now 2–0 in the conference while being 3–1 overall. We still only received honorable mention votes, and people were still making light of our schedule. We did not talk about the rankings much. The boys and the coaches still had the blinders on, thinking only of whom we would play next. It would be the midway point of the season, and we would travel to Monroe County to play 3–1 Monroe Central.

As the coaches prepared for week five there was concern about this team, which was senior dominated, and the fact they had a very talented coaching staff. The coaching staff at Monroe Central was in their second year together at Monroe Central. They had been together for years at a Muncie school, a big school where they were quite successful, and they brought to Monroe Central a change in attitude and a change in performance.

It was a long bus trip to Monroe Central, and when we got there it was already raining. The field was wet but very well kept. The conditions were bad, but at least the field was playable. I have only known the head coach and defensive coordinator a short time, but they are two of the great men I have known over the years. They are respectful, and their players are a class act on and off the field. I watched them during the pregame, and I was very impressed with their skilled athletes and how these two coaches have definitely had an impact on the quality of the Monroe Central program. I knew we were in for a challenge as we headed back to the locker room for final instructions to our athletes.

The game started out with the rain coming down in sheets. It wasn't cold, but it was a nagging misty rain as the game started to unfold. During the first half, our offense moved the ball at will, only to fumble the ball or get a costly penalty. We were in their red zone several times and could not produce any points. Then midway through the second quarter, they caught us with a seam pass, and a great pass from their quarterback to the receiver made the score 7–0 at half time. It was a long walk back to the locker room at the school, so I decided we would stay close to the field and advised the seniors to take the team to their baseball dugout for our half-time meeting. The coaching staff walked behind them, and there was nothing said. I cannot ever remember our staff being that quiet leaving the field at half time. Usually our coaches are already running things by me and with each other on what needs to be handled when we meet the team; tonight there was just silence. The dugout was so dark that I could not even make out our players' faces. Again, there was nothing coming from the boys, and the silence seemed to be contagious. Often at half time when a team is not playing to their potential, fans think the coach screams and threatens the players, singles players out, and then challenges their manhood. There was a time when I might have been that coach, but not with this team. We had made a commitment to our motto, a Team of One, and if I reacted in a negative manner, it might not pay off. The boys had their heads down, and so did the coaches. We had beaten this team pretty good the last few years, and the boys and coaches were embarrassed. I stood in front of the team awhile, and I sensed they were ready to get a tongue-lashing for the lack of focus during the first half. I was angry about one thing—they had their heads down.

I then addressed the team quietly. "Boys, the first thing that is going to happen right now is that each and every one of you will get your head up. We did everything right this first half except finish. There is nothing wrong with you! Right now you look like a team who is playing not to lose instead of playing to win! Coaches do not need to change anything; our plan is fine. What we need to do right now is have the seniors to take control and show they are capable of dealing with adversity under fire. You will win this game in the second half. Let me tell you why. You boys have been focused all season, and tonight is not the night that we give up our mission. Seniors, you lead! Underclassmen, you follow! Coaches, you coach, and let's make this first half a bad memory!"

Not the boys but the coaches immediately caught their breath. The coaches started talking to the boys, and the boys were communicating back. I really felt they would be fine in the second half. Coach Kennedy informed us it was time, and we headed back to the field with the heads up and a bounce to the legs. At this point, this game might get interesting.

When we got the ball to start the third quarter, the momentum change was started by our sophomore running back, Dillon. Dillon had a brilliant run that set up our first score, and now the boys were totally focused. We went on to win 24–13, and it truly was a great win for us and a moral victory for Monroe Central. We left respecting the Monroe Central team and coaches with our fourth consecutive win, and they left showing that their program had made sizable improvement. We were now 4–1 on the season and gaining some ground in the rankings but still being criticized over our strength of schedule.

We would now head into a conference matchup with the school where I was the head coach for twenty years. This game was important because it was a conference game, and if we win it, then the showdown with Sheridan in week nine would be for the championship, as it was last season. This game would also be our school's homecoming, and although Clinton Central was struggling, they had a handful of outstanding players on the team. The Clinton Central boys would play extremely hard, as this game has become a solid rivalry between the schools over the years.

We were now at the halfway point of the season, with a record of 4–1. We had moved up to eleventh in the state rankings. Josh was back now, but Ryan would need to sit out two more weeks before returning against Sheridan (at least that was our hope). Our senior running back, Garrett, was now in a position where he might challenge to set a school rushing record. Garrett has overachieved the last two years, but his offensive performance was a complete surprise. Everything Garrett had done thus far was due to his outstanding work ethic and determination. The other running backs, Dillon and Cody, were also playing well. Our receivers each brought something different to the offense and each one of them—Jade, Seth, Bryce, Cale, and Colten—were having a great season. Our quarterback, Cody, was also having a great year. Defensively, Coach Perez had the boys playing extremely well. Our defensive front, including Darius, Ryan, Lake, Dillon, and Bryce, were a force for any offense to deal with. Each week they were gaining confidence. Our inside linebackers, Garrett and Cody, were making plays and flowing to the ball well. Our secondary, including Davee, Cody, Seth, and Colton, were also playing at a very high level.

The first half of the season saw us start with a loss and never look back from that point to now. Clinton Central was the fastest team that we would see up to this point, and they also had three players who were as good as any school in class 1A might have. This game would be an important challenge, offering us a different struggle to prepare for.

It was now week six, homecoming week, a conference game, and yes, a strong local rivalry to contend with. I was still teaching at Clinton Central, which would make this an uncomfortable week for the boys and me at Clinton Central. One year ago we were fortunate to beat Clinton Central at their homecoming. This year they would be coming to Tri-Central to play us at our homecoming. The administration, community, and students at Clinton Central had not made a big deal with my coaching transition at Tri-Central. I kept football off the topic list in my classroom for the most part, other than wishing the boys luck each week. I kidded the boys that I would wish them luck all season except when they face Tri-Central, and everyone involved smiled and then would be done with it.

The talk forums still had not given us much credit as we entered the sixth game of the season. The thing is, I understand. Tri-Central has never been a postseason threat, and since we play—according to others—a weak schedule, it gives merit to people's view of our program. Talk during the week was centered on Clinton Central playing one of the most difficult schedules in class 1A, which might give them the edge over us. I believe it doesn't matter *how much* a team wins or loses by, the prominent focus after a game is *whether* you win or lose.

Another factor with our team not getting hyped up over the lack of respect in the polls and public opinion was that, frankly, we believed in us and planned to stay on the path of taking each game one at a time. A major part of this reasoning centered on our team concept that any team can rise up and beat you if you look past them. Plus, we enjoyed the underdog role.

Practice now was routine in preparation and our focus on detail. Coaches put the final touches on the plan Monday night, and for the rest of the week we would tweak parts of it until we were satisfied to present it on Friday night. This week, coaches were very concerned with Clinton Central's speed at the specialty positions. Their line was somewhat suspect, but their backs on offense and their defensive linebackers on defense were as good as we would see all season. It was easy to notice that the Clinton Central boys were eager to get a shot at our team, as they were extremely quiet during the week around me.

At practice on Thursday evening, our offense was going through plays, and as I always have done, I headed into the locker room to put the keys to the game on the whiteboard. At our team meeting, and when they arrive on Friday evening, they will see them, remember them, and plan to orchestrate them.

The boys came in, and we talked briefly about homecoming festivities. Then I presented the keys to the game. All eyes were on the board as I went through what we had to do to be in position to win. I reminded the boys that this game was very important as a rivalry game against us. Clinton Central would play hard for four quarters, and we needed to be ready to play hard for four quarters. To conclude the meeting I asked them, "How many points do we need to beat them by?"

In unison they yelled, "One!"

Ever since I started coaching, I have always preached to teams that running up the score is just wrong, and the most important thing they must never forget is that as long as you score one more point than your opponent, you win. There is a great deal of speculation over point spreads but I believe in high-school football it is not an issue at all. I will admit that there are games that get out of control, and the score gets out of hand; those things happen. As long as the coach is not trying to run up the score, respect is never lost. The coaches met one last time, and everyone decided to watch more film before the game to make sure we had not missed something.

Friday was finally here, and the atmosphere at Clinton Central was quite reserved. I was testing all day in my classes, so there was not much time for rhetoric; I was focused totally on my classroom and my students. When school was dismissed I jumped in my truck, changed my tie to the navy-blue tie I wear at every game, and started off to Tri-Central. I arrived at 3:45 p.m., and parents were already there, laying out blankets to reserve their places in the bleachers. This started during my third year at Tri-Central, and it truly made me feel good. People actually knew that the bleachers would be filled, and they wanted to come out early to reserve their spots. Each year the community has come out earlier to set up, and this year half the bleachers were already covered with blankets at 3:45 p.m. for a game that would start at 7:00 p.m. As always, Coach Arnold was already there, getting markers out, getting headphones ready, checking kits, and folding towels. He stopped when I walked in to say hi, and I asked him if he was ready for the game. He just laughed as he always does and said, "Coach, you know I will be ready."

He finished his tasks, and we sat down to talk about the plan. Coach Arnold is an outstanding coach because he prepares so well. We talked briefly about the offensive game plan as coaches and players began to arrive. By 5:00 p.m., the team was all there. Some boys were finishing up shaving.

I have a rule that boys must be clean-shaven on Friday night and their hair must be trimmed. I do not allow earrings inside the field house. One might think this is a little too much old-school philosophy, but I feel that where there is sacrifice, there is commitment. Our boys know the rules, and each week many do not shave until Friday when they come into the field house and shave together. The team unity and respect for one another and the team is very special.

The boys got ready, and we went through our normal pregame. The focus seemed great, and everyone looked ready as we left the field. Our coordinators went through last instructions before I spoke to the team. I went over the game plan one more time before we went to a knee and said the Lord's Prayer together. After we had finished our prayer, all stood up and waited for my final thoughts. I hesitated, I started to speak, and then I simply smiled and started a slow clap. The boys instantly smiled and joined in the clap until it was pulsating the locker room and I yelled, "WIN!" Which was echoed, and we proceeded to the field. The boys organized their two lines to take the field, with seniors in front.

As we walked, I began the ritual. "This is our field, this is our night, hit, no stupid penalties, hold on to the ball, hit, no turnovers, play together, win together! Now go take our field."

With that, the boys took off to run through the band while they were playing our school song and then through the student tunnel to the middle of the field. It was game time!

Clinton Central had a small following. Our bleachers were overflowing. There were people about three deep along the field fence. It was great to see so many of the Tri-Central community come out to back our team and enjoy homecoming events. Our boys were ready. We dominated from start to finish, with twenty first downs and thirty-five points, while the Bulldogs of Clinton Central were held to two first downs and zero points. Coach Arnold wanted to work on our passing game, and our junior quarterback, Cody, had a great night, throwing for over 280 yards with three touchdown passes. Our boys were very respectful to the boys of Clinton Central after the game, as were the Clinton Central players. We were now 5–1 on the season and in position for a rematch with Sheridan for the conference championship in week nine. There was little time to think about week nine, as all of our attention would go to the Anderson Prep Academy, who would be our week-seven opponent and our senior night.

The following Monday the polls came out, and for the first time this year, we were ranked in the top ten. We were number ten, but this showed that people were starting to notice Tri-Central somewhat. We were ranked number ten the year before, only to fall from the top ten after losing week nine to Sheridan. The game would have to wait; we had two opponents to get through before we played them.

We were still healthy, and that's important at this time in the season. Ryan, our offensive guard and defensive tackle, started practicing today. For the first time we were complete as a team, although it would be two weeks before Ryan would be available. It was extremely difficult for Ryan, and now that he could practice, it became more difficult. Ryan is an outstanding player, and our line coaches were looking forward to getting him back into the lineup. The boys who carried the load while he has been injured have done a remarkable job. Both Tanner and Wyatt on the offensive line did everything we asked and became better with the experience they were getting each week. On the defensive side, we already had three outstanding defensive linemen with Darius, Lake, and Riley. Ryan will give us depth on defense as the schedule gets tough in the tournament series; we will be able to rotate down linemen.

Week seven would be our last home game of the regular season. This is the traditional night to honor the seniors by introducing them individually and saying a few words about them. This would be a difficult, emotional evening, as this group of seniors have been so instrumental in the Tri-Central program turnaround. These boys represented everything coaches look for out of seniors. This group of boys stuck it out during the good and the bad, always believing in each other and their coaches. The level of respect and unity developed on this team was a true compliment to each of these young men. It would be nice if I could take all the credit for the transformation at Tri-Central, but it would be an injustice to the community, administration, coaches, players, and yes, the seniors. It took everyone involved to create something special and unique. This community seemed to be on the verge of something that might be unforgettable, depending on variables yet to be identified.

We had another great week of practice leading up to senior night, and the pregame introduction of the seniors was very emotional for everyone. The team we were playing was coming into Tri-Central with a current record of 2–4 but had won their last two games. Anderson Prep was going through some tough times, as their team was short on numbers with several boys injured.

Their coaching staff is made up of great leaders, and they coach the boys very well. I believe if the coaches are allowed to continue to develop the program, their program will be exciting to watch in the near future. The boys on the team are very athletic and fast. The program is still developing—they have only played varsity football for a few years.

Our boys came out early and put the game away, winning 52–0. They played well early, and since we were up big, the younger boys on our team finished the game in the fourth quarter. There was an interesting development late in the game that stood out for me as the head coach.

With about two minutes left in the game, Anderson Prep was in position to score inside our red zone at the ten- yard line with a first and goal. We had shut them out all night, and it would be up to our junior varsity to hold them. A score at this point in a 52–0 game was not a big deal to me, but to our defensive coordinator and the team, it was important for these boys to hold Anderson Prep. It was exciting to watch our varsity players cheering on our junior varsity players. The boys held as the clock ran out. The varsity boys ran to the field and congratulated the younger players with hugs and high fives. This was another one of those moments I cherished as I stood quietly on the sidelines. Our program had come a long way, and with this display of respect from the older boys to the younger boys, it truly made me think that we were close to becoming what we have inscribed on our practice fence: A Team of One!

Our football team was now 6–1 heading into week eight and beginning to get more respect in the polls. We were now ranked ninth in class 1A. This was now the longest that we had been able to remain in the top ten of our class in the school's history.

Our focus began over the weekend toward Wes Del High School, as we would be playing them on Saturday afternoon. I really do not like to play on Saturday; it changes our routine. On the plus side, we would all get to go and scout Sheridan, who would be playing the top team in our class, Linton, at Sheridan. On the downside, every class-1A team in the state would now get to come and scout us on Saturday night. Wes Del is a small school situated in Delaware County, which is close to Muncie and one of our longest road trips. Wes Del was currently 5–3 on the season with a new coach and a new excitement surrounding football.

I was impressed as I watched them on film; they have a large squad with mostly underclassmen playing. I feel their new coaching staff has made it clear that they are going to focus on fundamentals, and I look for them to become a team everyone in class 1A will notice.

Our week of preparation was focused, but the boys were already becoming restless about week nine, when we would face Sheridan. I did not want to talk about Sheridan, although I had been watching Sheridan game film all season. The best way to look at it was that I did my work, and watching Sheridan and studying them throughout the season was kind of a stress release and my recreational release. Anyway, it was important for me as a head coach to be ready for any questions presented to me by players, community, and coaches about them when that game week came around. This week was a nonconference opponent. The Sheridan game would mean a great deal more, but we could not lose focus and lose a game that we should win.

Practice went well all week. Ryan was just about ready to get back into the lineup, but he would have to sit out one more game. Ryan was frustrated and wanted to play this week; he felt he was ready to jump back into the left guard position. I told him that we all were excited that he would be back next week, and I tried to get him to relax a little by saying he would be our secret weapon against Sheridan. Ryan just laughed and continued to be a great example and do his part to lead from the sidelines.

We had a light practice on Friday evening. We told the boys they had to get showered and out quickly so we could go scout Sheridan. The team did as we requested, and we were off to watch the top game of the week in class 1A at Sheridan.

When we arrived at Sheridan, a large crowd had already gathered for this memorable game. Linton was coming into Sheridan undefeated and ranked number one in class 1A; Sheridan was coming in at 4–3 and ranked tenth right behind us. The three Sheridan losses were against very good bigger school programs. Sheridan is a great place to play, as the atmosphere is everything high-school football is supposed to be. Sheridan has played in eleven state championships and won nine. Linton has won eight regionals but has yet to make it to the premier game in the state. Both teams were very mechanical during pregame as people continued to flood into the Bud Wright Stadium. Coach Wright is one of the few coaches to have the game field named after him while he is still actively coaching.

The game was a hard-hitting, fundamentally sound contest from the start. Early in the contest, Sheridan had a couple of key players injured, which seemed to change the course of the game. At half time, Linton had a commanding lead, up 26–0.

On the first possession of the second half, Sheridan's all-state running back broke loose and scored on a forty-yard run. Unfortunately for Sheridan, offensively that was it. The final score was Linton 26 and Sheridan 7. The good news for Sheridan was that their defense did not allow Linton to score in the second half of play. Sheridan has always been a defense-first program, and Coach Wright is in a class by himself when it comes to preparation. Most of our varsity team was there at the game, and the boys really did not watch the game as you would think typical high-school boys would. They were coming up to the coaches and discussing formations and personnel as if they were coaches. It was exhilarating to see the focus of our team and how knowledgeable our players had become. We all left late in the game to get some rest for our long adventure to Wes Del and our quest to continue our winning streak.

As I drove the bus toward Wes Del, I thought about how important it would be for us to avoid injury and find a way to score one more point than Wes Del. This was their homecoming game, and we would be prepared for that as we were for everybody's homecoming. I knew they would come out extremely excited thinking, they had nothing to lose. When teams come out loose like this, good things can happen for them, or things can go bad fast.

When we arrived I got an opportunity to have a conversation with their young head coach. I was really impressed with his respect for our program and his genuine personality. It was easy to see why they were having success in his first year, and I know he will develop the Wes Del program into a force in class-1A football. Pregame went well, and as I was coming off the field for last-minute team instruction, there at the gate was my longtime friend and greatest coaching adversary, Coach Wright, along with his staff. I stopped, and we talked briefly about his game the night before and our teams. I felt several of his assistants were less genuine about our program than Coach Wright was. I felt this sense of arrogance projecting from them and saw smirks on their faces as Coach Wright and I talked about Tri-Central football. I have often felt members of his staff liked to apply the "big me and little you" concept, which has often bothered me, but Coach Wright's candor dispelled it.

I have known Coach Wright for twenty-six years, and what you see is what you get with him. I have the greatest respect for him as a coach and as a man. He has always been a straightforward guy who began coaching when I was eight years old. It was time that I get to the team, and Bud and I said our good-byes. He wished our team good luck.

In the first quarter, our team came out and went right to work. I felt Wes Del was better this season, but we were also better. Wes Del came out with a great deal of confidence, and that confidence was met by an experienced senior-dominated team. Wes Del was very fundamental and played well, but our boys had been improving each week and dominated the game defensively while running the ball consistently on offense. The game would end with us gaining our seventh consecutive victory by a score of 34–0. There were several future opponents in attendance, and our boys performed well for them to see. This team of boys at Tri-Central was focused. They truly believed now that we could play with any school at our level.

The boys never bragged about beating the teams we were beating. I did not see that arrogant attitude with any of the boys. What I did see was a group of boys, along with their coaches, who believed in one another and understood the reality that each and every week this team must go out and prove something. This proving something wasn't necessarily directed to the Indiana football community but rather the need to prove to one another that we were worthy to hold our heads up and be extremely proud of our program.

As our buses rolled out and headed back to Tipton County, the boys were talking about meeting on Sunday to see how the Indiana State Football Tournament would draw out.

The moms' club had reserved the local pizza parlor in Sharpsville on Sunday afternoon for us to gather and listen to the IHSAA give out the tournament draw for our class. Indiana has an open-draw system with no seeds, so the luck of the draw is very important. It is feasible that two undefeated teams could play in the first round in any sectional. Everybody was at the team party, having a great time together eating and laughing. There was a feel of stress among the team as we waited to hear our fate in the tournament. When it was finally time for us to hear what was going to happen, we realized that the pizza parlor television could not get the channel that was broadcasting the IHSAA sectional draw. Immediately our quarterback, Cody (who lived a couple of blocks away), told everyone to head to his house. Fifty people got up and headed to Cody's house to listen to the draw. When I arrived after helping clean up from our party, his house was packed. I stood outside and waited for the news from the boys. We were hoping not to have to face Sheridan, our immediate concern in the tournament, until the championship game. We were not going to take anyone lightly, but they were the best team and defending champions in our sectional. The announcers finally came to sectional 44, which included us. It got quiet, and after the selection I could tell the boys were somewhat disappointed by the draw. Our route to winning our first sectional since 1991 would involve defeating three teams from our conference that we have already played. Our first-round opponent would be Clinton Central, whom we played in week six. If we won, then we would most probably face Sheridan, whom we were playing in this last week of the season. If we could get by Sheridan, then we would probably face Clinton Prairie, whom we played in week four. It is difficult enough to beat a team once during the season, and now we would be faced with the task of having to defeat three teams we'd already played, and all three were conference rivals.

Everyone went their way. As they were leaving, I told the boys that the tournament would wait; our only priority at this time was week nine and the Sheridan Blackhawks. The boys agreed, and now all attention would be on our target team for the season—and to add to the importance, a Hoosier Heartland Conference championship.

This was the fourth season that I gave the boys a target game as a goal to prepare for. During the 2009 season, the only goal was survival. In 2010, our goal was to defeat Taylor, and we did. In 2011, our goal was to defeat Clinton Prairie, and we did. In 2012, our goal was to defeat Clinton Central, and we did. It was now 2013, week nine, our record was 8–1, we were undefeated in conference play, and we were state ranked eighth in class 1A going into the final week of the regular season. Sheridan was coming into this game with a record of 4–4, state ranked tenth in class 1A and undefeated in the conference. The stage was set for all the rhetoric on high-school football forums to begin, comparing teams.

The talk all week followed a familiar pattern. Sheridan has the toughest game schedule in the state, and Tri-Central has one of the weakest. Coach Wright has dominated Coach Gilbert's teams over the past twenty-five years. Coach Gilbert has only beaten a Bud Wright team three times over the years and never at Tri-Central.

Last year Tri-Central and Sheridan were fortunate to play this game on Championship Saturday at Lucas Oil Stadium, which is home to the Indianapolis Colts. We came into the contest 8–0, with Sheridan having the exact same record, and Sheridan defeated us 22–14, winning the conference. The only teams to win our conference over the past ten years were Sheridan and Lafayette Central Catholic. An interesting fact is that over those ten years, Central Catholic won four state championships while Sheridan gained four appearances, winning three. It was clear that history-wise, most people agreed that we had little chance to win this game. This game would be the spotlight game in class 1A this week, and football fans were giving us some praise on all that we had accomplished over the past three seasons, but most agreed that Sheridan would probably flex their traditional muscle and win another conference.

That being said, when I arrived at practice on Monday, somebody must have forgotten to tell our team that we were supposed to lose this week. Every boy was focused and truly believed that it was time for us not just to play respectfully but, if given a window of opportunity, to seize the moment. A win would create some tradition for ourselves and begin our own legacy at Tri-Central.

The thing that excited me most was that we were finally going to be at full strength. Ryan was more than ready to play. We all were glad to see that he could now physically contribute toward our team success. Practice was exciting. Boys were flying through drills, and the coaches were spending most of their time encouraging and praising the efforts they were seeing at practice. At the conclusion of practice each day we had a very short team meeting on the field to reinforce what was taught during practice and give boys direction for the upcoming game. Each night I would speak about taking advantage of the moment that we all worked so hard to be in position for. On Wednesday, I told the boys that this was a special week, and I thought we should make it memorable. I told them that it would be completely up to them, but on Friday, instead of wearing their jerseys as was our tradition, each boy should wear a white T-shirt and allow the student body to sign that T-shirt and write a note. I said it would be all or no one. This was not an activity that could be taken lightly. Each boy, no matter the class, was responsible. We were a Team of One, and we must demonstrate this fact. This was not the first time we'd done the I Believe shirts at Tri-Central. We had done this a couple of times before big games in the past. The difference this time was that the boys would write "We believe" on the shirts to let everyone in our school community know that we were asking their help and support on this singular Friday night.

The boys were excited. Everyone thought this was a great idea. I left the team to allow them to discuss the process and give the older players a chance to explain to the younger players the importance of what we were trying to do. I stood with the coaches away from the team to watch these thirty-nine boys huddle together, and it became apparent that these boys had a special bond that did not happen often.

It was finally Friday, October 18, and it was hard to focus on my classes at Clinton Central. It was probably a good thing that I was testing all day, allowing me to stay busy grading. When the final bell rang at 3:09, I was off for Tri-Central.

When I arrived, most of the boys were already there. The first thing I had to do was go and get a bus and move it to the field house to load player equipment. I imagine there aren't many football programs in which the athletic director and the head football coach drive the buses on away trips, but I don't mind, and I know Mr. Rhew enjoys driving us.

I moved the bus and walked into the field house and there were around five boys at the sink doing their weekly ritual of shaving to get ready to represent our school. I met with the team to go over our keys to the game one last time. My major concern was staying in the game. I told the boys that we were playing an outstanding defensive team, and much of Sheridan's success has been due to being opportunistic. Sheridan never went into a game without truly believing that they would win. I said that we could not drop our heads when bad things happened. We had to stay focused. If we were close, then we'd have a chance to win.

All the boys listened, and their eyes were wide open. I told them that it was time to head to Sheridan and do what we knew we were capable of doing. Boys quietly got up and headed to the buses.

I drive the varsity players, and Mr. Rhew drives the freshman players on his bus, along with the equipment. I have two coaches who ride with Mr. Rhew; I am the only coach on my bus. The rest of the staff drives to the game together. Coach Perez and Coach Tolle usually get off work a little later and they come together from work.

When we arrive at Sheridan, the Blackhawk football team is on the field, throwing balls, kicking, and punting. We head straight to our locker rooms. Again, our team seems relaxed and they are very quiet. As they change, boys are shaking hands with each other and quietly conversing in the locker room.

Playing at Sheridan can be very intimidating to say the least. They wear all-black uniforms with white helmets, and their football complex does not resemble most 1A schools. Football is very important to the Sheridan community. The town really does shut down, and everyone goes out to the game on Friday night.

Our pregame is routine, and the boys look sharp. Sheridan also looked very sharp during their pregame workout. Coach Wright and I talk for a while and he shares that he is impressed when he watched our team on film. He commended me for the turnaround at Tri-Central, and I thank him. I told him how impressed I am with his running back/linebacker—that I think he is the best running back we would see all season. We continue to talk about kids for a while, and then it is time for us to head back to our teams and go to work. We shook hands, wishing each other good luck. For the next two and a half hours, the pleasantry would be over; we are now adversaries. We finished pregame, and the boys head back to the locker room for final preparations.

Our routine was about to start. Coach Hatcher went right in to finalize our special teams, followed by Coach Perez and his last-minute instructions. Coach Arnold then talked about offense one last time. When Coach Arnold was done, I decided to wait and spend a little time with the boys to allow them to absorb everything. It was clear that they were nervous but ready. They wanted to get out of the locker room and get this game underway.

I said, "Keep your heads up, create your opportunities, hit, take care of the ball on offense, force them to make mistakes, and do not allow big plays. Keep us within reach this first half so coaches can adjust and coach at half time, and most of all, play together, play to win and play as one! This is our time! We must seize the moment! There are no second chances and absolutely no regrets! I am proud of you, your coaches are proud of you, your parents are proud of you, and your community is proud of you! It's time!"

We headed to the field. The crowd was electrifying on both sides. We have a tremendous following, and as we got closer to the field, we could feel something was about to happen.

As the game started, both teams were ready to get after it. Sheridan knew we were improved, but they still believed that they could dominate us. Our boys had incredible faith in each other and a chip on their shoulder with something to prove. The hitting on the field was off the charts. Both teams played incredibly hard. When the first quarter was over, we were ahead 13–7. Our offense was clicking, and Cody, our quarterback, was playing outstandingly, connecting with Bryce and Jade while Garrett, Cody, and Dillon were getting hard yards. The Sheridan running back was also proving everything I said before the game to his coach. He is fast, strong, and determined. I felt our offensive line had control the first quarter, and I was hopeful they would only get better as the game went on.

The second quarter started to slip away a little as we struggled to stop their all-state running back. Sheridan won the second quarter, and at half time the score was tied at 20–20. We seemed to hit a point offensively in the second quarter where we could move the ball but were unable to sustain drives due to penalties or missed assignments.

Coach Arnold was not happy going into half time. As we jogged off the field, I approached Coach Perez and asked him if everything was all right. We had not had a team score twenty points on us all season in the first half. Coach Perez didn't even look at me and responded that everything was fine. I needed to back off and allow my outstanding defensive coordinator to take control.

I have always been able to sense when it is necessary for me to step in and give suggestions, and this was not one of them. I stepped in at half time against Monroe Central because I knew I had to show confidence by leading. Tonight, the biggest game of our season thus far, perhaps the most important game during my tenure, I needed to back off and let these men, whom I had chosen to lead, lead! This might have been one of my best decisions during my tenure at Tri-Central. We would either find a way to win or face defeat together with no regrets. When I got back to the locker room, Coach Hatcher was already making adjustments with the boys on special teams. When he finished, Coach Perez, in his quiet but assertive voice, told the boys what needed to happen if we were going to stop Sheridan's offense. He was most concerned with our pursuit angles and lack of solid tackling. He emphasized that we must swarm to the ball. Sheridan was one dimensional, so if we stopped the run, we'd win. When he finished with his adjustments, it was time for Coach Arnold. Coach Arnold commended the offense on scoring twenty points. He then discussed with them our missed opportunities during the first half. I think everyone in the room sensed that he was agitated. He tried to hold it in, but finally he let it all out. He told the boys that on the way in, some Sheridan fans were standing by our gate— the locker rooms were close to the entrance to the stadium, and people were still in line to buy tickets—chuckling about our team in an effort to get a reaction.

Coach Arnold heard the arrogance about how we would not have a chance in the second half, and it would be like last season when they came out in the second half and beat us. His speech to the boys was from his heart and years of Sheridan dominance. They had the tradition and the success, our job was to play close for a while and then step aside. His speech moved everyone in the room. Coach Kennedy came up to me and said we had two minutes to get back to the field before we would get a penalty for delay of game. There was nothing for me to say. There have been few half times in my career where my assistant coaches have taken complete control. I was extremely proud of all the coaches during this half time, and I truly believed we now had a chance, thanks to them, especially Coaches Arnold, Perez, Tolle, and Hatcher.

It was clear Coach Arnold had truly moved the boys with his speech. I gave Coach Arnold the look, and he finished his motivational speech. All of our boys were seeing red, and it was clear that they would not be denied on this night. Our team had to run to the field to get there on time, and we did.

As the boys were going through their three-minute warm-up before starting the second half, I did not see a great deal of stretching. The boys are walking around slapping hands, hitting shoulder pads, and quietly talking.

It was clear from the start of the third quarter that one team would dominate the second half, and it surely was a surprise to the Sheridan community that it was Tri-Central. Our defense did not allow their offense anything in the third quarter. Our offense went to work and gave Sheridan a clinic on fundamental football with a purpose. Our boys outhustled, outhit, and took command of the game. Every close game has a single play that can be looked at in the aftermath as the defining play to shift the momentum. Sheridan had the ball on their forty-yard line, faced with a fourth down and ten yards to go to get a first down early in the fourth quarter. Tri-Central was up at the time 26-20. Coach Wright decided to go with a fake punt. Our boys stopped Sheridan, and we took over on downs. During the ensuing drive, we scored and went up 32–20. We continued to dominate the game, and with one minute left, we had the ball, trying to run out the clock. Our running back got stood up, and there was no whistle. The next thing we saw was a Sheridan player running down the field with the ball. The boy scored on this confusing play, and now the score was 32–27. Sheridan kicked the ball short, but we recovered the ball, and the clock ran out.

We won. We defeated Sheridan at Sheridan, and now, for the first time in over twenty years, we were Hoosier Heartland Conference champions! We now had won our target game four straight years!

As the boys and coaches hugged, the fans were coming onto the field, and all I could do was stand, watch, and listen. Everything seemed to be happening in slow motion, an incredible feeling that is very difficult to explain. We had been continually an underdog, with very few people around the state believing that we were for real. It was clear that these great young men from this small rural community in northern Tipton County have proved themselves worthy.

Coach Wright and I met and shook hands, and Coach Wright was extremely respectful toward me and our program. He was going out of his way and congratulating several of our key players. The Sheridan coaches were reserved but show good sportsmanship as our teams formed lines for the traditional handshake. As we shook hands with the Sheridan boys, they all said, "We will see you in two weeks." If we both won our first-round sectional game we would meet again at Sheridan for the rematch.

When the handshake was over, our boys gathered at the end zone so parents could take pictures of our conference championship team. The happiness and excitement was tainted by the Sheridan boys, standing at the fifty-yard line with arms crossed, staring at us. We all felt a little uncomfortable, and I questioned their motives. I have lost in championships over the years, and I would always get my boys off the field so the winning team could enjoy their victory, so when the Sheridan team stayed on the field staring at us I felt they must be trying to intimidate our team. We enjoyed our time on the field anyway then got together. Darius led the team in prayer, and then it was time to head to the locker room, where all the Tri-Central fans and families were waiting.

Everybody who stepped on the field contributed on this night. Ryan (who was playing his first game of the season) was outstanding all night long. Cody, our quarterback, threw for two touchdowns and ran for two behind an offense that blocked well all night but played extremely well in the second half.

Teams that have regular success become comfortable with winning. A school like Tri-Central that has only won twenty games between 1995 and 2009 while losing 128 games understands there is no comfortable feeling yet, just jubilation.

It was pandemonium in the locker room. I did not have time to enjoy the moment, as media personnel could not wait to talk with me; they knew Saturday papers would be easy to sell with this story as a headline. I finished with the area reporters, but I knew I would have one more reporter come see me—our local reporter, Gene. Gene is eighty-plus years old and has reported for Tri-Central football for as long as I can remember. Now he had an unfamiliar story headline about a school that paid its dues in high-school football and now had something to show for it. Gene and I talked for quite a while, and I told Gene to make sure and talk about the staff and kids, who all came together to make this happen. After Gene and I finished, I headed to the locker room and told the boys that it might be nice if we got showered and headed for home sometime before dawn.

I was approached by Coach Arnold, who said someone needed to talk to me outside. Some of our fans wanted to know if they could get local fire and police departments to lead us back to Tri-Central.

It was something I had never been involved in before. The parents followed the buses, and a fire truck and a police car met us on US 31 and led us all the way back to Tri-Central. When we arrived at Tri-Central, the parking lot was full. I could not remember the last time I shook so many hands of happy people.

I made my way back into the locker room, and all of us coaches sat around for quite a while going over the game, sometimes just sitting quietly, smiling at each other. I told the guys finally that we needed to call it a night. We now must prepare for our first-round sectional opponent, Clinton Central. We were now 8–1 and conference champions. Record-wise we were at the same spot we had been in 2012. As I drove home, my major concern as I thought about this great accomplishment of meeting our team goal now four years in a row was letdown. For us to win the sectional, we would have to play three teams we had already played and beat during the season, and all of them were rivals and conference teams. After winning such a big game, I was nervous about how we would react.

CHAPTER 11

2013—Tournament Run

When I arrived at practice on Monday afternoon, I was expecting the boys to still be reliving the Friday night game with Sheridan. I was pleasantly surprised to see that the team and coaches were already focused on our task at hand. We were 8–1 and ranked number eight in class 1A in the state of Indiana. I walked from my pickup to the field house, and our players were going through their normal Monday routine of wind sprints. The boys were all sweating, and Coach Arnold was directing them as they work incredibly hard. The tournament has never been kind to Tri-Central. Since the tournament began, we have only won twelve sectional games in the twenty-eight-year history of the tournament series. As I reached the field house, the team finished their Monday running and headed into the locker room for drinks and to get dressed for practice. Our first-round opponent was Clinton Central, whom we defeated convincingly in week six of the season. Clinton Central had always been a school rival, but since I still taught there, the rivalry had gained more attention. I knew they would work hard in their preparation for us, as they had ten seniors and three outstanding offensive/defensive backs. Our team had made positive strides all season, but now we would be faced with the team losing out of the tournament.

We had a great week of practice, and the week went fast. Before I knew it, it was game day. The game would be played at our field, and when I arrived at school at 3:45 p.m., people were already saving their spots in the bleachers.

Coach Arnold already had all of our field preparations done. I have never had an assistant who did all that he does. He never says a word or complains in any way. He is an outstanding coach who one day will become an outstanding head coach. The players began to arrive along with the coaches around 4:30. The boys were going through their shaving ritual, and the coaches were making small talk and casually discussing our game plan.

I met with the team at 5:15 and went over expectations and direction. The boys seemed focused, as they had been all season. This group of boys was not arrogant. They did not *expect* to win. They went into every game as if it were the last game of the season. I attribute much of our success to their team unity and respect for all the teams they played. It is this singular focus of urgency that defined this team all season.

We had a normal pregame, and the boys worked hard. We came back into our locker room for prayer and final preparation and headed out to play. When we walked out of the locker room, there was a sea of blue and gold. Our side of the field was filled, and people were standing along the fence two and three deep. On the other side of the field, Clinton Central had brought a small crowd. I thought to myself, "Six years ago, when I was at Clinton Central, this whole crowd thing was reversed." During my tenure at Clinton Central, we had a huge following, and Tri-Central did not. It was hard for me to fathom the turnaround at Clinton Central, and it saddened me. I worked hard for twenty years to make Clinton Central a quality program, and now it looked as it did when I arrived there.

The game was never in jeopardy of being close. We came out and scored twenty-one points in the first quarter and never looked back. Our defense held Clinton Central to only five first downs while Garrett (our senior running back) ran for over 140 yards. The boys were poised and played together all evening long. Our offensive line dominated the line of scrimmage, as did our defensive line. The clock ran down in the fourth quarter, and we won 35–6 to move on to the second round of the sectional in the tournament. We were now 9–1 and would face Sheridan in the second round of three in week eleven.

I was very proud of the boys and their effort, especially since we were able to continue to play injury-free. All the boys were definitely on a mission. They prepared as one, and they definitely played as one. It was evident each week that every boy who stepped on the field excelled. We had no superstars but rather a group of boys who seemed to be out to prove something—first to themselves and second to everyone else.

The talk on the fan football forums started to heat up quickly. After the game, people were already talking about the rematch of Tri-Central and Sheridan that would be played at Sheridan. The legendary Coach Wright and his Sheridan Blackhawks have never been beaten twice the same year by the same team during his long forty-nine-year history.

The Sheridan boys made a statement after the conference championship game two weeks prior when they stayed on the field to stare at our boys after we defeated them. It was clear that this game was going to be quite an obstacle for us, as it was predicted before the season that Sheridan would represent the north in the state championship. Sheridan had always been my nemesis in the tournament. Over the years at Clinton Central, I had many outstanding teams but could not beat Sheridan in the playoffs. I have never had a team beat them in the playoffs, but during three seasons I had teams beat them during the regular season. The one year that stands out was 1990, when the Clinton Central boys I coached beat Sheridan decisively in the regular season and then lost in a close game during the playoffs. Our team goal this season was to beat Sheridan, but now we were faced with having to defeat them twice; no other program had been able to get that job done. This would be the most stressful week of the season for me.

I focused each week on the game at hand, but quietly I studied teams that we might face. During the week of the Clinton Central game, I spent a great deal of time studying film on them but then made time to begin the process of preparation for Sheridan. Each of my assistant coaches worked diligently in preparation for the opponent at hand, and they all did a magnificent job in putting together the game plan. We all had worked long enough together that we seemed to think in similar ways. The coaching staff knew the complications of playing Sheridan a second time, and when we all came together on Monday, it was clear that everyone had done their homework. We all knew it would be difficult to stop their all-state running back, so we needed to focus on slowing him down and stopping everyone else. They had a young man playing quarterback who had only played a couple of games, but we did play against him in week nine. This young man was an outstanding athlete, and we had to focus on him. The results of the first encounter with Sheridan saw our offensive and defensive lines control the game. We would need our line to continue to step up if we were to have a chance.

Coach Tolle, our offensive line coach, does an incredible job teaching and preparing our linemen. Coach Tolle is always scheming and looking for ways to give our linemen better angles. Much of our success has been due to his work ethic, leadership, and knack for motivating our line. As our team has jelled, and everyone has made an impact, the same can be said of our coaching staff. There are no superstar coaches among us, and my role as head coach has become more figurative, which is a tribute to the men I coach with.

All week long the talk was that Sheridan would take care of business and that they would continue their incredible story of success. Going into this game, we were ranked number eight and Sheridan was ranked number fourteen in class 1A.

Thursday night at the conclusion of practice, the boys gathered around me. I asked them if they wished to do anything special on game day as we did in week nine when we played Sheridan. The answer was a unanimous no. The boys had practiced hard all week and were excited about playing Sheridan again. They really wanted this opportunity to make a statement. I was impressed that they now wanted to treat Sheridan as any other opponent and not get caught up in the rivalry hype.

Friday was a busy day at school, which was a good thing, as I was somewhat stressed about the game that evening. You wouldn't think an old coach who has coached 358 games could get stressed, but I was. The day went fast, and before I knew it, I was headed to Tri-Central to prepare a bus for our second voyage in two weeks to Sheridan.

When I arrived at the field house, the boys were shaving. The staff was present except Coaches Tolle and Perez, who would meet us at Sheridan. Before we left, I had a brief meeting with the boys to go over one more time our game plan and keys to success. The boys seem relaxed and confident. They knew that Sheridan would be ready and that we would need to play a great game to beat them.

When we arrived at Sheridan, Coach Wright meets me as we approached the locker room. He said that we had a very good team, and he was impressed with our line play. Coach Tolle and Perez were just now arriving, and I would have loved for Coach Tolle to hear the accolades Coach Wright was sharing about his line, but I would tell him later. Coach Wright and I talked a long time about our programs. After a while it was time for both of us to go to work, so we wished each other luck and went our separate ways. From that point forward, our friendship would be put on hold until the handshake at the end of the game.

Sheridan teams are always intimidating and play with a great deal of confidence. They always play good hard-hitting football, show respect on the field, and exercise sportsmanship. The major stress I was feeling was due to the fact that I had never had a team beat Sheridan in the tournament, and Sheridan had never lost to the same team twice in one year. It was important that I hide my feelings from the team, but we were such a close group, I was sure the boys knew.

The boys went through pregame focused and looked ready. Boys were slapping hands and shoulder pads all during warm-up. The team unity was set for a game that could define this season and raise our football program to new heights.

Sheridan also looked ready. Sheridan was much more vocal than we were during pregame and definitely wanted our boys to know that we were on their field, and they were not going anywhere. We headed to the locker room for our final meetings and prayer. The bleachers were filling up fast.

After all the coaches said their piece, it was game time. We all dropped to a knee and thanked God for this wonderful opportunity to play this great game of football. I reminded the boys how important it was for us to come into the locker room at half time still in the game. I encouraged them to keep their heads up when bad things happened and fight harder. I wished them all luck, and we were off.

As we came out of the locker room, we saw that our stands were overflowing. I could not believe how many people had come to support our team on this night. As we approached the field, I did my normal ritual of talking loud and fast, directing the team to our objectives of holding on to the ball, no stupid penalties, and hit! When the boys took the field, Sheridan also did, and the excitement was electric. This was what high-school football was all about and, win or lose, the boys who played tonight would have the memories of playing in front of a huge crowd.

The game started out living up to the hype. At the end of the first quarter, both teams provided great defense, and the score was 0–0. There weren't huge offensive mistakes for either team, but both teams were playing rather conservatively, and both defenses were making plays. It would be the second quarter that would define the direction of the game. Coach Arnold started throwing the ball more in the second quarter, catching Sheridan off guard. Our receiving corps was making plays behind solid line blocking, giving Cody time to throw. Cody made some great decisions and threw the ball well. Cody would throw to Bryce for one touchdown in the second quarter, and Garrett would rush for the second, making the score at half time 14–0 in our favor.

I remembered heading into the locker room two weeks ago, asking our defensive coordinator if he had a plan when Sheridan had scored twenty points by half time. Tonight as we were heading in, I jokingly asked Coach Perez if he had a plan, and he never even looked at me. "We are fine," he said.

But the game was not won yet, and there was still much to do to secure the victory. Sheridan always had the capability of coming back and, if given an opportunity, to win. The half-time meetings went well. Coaches and players discussed second-half strategies. The boys seemed eager to get back on the field and finish something that had not been done by anyone else in Indiana football history— beat Sheridan twice in one season.

The second half started out with Sheridan scoring early in the third quarter. The score never fazed the boys, and Coach Arnold orchestrated a long offensive series, with Cody making the decisions on the field. Cody found our sophomore wide receiver in the end zone, and we went up two touchdowns again. This seemed to take the air out of the Sheridan Blackhawks. From the midway point of the third quarter on, Tri-Central would dominate the game in all facets of play. The final score was Tri-Central 35 and Sheridan 7. The boys had done something incredible by beating Sheridan twice in one season and now would advance into the sectional championship game for the second year in a row.

When I met Coach Wright in the middle of the field, he had nothing but praise for our program and congratulations on the great victory. It would be a personal triumph of sorts, since this was the first time in my long coaching career that one of my teams beat Sheridan in the playoffs. The boys were very excited, and the Sheridan boys showed outstanding sportsmanship.

The Tri-Central community had lived year in and year out with a lack of success, watching the boys of their community not only getting beat but beat up each and every week during the season. Now they were getting to enjoy success that had been long overdue and the pride that showed through cannot be expressed in words.

I took care of my head coach responsibilities with the press and headed back to the locker room, where parents and fans had accumulated to greet the boys as they came out of the locker room.

Coach Wright approached me. He told me that he felt this might be our year. He commented that our team was very good and must stay focused, but we would have a chance at making it to the state championship game. He had never said anything like this to me before. I told him that we were taking each game one at a time and not thinking ahead. Privately, I did not think at this time that winning a state championship should be a possibility or focal point. My main focus was winning a sectional title and then seeing what happened. I look back and this great man from Sheridan saw something in the boys that perhaps I had not recognized yet.

The excitement after the Sheridan victory was meaningful for the entire community. After making sure the locker room was clean, Coach Arnold and I started for the bus. A large crowd of parents and fans were still by the buses, congratulating and having a good time with the boys. Mr. Rhew came up and said that the local fire departments and police would be escorting us back to school as they had done two weeks earlier when we defeated Sheridan to win the conference championship. The ride back to school was long, as we had quite the caravan of followers. Horns honking along with police and fire department lights and sirens made the journey back to school memorable for everyone involved.

When we arrived at the field house, the parking lot was full of community members, students, and parents. It was a magical night in northern Tipton County. When I was able to finally make it into the locker room, our coaching staff was all seated in the office, and every one of them looked exhausted. Coach Tolle piped up and said that we would be playing Clinton Prairie in the sectional championship in week eleven. We had beaten Clinton Prairie decisively in week four, 54–0, the first time we met. The game got out of hand early when their star player was injured in the first quarter and could not return. Clinton Prairie is a longtime rival, and their head coach is very talented. We all realized that this game would be different as the stakes were different. We talked about our victory over Sheridan for a long time and decided to worry about Clinton Prairie tomorrow. Everything would be for naught if we had a letdown next week. Coach Perez looked up at all of us half-jokingly and said, "That will not happen!"

The next morning I got up and headed out to do my radio show in Kokomo. I struggled getting to sleep after such an important victory for our program, but it felt as if I was still working off adrenaline from the night before. I did the show and headed to Tri-Central to watch the game with players and coaches. The boys all showed up, and we went over the game with the boys, discussing situations as they developed during the game. When we finished, the staff gather to go over direction in preparation for Clinton Prairie. No one, from players to coaches, acted arrogant in any way about playing Clinton Prairie, and this attitude is what has been a major part of what defines this team. The coaches all shared their responsibilities for preparation for this sectional championship game. Our team was now 10–1. With a victory against Clinton Prairie, this team would have the best record in school history.

Practice during week twelve went as it had gone all season. No one talked about what we had accomplished. Everyone was focused only on the game we were about to play. Clinton Prairie was on a four-game win streak and won their last game in a shootout, showing that their offensive performance had improved all season. Their 250-pound fullback, an outstanding player, was back. Coach Perez worked hard on pursuit drills during the Wednesday defensive practice.

Every week Coach Perez drills the boys as a team on pursuit but his intensity has been on the rise during the tournament. The boys work extremely hard and do everything he asks of them. Offensively, Cody, our quarterback, has improved each week during the season. Cody set a new school record for touchdown passes and is orchestrating our run offense with equal proficiency. Garrett, our senior running back, is having an all-state season. I did not know at the start of the season if he was the guy we needed to lead our run game, but he proves it each and every week. Garrett not only excels, he also set a new single-season rushing record. Garrett has a great personality, and all the boys care a great deal about him. He has a way of getting everyone to play better. Early in the season, we worried about our two sophomore backs. Dillon and Cody have been outstanding at running back all season long. They, like Garrett, become better and play with more confidence each and every week. Dillon plays outside linebacker on defense, and Cody is one of our middle linebackers. Both boys are impact players for our defense. The greatest surprise has been Colton, our young free safety. Colton has become one of our top defensive backs and one of our best tacklers. Seth, our flanker and strong safety, has been our passionate leader both on and off the field. If something needs to be done, Seth gets it done. He possesses outstanding character and is driven to win in all that he does. Davy, our cornerback on defense has also played consistently all season, as well becoming a solid tackler. Jade, our big tight end, has also had an all-state season. Jade has great hands and a desire to achieve both in practice and in games. Jade has such a wonderful personality, and he often brings the comic relief when needed. Keith, a special-team performer, also has led by his great personality. Keith does not get on the field a great deal but never complains and when called on does a great job. Keith demonstrates character and leadership from a different but needed perspective. The true heart of the team is our offensive and defensive lines. Our offensive line is a product of Coach Tolle, and each week Brandon, Nick, Ryan, Darius, Josh, and Wyatt are ready to play and have a plan for execution. Our defensive line is coached by Coach Hunter, and Lake, Riley, Ryan, and Darius truly make a difference. No team all season long has had an answer for our offensive and defensive lines.

The week seemed to go fast, and it was already Friday. The game would be played at Tri-Central, and it was difficult making it through the day in anticipation of the upcoming game. I was busy in my classroom all day, and when the final bell sounded, I was in my old 1992 Ford pickup headed toward Tipton County. When I arrived, and Coach Arnold had everything ready. I walked out to the stadium to look around and relax for a little while and the bleachers were already over half-covered with blankets as our fans continued their tradition of reserving their spots for the game. As I stood for a moment out at the field, I thought to myself, "This school went seventeen years without a win in the tournament, and between last year and now we have won four sectional games, we're in our second consecutive championship, and this year we have a chance to win. The progress and development of this program is really unique and special. It is the cooperative effort between all coaches and players along with the community support that has made this turn around. This program, which has been considered throughout its forty-three-year existence as one of Indiana's worst high-school football programs now has an opportunity for redemption."

The talk in the area was a little more positive toward our program, but most still believed that we hadn't played any real good teams (except Sheridan). The verdict was still out on how good we really are. We were favored to win this week, but the consensus around the state was that this would be our last win. We were excited to be in this position and have the opportunity to make local history with a win tonight, and as the boys showed up, it was clear that they were focused and ready to make history.

Both teams came out of the locker room ready to play. The outcome would never be in question, as we systematically defeated Clinton Prairie 32-0. Clinton Prairie played very hard, and their 250-pound fullback was hard to stop, but our boys never faltered in their relentless defensive attack. The game moved slowly, and I was hopeful that we could get through the game without injury. We were successful coming out of the game injury-free, but this long season had definitely been hard on our players' bodies. The program made huge gains, and this victory made school history, giving the boys the best team record at 11–1. Our principal gave the boys the trophy before a very proud community. As I finished up my interviews with the press, I was told that South Adams had won their sectional. We would be faced with traveling to Berne, Indiana, to play South Adams at their field for regional competition.

I arrived back at the locker room, and everyone was excited about winning our school's second sectional championship in forty-three years. We had to play teams over the last three weeks that we'd played during the season. I commented to our coaches that it would be nice to prepare for a team we had not played. All agreed, and after a light discussion about the game, everyone was ready to head home, rest, and start preparation for the regional championship.

Saturday morning in Tipton County was pure excitement; both the county schools had won sectional titles the night before. Tipton High School is a traditional powerhouse in football and year in and year out one of the best programs in class 2A. This was the first time both schools had won titles on the same evening, and the area football fans were excited for Tri-Central. After my radio show, I headed to the field house, and when I arrived the boys had already begun watching the game with the coaches. The boys were all quietly watching the game as coaches shared their observations on the performance. Our coaches do a great job of instructing during film sessions and work diligently not to embarrass the boys as they critique performance. When the video was over we talked briefly about our next opponent. Then we told the boys to have a great weekend so we could begin to study South Adams as a coaching staff. The boys left with a sense of confidence that had become stronger and more noticeable each week. The boys did not act arrogant, just confident. They were excited about where they were and willing to do what was necessary for all this to continue. I really think the driving force of this team was simply that they were not ready for this to be over. They liked one another and their coaches, and they looked forward to our time together. Coach Hatcher got the South Adams video ready for us to simply sit back together and watch with little or no rewinding of plays. We needed to get a general idea of their team and how they play. There would be plenty of time over the course of the weekend for each coach to privately watch plays over and over, according to their responsibilities.

South Adams is located in Adams County directly east of Tri-Central, about two and a half hours away. The game would be played at South Adams, who brings in a record of five wins and seven losses on the season. It must be noted that they played the second-toughest schedule in class A, as most of the teams they played were much larger than they were. We watched them play together, and we were impressed with their fundamental skills and how hard they played. We did not make any decisions about South Adams at this point, but we all said our good-byes and headed to our families. We would discuss things with each other over the weekend as necessary. We have had a great deal of success working like this. I have required coaches to all meet together at times over the years, but as this staff developed, I felt this direction I chose was best for us, and it has paid off. The main reason I went to this form of preparation is that almost all the staff have several children, and I believe my coaches are able to focus better at home when they can make time and concentrate. I am truly blessed that each man carries his responsibilities with a passion similar to mine. On Monday, everyone would contribute, and the plan would come together as the week developed.

My primary job is first to watch all facets of play of our opponent. I next cut all offensive plays of our opponent. This is the toughest job, and one that I feel is my primary responsibility as head coach. I will then watch their defense and take notes about what I think we should focus on against our opponent. Next, I watch special teams, looking for key personnel that we do not want to touch the ball. Finally, I will prepare the first installment of our weekly practice plan, which involves Tuesday, Wednesday and Thursday. I will not finalize the practice schedule until all three of my coordinators have added what they feel they need in terms of drills and time. Coach Arnold only watches the opponent's defense. He will develop a game plan to challenge their defensive alignments and discuss it with Coach Tolle and me on Monday. Coach Perez deals only with cutting offensive plays to prepare a game plan for our defense. Sometimes he will cut plays like I do, but he knows our defensive package so well that I prefer he watch and set his plan of attack while I do the busywork. Coach Tolle primarily works with Coach Arnold and develops the offensive-line schemes to challenge our opponents' defense. During

the course of the week, Coach Arnold and Coach Tolle work diligently together in putting their plan of attack together. Coach Hunter
only watches the offensive linemen to prepare his defensive linemen
for the athleticism they will be facing. Coach Hatcher has a great
deal of responsibility, as he will dissect all of our opponents' special
teams and prepare a plan for Coach Kennedy and me to go over on
Monday. Coach Kennedy watches special teams and defense to help
our offensive coaches. Coach Johnson watches line play to add to
the plan for Coach Tolle and Coach Hunter. Coach Blades watches
offense so he can give advice to our offensive coaches. This form of
preparation gives much of the responsibility of the head coach to
the assistant coaches. My philosophy is built on the fact that men
need to contribute, men need to be needed, and men need to have
a vested interest for a staff to come together and develop a plan
that is not just a reflection of the head coach but of the entire staff.
We worked all weekend long, with Coach Arnold and Coach Perez
speaking several times with me on the phone.

During the football season the weekends are short, as most of a
coach's time is spent on preparation. I believe in what Coach Woody
Hayes (legendary Hall of Fame coach from Ohio State University)
said: "A coach may be smarter than I am, but no one will outwork
me." I have coached my entire career believing these words and living by them. And as times become difficult, I can always look up at
a bust of A. Lincoln on my desk to remind me that the true test of a
man is his commitment to perseverance. All these things I believe in,
and I try each day to share the importance of the qualities of character, work ethic, determination, passion, empathy, and focus to the
young men I work with. I believe a coach's ultimate responsibility is
to prepare young men to become good American citizens who will
contribute to the greatness of our beloved country.

When I arrived on Monday afternoon, the team was just finishing
up conditioning. Coach Arnold had them all huffing and puffing, but
no one seemed to mind. When they concluded, it was time for them
to head into the locker room, get a drink, and then get dressed. The
boys were set in a routine, and as they finished getting dressed they

got their chairs out for our brief meeting before we went to the field to go over the South Adams scouting report.

When all the coaches arrived, we met and discussed South Adams and the unique problems they presented to us from the games we watched. I gave Coach Perez all of their offensive plays that I had charted, and he thanked me and commented that he was impressed with how well South Adams played together. Coach Arnold spoke up and discussed some of the things he wanted to focus on this week and how important it would be for us to be able to run the ball right at them. He felt if we ran right at them, they would probably load up the box and allow us to use our play-action passing game effectively. Coach Hatcher then shared what he wanted to do on special teams, and we were now ready to meet with the team.

I started the meeting by congratulating the boys on becoming the winningest team in school history. I went on to tell them that although our school played in a regional championship once back in 1991, we did not win. I said that although South Adams had a losing record coming into the game, that fact was quite misleading. We would need to play fundamentally sound football and mentally alert game management. We would be playing on the road, and their community would be out in force to watch their team play. I advised the boys that they were on quite a run and that their schedule was one of the toughest schedules in all of class 1A. The boys listened and agreed with what I was saying, and I asked if any of them had anything to say. Several of the boys admonished the team to stay focused and work hard during the week. They discussed the fact that we had a real chance to make this season even more memorable if we continued to play hard together. At that, we ended the meeting and went to work.

I got home around 7:30 p.m., and my wife had just arrived from her job. We sat down and ate leftovers. We were discussing our day when the phone rang. It was Coach Arnold. Coach Arnold seemed a little upset as he told me that I need to get on the Internet and listen to the interviews coming out of the South Adams camp from the players and their local news media. Players and news media were talking about our team schedule and saying that we would struggle against them.

I said, "That is great! I'll watch the videos, and if they are what you say they are, I want to play them for the boys before we take the field on Tuesday to use as motivation."

He just laughed and said that he thought the South Adams boys were just talking up their chances and that there was nothing nasty to it. I watched the videos, and he was right. The boys talked about how they were ready to hit us and win regionals. When I arrived at practice on Tuesday, Coach Hatcher already had the videos ready when the boys sat down for a quick meeting before practice. I told the boys to watch the videos and decide for themselves what they thought of the South Adams players basically calling us out. Most of the boys laughed and said they had already seen the tapes. We showed them anyway, and it was kind of neat how the boys responded. They didn't rant and rave or swell up over what was said. Seth and Darius spoke up first. "We will see." Garrett said that we just needed to take care of business. I was impressed at how the boys responded and then watched as they went out and had an outstanding practice. As a matter of fact, the entire week went well. The boys were flying around and working hard, preparing to play South Adams.

It was finally Friday night, and we were off, headed to Adams County to play South Adams High School. It was week thirteen, and we now had a record of 12–1. When we arrived at South Adams, it was cold and damp. South Adams had a beautiful venue for a high-school football game. Their coaches were respectful, and their players demonstrated sound discipline and sportsmanship. I knew we were in for a game.

We came out in the first quarter and marched the ball down the field, with Cody giving it to Garrett behind our outstanding offensive line. We used most of the first quarter before we scored, making the game 7–0. In the second quarter, we had a miscue, and our punt got blocked. South Adams got the ball on the eleven-yard line. They would go on to even the game up 7–7. Each team traded defensive stands, as both teams had outstanding defensive teams and schemes. We got the ball back and moved it out to the forty-three-yard line, and we were facing a fourth down and three yards to go for a first down. I asked Coach Arnold to go on a long count to attempt to draw South Adams off side, but they were too disciplined, forcing us to take a time-out. I knew exactly what I wanted us to do. I told our special-teams coordinator, Coach Hatchett, that we would use our fake punt. Coach Hatcher asked me if I was sure, given where the ball was located, and I said yes. We used the fake punt and fooled everyone from Adams County as Cody (our running back) scooted for thirty-one yards and a first down. Right before half we went up 14–7. We had stopped them consistently throughout the first half, with outstanding play coming from Ryan, Lake, Darius, and Riley up front. Seth made several big defensive plays, as did Cody, Cody, and Garrett. Offensively, we were averaging five yards a carry, with Garrett leading the charge along with our quarterback, Cody.

The third quarter saw neither team making it into the end zone. Both teams played outstanding defense. During the fourth quarter, our passing game began to help our cause. We scored twice via the pass and sealed the victory. The game was over. We were now 12–1, regional champions, heading for the semi-state game, one game away from the state championship. We had a wonderful following to the regional game, and the excitement was memorable, as it was after every game during this run. We again had a parade back home, with local police and fire departments leading us with lights and sirens. The boys were experiencing an incredible string of events that each of them would remember forever.

When I finally returned to the locker room, word reached me that we would be playing Winamac High School in the semi-state game the following week. Winamac was undefeated at 13–0 and had one of the top offenses and top defenses in the state of Indiana, regardless of class. On top of all this, we would be playing the game at Winamac. I told the staff we needed to enjoy tonight and worry about Winamac tomorrow. We had all spent a great deal of time in preparation each of the last thirteen weeks. The preparation had intensified over the past three weeks, and it was clear our staff was tired. There was no doubt, though, that come tomorrow, preparation would begin and we would probably spend even more time getting ready for Winamac. We would have all winter to recover from this historic season. The true joy of all of this for me was to stand back and watch our community and players enjoy something that up to this moment had been only a dream. The community had been patient for over forty years, and their pride in the team accentuated our motto Team of One.

CHAPTER 12

2013—Semi-state Championship

I no longer needed to go to a radio show, because the focus in Indiana during late fall transitions to basketball. I received many texts congratulating me and our team on our recent success. The papers did a great job of distributing praise to all the boys and the entire coaching staff on winning the regional. We were now one game away from playing on the ultimate stage for high-school football—the state championship at Lucas Oil Stadium, home of the Indianapolis Colts. Standing between us and that game was an undefeated and unchallenged Winamac Warrior football team. Winamac High School was having an incredible season to remember. Their offense was dominating. They were ranked third in points scored in all of the state, outscoring their opponents 206–7 in the first quarter alone. Their defense was equally impressive. They ranked sixth in the state, giving up fewer than two touchdowns a game. They would enter this game ranked number one in the coaches' poll and number three in the press poll for class-1A teams in the state. Football enthusiasts have claimed all year that our schedule was soft, and we have not had to play the best in our class yet. It was obvious at this point that this game would define how good we have become, but it would also defend our schedule that so many people chose to insult.

When I arrived at our team film session, most of the team and coaches were already there. Video of our regional victory the night before was already running. The coaches shared concerns observed during the contest. The boys were focused and asking questions when puzzled about situations that occurred. Most of the rhetoric during the film had to deal with offense. Coach Arnold and Coach Tolle broke down concerns and reviewed plays until all who performed understood their mistakes and saw how to remedy the schemes and assignments in preparation for the semi-state game against Winamac.

Coach Perez was less critical but made sure that the boys realized that we could not allow ourselves to break down defensively. He then shared a few things he felt we needed to shore up this week defensively. At this point, it was now my turn to discuss the regional game and give the players some insight about the week ahead.

I started out by congratulating the boys on an outstanding victory that allowed us to become the winningest football team in our forty-three-year school history. I told the boys that I was extremely proud of them, and I also shared with the coaches, in the presence of the team, how proud I was of them and the incredible job they all did in planning and coaching the team. The boys rewarded the coaches by giving them all an ovation.

I told the boys that we had a great deal to be excited about because our community was living the moment with us. We were now on a mission, a mission that would take us to a place none of us had ever been, and no matter what happened, none of us would ever be the same. We must focus on continuing this journey and not concern ourselves with anything else. I continued, "Boys, we are now one game away from playing at Lucas Oil Stadium for a state championship! The stakes are higher, and so is the competition. At this point, for us to win the class-1A state championship, we will need to defeat the top two offensive teams in the state, regardless of class. We will need to defeat two of the top defenses in the state, and as you all know, both teams have spotless records that currently stand at 13–0. The only game we can think about right now is this game against Winamac. Please don't think ahead. Live this moment, prepare for this moment, and Friday night, perform for the moment. Winamac is big. Winamac is fast. Winamac is a physical team. We are playing Winamac at their home field in front of a hostile crowd. This will be the largest crowd you all have ever played in front of. We will be forced to play above our level of performance come Friday night to have a chance to win. We must spend our week of preparation concentrating on what has got us to this point. Fundamentals, ball control, attacking pursuit, aggressive tackling, and not allowing Winamac to score quickly are the keys for us to win. Enjoy the regional win this weekend and come prepared to work hard on Monday."

The boys headed out, and the staff stayed behind to start discussing Winamac. Winamac looks very good on film—fast and athletic. They play very physical football. Their quarterback is very athletic, and he throws the ball well. We watched them play together, and we talked about week fourteen preparation. I told Coach Perez that I would diagram plays to have ready for him on Monday. He said he would do the same, and we divided up the games between us. Coach Arnold and Coach Tolle talked about offensive strategy; they planned to talk all weekend and put a preliminary plan together for Monday. Coach Hatcher had already started preparing for special-team play. We talked about the Winamac kicker being the best kicker in class 1A, but their punter had not had much work this season due to their outstanding offense. We agreed that we needed to force them to punt. We discussed what we wanted to set up to prepare for them. We all said our good-byes and headed home to our families and a long tedious weekend of preparation.

The week was extremely busy in preparing for Winamac. We never talked much during the week about what we had accomplished or what would lie ahead if we won this game against Winamac. Instead, the focus was centered on a game plan that involved running the football and mixing in some play-action passing while remaining fundamentally sound on defense. The senior class had become great leaders over the season. Their leadership would be tested come

Friday night when we traveled to Winamac. Each one of the boys offered a different type of leadership, and as we progressed in the tournament, each young man stood out in his own way.

Seth and Garrett are our motivational leaders on and off the field. Both of these young men play the game with incredible passion and prove time and again during the season that they can motivate teammates by their work ethic, character, and determination. Both of these boys are our leaders defensively and go-to guys on offense. Darius is our go-to guy up front and our spiritual leader. Darius stands out on our team as a lineman playing both offense and defense. I remember when this young man was a freshman and how he almost made the choice of walking away. If that had happened, I do not believe we would be where we are right now. Darius has had to overcome so much in his life, and it is clear that he plans to seize this moment and create a legacy in our school district. Nick and Brandon have been our rocks for four years. Both of these young men entered high school with little speed, and both were short on talent. Their contribution has been steadfast as the guys who never missed any workouts in the weight room or on the football field. They both lost a great deal of weight during high school to make themselves into two of the finest linemen I have been blessed with having the opportunity to coach.

Josh, Jade, and Keith all do an outstanding job accepting their roles, and they all have developed into fine athletes. Josh came back his junior year, and we had no place for him in the backfield. He was willing to play offensive tackle at 150 pounds. Josh has played like a 250-pound boy the last two years, and he has helped to define this team. Jade really did not have a great deal of impact on the team until this season. Last year, right before the sectional championship on a Thursday night walk-through, he broke his ankle horribly in a freak on-field collision. It required a serious operation to fix. I never thought he would return this season because his first love is baseball. He did though, and he has had an all-state season. At left end, he became an outstanding receiver and also an outstanding blocker. Keith has had the toughest situation of all the seniors, because he really only gets to play on special teams as our deep receiver. Keith has a great presence and is as respected among his peers as if he were a full-time starter. Davee transferred to Tri-Central right before his junior year, and he has done a great job at defensive cornerback. Davee has had to deal with much adversity in his life, similar to Darius, and he has responded by demonstrating outstanding character and a willingness to get better at playing football each week. With two years of varsity football experience, it is impressive how Davee has responded in such a short time. The last senior on the list is Ryan, an offensive and defensive lineman. Ryan missed most of the season with a knee injury, but when he returned, it was if he played all season. Ryan has raised our level of play throughout the playoffs. It is easy to see that each of these young men has a tremendous impact on why we are now preparing to play for a semi-state championship.

The juniors have also had a great impact on why we are still in the tournament. Our key junior performers are Cody, Bryce, Cale, Caleb, Riley, and Lake. Cody has become an outstanding quarterback while being one of the top defensive backs in the state. Cody plays like a senior. He is extremely competitive and plays hard every play. The boys like Cody and have nicknamed him "Cody Football" due to his knack of getting out of tough situations and making plays. Cody has a great work ethic; he is usually the first to workouts and the last to leave. Bryce has become an outstanding offensive end and outside linebacker. Bryce has matured over the last three years, and he has earned everything he has achieved. Bryce is a player who can make big plays. Cale plays tight end, and he also has earned everything he has gained by never missing weight-room workouts and accepting his role by playing at a high level when called upon. Caleb is our kicker. Caleb catches my wrath more than anyone else on the team, but he never falters and never gets mad. Caleb has become a better kicker as the season has progressed. Riley is an outstanding defensive lineman. Riley came back out this season, and at the start of the season I never felt he would help us. It did not take long during summer camp for me to notice Riley. Riley came into this season with something to prove. I do not think he necessarily had anything to prove to me, but rather to himself. Riley has played with inspiration all season long, and in this tournament run, he has been outstanding. Lake plays nose tackle for us on defense. Lake has been an outstanding player for two seasons. Lake plays our most important position on the defensive line, and thus far this season, no one has been able to block him. Lake is a quiet, good-natured young man whose personality changes on a football field. Lake transforms himself not in any showy way but quietly, by making plays. These juniors work well with the senior class, and it is easy for anyone to see how much these boys care about one another.

The sophomore class has five boys who play regularly on the varsity team. The sophomores are Tanner, Wyatt, Dillon, Cody, and Colten. Tanner and Wyatt were instrumental while our two senior linemen recovered from injuries. Wyatt did a great job coming in and playing varsity as a sophomore at right tackle until Josh was able to return about halfway through the season. Tanner played guard until Ryan was able to play, gained valuable experience, and did a respectable job. The coaching staff felt confident that Dillon and Cody would play consistently all season, but we were truly surprised how good both of these boys have become. They split time at left halfback on offense, and both start at linebacker on defense. Both boys get better each week, and during the tournament, they both are playing well above their class in school. Both boys play with a great deal of passion and understanding of the game and their assignments. Colten was the greatest surprise. Coach Perez early in the season did not know if he wanted to stay with Colten at free safety, but he allowed Colten the opportunity to learn the position and he, like the other two sophomores, is now playing as if he were a senior. He also gets better every week. He has become one of our leading tacklers on the team, and he has caught several key touchdown passes on offense. Colten has played above his age level all season long and he, like Cody and Dillon, has become an impact player on the team this season.

I have refrained from developing this story around individual players because of the motto Team of One. We have established at Tri-Central, through the compliance of players, parents, community, and coaches, this singular idea that true success comes when everyone has a vested interest to defend and work hard toward the same goal. The entire football community has bought into this Team of One phenomenon, and it has paid off up to this point. We are now going to be faced with our greatest challenge during week fourteen. We will be taking our Team of One ideology and seeing if we can meet the challenge facing us as we attempt to defeat one of the best football teams in the state of Indiana.

I wanted the week to be as normal as possible for the coaches and players. I was approached about having a pep session for the boys, but I respectfully declined as I had done throughout the tournament. I told parents that a pep session would be possible if by some chance we defeated Winamac and were to play for a state championship the following week. This would be the last week of a normal practice schedule, and I wanted the boys to engage in routine, preparation, and unity as we prepared for Winamac.

Parents did not question me. I did not give a great deal of explanation as to the whys or why-not's of not allowing a pep session. They just said "OK, Coach," and that was that.

The boys were extremely focused; drills were smooth, and mistakes were minimal. There have not been any team issues during this tournament run, and I have been proud of the due diligence of players and coaches.

Parents were now coming out more to watch practice, which was awesome. I have never had closed practices, and it was neat to see community members and parents come out and give moral support. Before I could even realize it, it was Thursday night, our last practice before a game in which we were huge underdogs.

The social-media commentary involving Indiana high-school football for the most part was in agreement that Tri-Central would probably lose this game by four or five touchdowns. There were a few Trojan backers who felt we might make a game of it, but condolences were already being offered. Football fans said we had nothing to be ashamed of because we have had a great season, and we should be proud of our accomplishments.

As the coaches were going through our normal Thursday runthroughs, I filled the whiteboard with information for our players for game day, and I headlined, for all of them to see, the keys necessary for us to win come Friday night.

When the boys came in for our Thursday night meeting, they all got their chairs out and sat in front of the whiteboard.

I said, "Boys, remember, we have a long drive tomorrow night (two hours) to get to Winamac. The game has been moved back a half an hour, so game time is set at 7:30 p.m. Your parents are preparing you a pregame meal, and you need to get out here to the field house right after school. We plan to leave for Winamac around 3:45 p.m. I want you all to know how proud I am of each and every one of you. I know the coaches echo what I am saying. You have come such a long way, seniors. When you first arrived as freshmen, we were not a very good football program, and you have been instrumental in turning this program into one each of us, along with the community, can be very proud of. We will be playing one of the best high-school football programs in the state of Indiana tomorrow night. They are bigger than us, they have a greater number of athletes, and they have not been challenged all season on either offense or defense. We are supposed to lose, according to all social media and computer rankings. Gentlemen, this is why we play the game. You have shown outstanding fundamental skills all season long. You have played with incredible passion all season long. You have played together, with no boys claiming to have a more important role in determining our success, but rather all of you have shared in the success. We never have to look to just one or two guys to stand out; all of you stand out each time we take the field. We do not have a great window of opportunity against this team, but those opportunities that present themselves during the contest must be acted upon for us to win. We need to get into their heads early both on offense and defense to make sure they realize that we couldn't care less about all the hype about how good they are. We are also good. We need to get them to begin to worry about trying not to lose as we worry about trying to win. Field position and turnovers in big games make a difference. We are playing on their field and believe me, often it is hard not to think that the officials will side with the larger crowd. So keep your mouth shut and your focus steady, and control what you can control. If we can slow down their offense while finding a way to score, we will have a chance to win. I wish each of you the best tomorrow, and win or lose, I will always be proud of this team and the remarkable legacy each of you leaves behind during this 2013 football season. You all have bought into the We Believe focus of this program and your motto needs to continue to define each of us as a Team of One."

I allowed the seniors to talk to the underclassmen about their thoughts on this game. I then allowed the underclassmen to talk. Each coach followed up by giving a message to the team, and then we were done. The general theme was to just go out and do it—that simple. Each of the boys who talk believed that we could and should win. It was clear that there was no doubt among the players. And just like that, it was game day!

It was a difficult day at school, to say the least. I took care of business, but my mind was far from the classroom. I have always prided myself on being a classroom teacher first and a coach second, but today was different. Neither my staff nor I had gotten much rest since we'd won the regional seven days ago. We prepared a game plan, we practiced that game plan, and we tweaked it all week, trying to give our student-athletes the best opportunity possible to pull off an upset over the heavily favored Winamac Warriors.

The day dragged, but finally it was 3:09 in the afternoon, and I was out the door, heading for Tri-Central. My first order of business was to get buses, because I (along with Mr. Rhew the athletic director) would be driving one of the two buses taking the team to Winamac. It was a cold afternoon. The sky looked wintrier than fall.

It was November, and I have never coached this late into the season before. I parked the bus at the field house and went in to see the boys. I told them to get their stuff on the bus then come back in for a brief meeting before we headed to Pulaski County in Northern Indiana.

When all the boys were back in their chairs in front of the whiteboard, I stood in my office with the other coaches so the boys could focus on all the information on the whiteboard. I watched as they read the goals, keys, and expectations for the game. I did not plan this to be a long meeting, and I definitely did not want to create drama or stress. We had a two-hour bus ride, and I wanted the boys to relax and save as much adrenaline as possible for the game.

During the course of the week, as in past weeks of the tournament, we did not talk about a state championship. We concentrated on the game at hand, and we tried not to focus on something that was out of our reach. If we won tonight, then the state championship would be in reach and worth talking about. Right now the state championship was not of interest. Instead it was the focus of the team to keep us in the game at half time if we wanted to have a chance to win the game in the second half.

I told the boys they needed to expect a huge crowd and for them not to get caught up with all the hype of the game. When it came right down to it, it was a game, and everyone on this team needed to concentrate on their jobs and remember to hit, play field position, and not turn over the ball. "Remember," I said, "Winamac has committed a great deal of penalties throughout the season, and our discipline will give us an edge if the game is close." I wished the boys good luck, and we all boarded the buses.

The bus ride was long. I watched as the boys relaxed quietly in their seats. I struggled through game scenarios in my head. I would not need to make many decisions tonight because my coordinators were outstanding, but in a game like this, I might be faced with two or three decisions that could win or lose the game. That is the role of a head coach. I have waited thirty-four years to have this opportunity, and it was my only hope that our boys could keep the game close and create doubt in the Winamac players' minds. They have dominated all thirteen teams they have played this season, especially in the first quarter, where they have outscored their opponents 207–6. If we could make them earn their points by driving the length of the field, we might have a chance to pull off the upset.

We arrived in this northwestern Indiana town at about 5:35 p.m., making the trip in an hour and fifty minutes. As we turn into Winamac High School, it started to snow. The snow was coming down in big flakes with a strong north wind making it feel like twenty degrees.

There were already people everywhere. It was 5:35 p.m., about two hours before the game, and Winamac's stands were already about a quarter full. The football complex was such that the home and visitor locker rooms were about forty-five feet away from each other in the same building. Not being able to have ample distance from the opposing team would make preparation a little more complicated.

I let the boys off and then went and parked the bus. As I walked from the bus to the football complex, it really began to snow hard. I didn't think we were going to get any accumulation, but it was cold. For thirty-four years I have never worn a coat on the sidelines. I have always presented myself as a head coach with a white shirt, tie, and long black pants, because I have always believed as part of my personal philosophy that I should represent my team, school, and community well. As I walk, I think that this might be the night that I wear a coat during a game. My only concern was how the boys would react to me changing a tradition that they have grown to expect and respect. I decided this was not a major issue, and I would make that decision at game time.

Coach Roth walked up, and we began to talk. Coach Roth and I have known each other for years. We coached against each other years ago when I coached at Pioneer. We met two times, and his teams beat mine each time. It was easy to see that he is respectfully confident about his team and their chances. I commended him on his fine team, and he said the same to me. I told Coach Roth that the only thing that I had not been able to prepare for by watching video was speed. He agreed. We have not played each other or seen each other live, so we would need to wait until the game got underway to know this particular answer. Coach Roth asked me questions about Eastern Hancock, and I told him that I would give him our game video if he defeated us tonight, and he thanks me. The boys were starting to come out of the locker room, so we said our good-byes, wished each other good luck, and headed off to our respective teams.

The boys lined up for us to take the field. There was a bitter cold that seemed to rip through my double coat, hood, and gloves. The boys seemed fine as we took our walk to the field for pregame. As we approached the field, we saw that the Winamac stands were already almost full. I could not believe it. I looked at our stands. There were about ten people there, and I wondered if our fan base would travel this long way to watch their underdog team take on this undefeated Winamac squad. Our quarterbacks and receivers finished their throwing session as our linemen made their way to the field. We do our traditional two lines into a huge circle to start our stretch session. As we were stretching, the Winamac team were yelling and jumping around. There must have been over fifty boys dressed. They walked the sidelines on both sides of us stretching and then taking off, screaming as they ran along the fifty-yard line looking at us and telling us how they were going to kick our butts. I had not seen this in a long time. Football has changed. There was a time when I would see this each week. Times have changed, and this tactic is not used much in high school sports anymore, but I was truly thankful that the Winamac boys did this tonight. As our boys were stretching, they looked up at the Winamac boys and listened to their taunts. Then they quietly went back to stretching. The one obvious thing that I commented about to my staff was the boys' eyes. There was a new determination in their eyes, and not one boy said a thing.

The pregame was the crispest I had ever seen. All the boys were slapping hands and focusing only on us. That is what a coach wants to see. The Winamac fans were excited and already cheering on their team. It was now around 7:00 p.m., a half an hour before game time. As we headed to the locker room for our last meeting and our prayer, our stands were about half full; the Winamac side already had over-flowed to the fence line.

Each of the coordinators gave last minute instructions to the players. Coach Arnold delivered a solid motivational speech. When he finished, I waited a little while to allow the boys to relax and think. There was not a sound from anyone. Then it was time for me to bring the boys together, pray, and get their adrenaline flowing. When I walked into the room all eyes were on me. I stood for a moment and looked around the room and then asked the boys to go to a knee and touch someone as we thanked God for this incredible opportu-nity he has seen fit to offer us. After the prayer, the boys stood up and waited to hear what I had to say.

"Boys we were never supposed to be here, but we are. We were not supposed to play with them, but we will. We are not supposed to win, but we shall! Our school has waited forty-three years for this moment, and it is time to seize that moment! Stay focused, play fun-damentally sound, hold on to the ball, and hit, *hit*, HIT! If we do these things together we will have a chance. Keep the game close at half time so coaches can coach! Play as a Team of One!" I took off my coat and gloves and told the boys, "Let's go to work!"

It was clear they were ready. We formed our two lines and headed to the field. As our lines developed outside of the locker room, I noticed something that would truly inspire all of us. "Look at that!" I said to the boys. "Look at our community following! Look at all those people there in front of you who believe in you! Let's take a walk!" Because it was a long drive to a school we have never played, because they had to get off work and drive for two hours, our fans have come late, but they were here and excited. Our stands were full and overflowing three and four deep along the fence, with a long line at the ticket booth working to get in before kickoff. I could not believe it. Our fans followed us during the bad as well as the good, and it looked as if most of the people who live in our school district were there and believed. I went through my normal rhetoric of "hold on to the ball, no stupid penalties, hit, play fundamentally, HIT, tackle, now take the field, and win!"

The boys stormed the field, as did Winamac right behind us. The noise was extremely loud as our captains went to the center of the field for the flip of the coin. When Winamac won the toss and elected to receive, the Winamac fans erupted in cheers. This meant we would immediately find out how quick Winamac truly was. Their offense had not been stopped all season long on their opening drive. Our work was definitely cut out for us.

We kicked off, and Winamac was able to start their first drive on the thirty-yard line. The first drive is always important to set the pace, and Winamac was a lot bigger in person than they seemed on video. The boys responded by holding Winamac and forcing a fourth-down punt. It was clear that Winamac was going to struggle with our speed up front, demonstrated by Dillon, Riley, Ryan, Lake, Darius, and Bryce. They punted the ball, and we were able to start on the thirty-nine-yard line for our first offensive series, which Coach Arnold started with a dive to the left side. The Winamac defense put all eleven players within seven yards of the ball, and they stopped us for no gain. I walked over to find out what our second play was, and Coach Arnold said he planned to do a play-action pass downfield.

I said, "Really? The second play of the game?"

He nodded. Cody brought the team up to the line of scrimmage for the play. He dropped back and found Bryce, our tight end, behind the defense and laid the ball out in front of him. Bryce grabbed the ball and ran to the one-yard line. On the next play, Dillon scored on a halfback dive, and we were up 6–0. We missed the point after touchdown, which in championship play can come back to haunt a team. The good news was that we had just scored first against a team that was supposed to dominate us. It was easy to see after we held them offensively and then scored in two plays that their players were in shock and angry.

We held Winamac on the ensuing offensive series, and they were facing a fourth down and four at midfield. They decided to go for it, and Bryce read the play and forced the quarterback out of bounds short of the first-down marker with Garrett's help. We got the ball back and moved it down to Winamac's thirteen-yard line before we lost it on downs. Winamac would now start a drive that ended around the thirty-yard line when Garrett intercepted the ball. Again we were able to get inside the red zone but dropped a pass into the end zone, keeping the score 6–0 to end the first quarter. We had three opportunities to score in the first quarter and were only able to score once.

During the second quarter, things became much more intense. We stopped Winamac around our thirty-yard line and started a drive. We had the ball on the Winamac thirty-yard line, and Cody threw for the end zone, but the ball was tipped and intercepted by a Winamac player, who started a return. He took off along the Winamac sidelines with guys in position to make blocks. He got to the fifty-yard line, and there was a pileup on the sidelines. One of our players came in and finished tackling the Winamac player out of bounds. A huge pileup occurred, and the next thing I saw from our sidelines was coaches grabbing players and yellow flags soaring in the air.

I waited to see what was going to happen. When the smoke cleared, the officials gave us a penalty for a late hit, they gave Winamac a penalty for excessive roughness, and gave the sidelines an unsportsmanlike-conduct penalty, which would move the ball back fifteen yards because the other two penalties offset one another. I was very upset with the chain of events on Winamac's sidelines, especially with Winamac coaches touching our players.

I asked the side judge if I might speak with the referee concerning the situation. The referee was gracious enough to start toward me to discuss what has just transpired and the decisions that were made. As the referee approached, I knew from my long career that how I handled this situation with the referee could make a difference in how he and his crew perceived me and my sidelines the rest of the game. I could tell that he was ready for whatever direction I chose to go. This crew would have never been able to reach this level of play if they were not solid in decision-making skills. The referee said, "Coach, this is what happened…" I listened to him explain the penalties and keep quiet.

When he was done, I got close to him and said quietly, "Please don't let any of their coaches touch my boys again."

The referee said, "Thank you, Coach. I will keep control of this game!"

I thanked him, and our conversation was over. The referee was correct. They immediately began to call the game much closer, which fit well into our scheme of play, because our boys usually play fundamental, disciplined football.

We would have one more opportunity to score in the first half and did not get the job done. As the first half ended, we were ahead 6-0. The first half was very physical, and I knew the second half would perhaps be even more physical. I walked alongside Coach Arnold as we left the field and asked if he was OK. He said yes. He was happy that we were moving the ball and controlling the line of scrimmage but upset that we were not finishing drives with scores. I thought the Winamac community was in shock after watching this little school from northern Tipton County play with their team, who has not been tested all season long.

When we arrived in the locker room, the boys were still quite focused, but I could see that they were somewhat tired and needed this time to rest. Coach Hatcher talked first about special-teams play, followed by Coach Perez and the adjustments he wanted to make for the second half defensively. While Coach Perez addressed the team, I had a meeting with Coach Tolle and Coach Arnold as they went over adjustments for the second half. Coach Arnold addressed the players with a praising but stern demeanor, telling the boys that we must finish our drives with scores if we planned to beat Winamac. He made it clear that Winamac was an outstanding team, but he emphasized the fact that they were playing out of control at times; if we took advantage of them and their lack of discipline, we could win the game. I said I was proud of them and told them they should leave everything they had on the field during the second half. We might never have an opportunity like this, and it was up to us to seize the moment. The boys seemed refocused and ready to give their best as we left the locker room for the field.

The third quarter is usually the most dangerous quarter of high-school football. Whichever team gains momentum in the third quarter has an edge to win the game. We would get the ball first in the second half. Our kickoff-return team took the field as Winamac prepared to kick the ball off to start the second half. Our boys were seasoned veterans, and they all knew the importance of field position. Sometimes things happen that are unexpected in a football game—just as things happen unexpectedly in real life—and we are faced with adapting to the situation. Our job becomes finding a way to work through adversity. Winamac's all-state kicker kicked a line drive that Seth attempted to field at the nine-yard line, but the ball got away from him. He went after the ball and tried to start up field, but he was tackled at the seven-yard line deep in our territory. The Winamac bleachers erupt in excitement because after ten seconds their team was in a game in which they'd played the whole first half being dominated by us. We have zero success moving the ball. The Winamac defense was on fire, and we were faced with a fourth down on our seven-yard line. We sent our sophomore punter back, and we all held our breath, hoping that this bad situation would not get worse. Dillon caught the ball clean and did a great job punting the ball down the field to our thirty-five-yard line with no return. We were able to escape, but Winamac was now in great field position and had all the momentum. Winamac had a holding call and were pushed back to the fifty before gaining ten of those yards back.

Still, our defense flexed; Winamac was facing a fourth down and ten at our forty-yard line. Coach Roth decided this time to punt the ball and play the field position game, hoping his defense could hold again and give them an opportunity to score and perhaps take the lead. Again Coach Perez's defense held strong. Up to this point, Coach Perez seemed to have an answer to anything Winamac wanted to try.

The boys were playing inspired defense, because they knew they had to stay strong and play together to work through this situation. Winamac punted the ball and downed it at our own five-yard line. Here we were for our second offensive series of the half starting near our own end zone. Coach Arnold went to our one-back offense and began to hit Garrett into the line fast. Cody and Dillon continued to work to the corner with our outside game. We were able to control the ball and picked up a couple of first downs. Then we got bogged down, and we were looking at a second down and twelve on our side of the field. Cody ran our veer option and kept the ball around the left corner of the defense. He was hit hard at the out-of-bounds line, and a yellow flag came streaming out from the line judge. Cody got up, dazed from the hit, but headed back to the huddle as the referee signaled a personal foul with a helmet to the head. This would give us a much-needed first down and take the wind out of the Winamac defense.

Coach Arnold worked his magic, calling plays as Cody orchestrated that magic at the quarterback position all the way down the field. There were three minutes left in the quarter, and we had the ball on the thirteen-yard line, facing a third-down situation. We had been down to the thirteen-yard line four times during this game, and we had only scored once, as the Winamac defense seemed to come together to stop us each time. This time Coach Arnold called a short play-action pass to Bryce, our tight end, into the right flat area. Cody faked the ball to Garrett and passed the ball to Bryce, who was able to score as Seth executed an outstanding block to free Bryce to get into the end zone.

We were now up 12-0, and I made the decision to go for two points instead of kicking the point after. I told Coach Arnold we would be going for two, and he immediately called in a play to Cody. It was if he was eagerly waiting for me to give him the go-ahead, because he felt very confident with the play he chose. The coaches on our staff had done an incredible job preparing, and it was clear that Coach Arnold was ready. Cody dropped back and threw a short pass to Garrett, our halfback, to the right. Our tight end and slot receivers ran in routes; there was no one to defend Garrett, and he scored the two-point conversion easily. We were now up 14–0 in a game that we were dominating defensively and scoring enough against one of the best defenses in the state.

Winamac got the ball back and started to move it when the quarter ended. At the end of three quarters, we were ahead 14–0 against this team we were not supposed to be able to play with. Our boys and staff made no big deal about our lead. Our only concern now was the fourth quarter. Winamac averaged forty-eight points a game throughout the season, and we all knew they were capable of coming back and beating us if we got lazy. When the boys came to the sidelines at the quarter break, Coach Perez reminded them, "The only thing important in our entire season is this next twelve minutes. We must remain focused and continue to play with passion."

Winamac was moving the ball as the last quarter started, and they moved the ball to midfield. At this point, Winamac began to throw the ball more and was starting to have some success. Winamac was able to move the ball via the run and pass to our thirty-yard line and they were in a first-down situation. Their outstanding running back gained five yards running outside our defense, and they now were faced with a second down and five at our twenty-five-yard line. Winamac's quarterback dropped back and threw a ball to the end zone, where we had two boys defending the receiver. Somehow the Winamac receiver made an outstanding play, catching the ball and scoring their first touchdown of the evening. The point after by their outstanding kicker made the game 14–7 with eight minutes left in the contest. The Winamac fans were all on their feet, and their players had new life. It was now a one touchdown game, but as our boys came to the sidelines after the score, they seemed focused and eager to get back into the action. Winamac kicked off to us, and Keith ran the ball back to the thirty-yard line. On the ensuing play, Cody gave the ball to Garrett, running a dive left, and he gained about eight yards, but as he was being tackled, he fumbled the ball. The place erupted again as Winamac recovered the ball.

This was a huge blow for our players. It seemed like Winamac was now in position to tie the game. Winamac pounded the ball into our defense. There is no easy fast score, but their running back did make it into the end zone, and the score was now 14–13 with five minutes left in the game. Coach Roth decided to go for the tie, and his kicker made the game 14-14. Just like that, in a game we had dominated for three quarters, we now were facing an undefeated team with new purpose and playing with tremendous passion. The boys came to the sidelines, and we did have some focus issues; the boys definitely were in disbelief. We told the boys to continue to play hard, as we could still win this game.

Winamac kicked off to us, and Keith was able to get us to the twenty-yard line on the return. Coach Arnold told the boys to just play assignment football, and we would be fine. Coach Arnold called in a flanker reverse to Seth, which was a great call and one we had not used all evening. Seth got the ball from Cody, made it around the corner of the defense, and broke into the secondary for about twelve yards when the unthinkable happened again. Seth fumbled the ball, and after a long discussion between the officials, Winamac was awarded the ball on our thirty-yard line. Here we were with five minutes to go in the game; the score was tied, and one of Indiana's top offenses had won control of the ball thirty yards away with a kicker who has kicked during the season field goals of forty-six, forty-eight, and fifty yards.

The Winamac crowd was now roaring, and we could hardly hear ourselves think, much less yell instructions to the players. This was a time when the boys would have to come through and play the game as they had been taught. On first down, they ran their all-state running back for five yards. It was now second down and five at our twenty-five-yard line.

Coach Perez does not like to blitz his linebackers much, but for some reason he decided to send Garrett this time, and Winamac missed him. The Winamac quarterback was sacked before he could do anything in the backfield. It was now third down on the thirty-yard line. Coach Roth decided to give the ball to his running back, and he only gained five yards, making it fourth down and five yards to go at the twenty-five-yard line. Coach Roth decided, with just under four minutes left in the game, to attempt to win the game with his kicker. As the kicker set up to kick the field goal, I called time-out, leaving my offense just one time-out. I felt it necessary to give the kicker a little more time to think about everything. The officials whistled the ball in play, and both teams hustled back to the field.

Winamac set up for the field goal again, but they decided to try to get us to jump by going on a long count. Coach Roth must have felt this would give them a first down and move them closer to the end zone so they could eat up the clock and win the game by scoring a touchdown or a field goal. His plan was outstanding except for one problem—his guys moved early, and now the kicker would be five yards farther from the goal posts.

During the time-out, Coach Hatcher and I talked to the boys about this very thing and told them not to jump or move until the ball moved. The quarterback was the holder, and he barked out signals. Winamac's guard jumped, bringing out the yellow flag, and instead of being a positive, it moved the ball back to the thirty-yard line. The kick now would be a forty-seven-yard field-goal attempt. The ball was hiked, and it looked to move to the right but fell about five yards short, keeping the game tied 14–14 with two minutes and forty-two seconds left in the contest.

We were now eighty yards away from winning the game. We had one time-out left against one of the best defensive teams in Indiana high-school football. It seemed as if everything from the high hopes of playing in a state championship to creating an Indiana high-school sports legacy was now all in front of us and within our control. Obviously, the only thing on our minds along the sidelines was how to systematically move the ball to a point where we could attempt a game-winning pass.

The most pressing issue at hand was that we could not panic. Coach Perez and his defense had done their job, forcing the second-most point-producing team in the state to a fourth-down situation. Coach Hatcher and Coach Kennedy coached our boys through the field-goal attempt, which came up short, and due to our special team's discipline, forced Winamac to an additional penalty. It was now time for Coach Arnold and Coach Tolle to do their magic with our offensive unit. Our players believe totally in our coaches, and it was now Coaches Arnold and Tolle's opportunity to take over the spotlight. I stayed away from Coach Perez when he was making defensive decisions. I stayed away from Coach Hatcher and Coach Kennedy as they made decisions and prepared our boys for the field goal. Now the most important thing for me to do was rely on these two coaches and the fourteen boys who would play in this, our final offensive series of this game—and perhaps the season.

I have stated throughout this book that it would be totally unfair for one person to take all the credit for what had happened at this small rural school in northern Tipton County. I now relied on these experienced, skilled coaches to lead these young men to victory.

Our offense took the field. Coach Arnold gave Seth the play to inform Cody. We tried running Garrett on a dive, but he was stopped immediately for a slight loss. It was now second down, and the clock was running. Coach sent Colten in with a play-action pass on second down. Cody dropped back to throw the ball, and Winamac had a blitz on. Two Winamac linemen were on Cody before he could get set to throw, and it looked as if he was going down. Cody spun around, losing his balance for a second, and then regained it just as the referee was getting ready to blow the play dead. Somehow Cody escaped and rolled right. Cody found Bryce fourteen yards downfield, and just like that it was first down.

Coach Arnold quickly got a play in as the chains were moved. The referee blew his whistle to start the clock and Nick hiked the ball to Cody, who gave it to Garrett. Garrett seemed like he had been shot out of a cannon, breaking into the secondary for an eight-yard gain. As the Winamac defender was tackling him, he grabbed Garrett's face mask as he took him to the ground. The referee marked off fifteen yards. Now we had the ball at the Winamac forty-yard line with about 1:30 left on the clock. Coach Arnold called another play-action pass, this time across the middle of the field, but it was hit by the Winamac linebacker and almost intercepted. It was now second down and ten yards to go. Coach Arnold called for a pass downfield that was defended very well, and just like that it was third down and ten yards to go. He called a short outside pass to the left, sending both the receivers to the inside and clearing the zone for our halfback, Cody, to hit the flat under the coverage. The pass was right on target. Cody not only got a first down but was able to get out of bounds to stop the clock. Coach Arnold called another drop-back pass, but this time Winamac was blitzing again. Cody got away from several defenders and picked up about nine yards before being tackled, and he was forced to call our last time-out.

Then there it was, a yellow flag lying on the field in our back-field. The official called us for a chop block, and that would negate the play. It was still first down, but now we were looking at a first down and twenty yards to go. There was now less than a minute left in the game. Coach Arnold attempted another pass to the end zone, but it was broken up. It was now second down and twenty yards to go at about thirty-five-yard line. Coach Arnold made an incredible decision that would put us in position to have a shot to win. He called a screen to our left. The ball was going to be thrown to Cody (our sophomore running back). Cody dropped back. Winamac never considered that we might throw a screen; five guys were attacking toward Cody. Cody dumps the ball out to Cody, and Cody is able to get the ball down to the sixteen-yard line and a first down behind the outstanding blocking of our linemen downfield along with our receivers. Cody (a sophomore) was even able to get out of bounds to stop the clock with sixteen seconds left in the game.

Coach Arnold called in a pass to our all-state tight end, Jade. This would perhaps be the last play for us before being faced with overtime. Cody dropped back to throw, and he let the ball go to the left corner close to the goal line. Jade made a spectacular catch. He was unable to score but did get a first down to kill the clock. The boys rushed to the line, and Cody took a quick snap to try a quarterback sneak of the ball into the end zone but whistles were blowing. I panicked, thinking we left early, but I did not see a flag. The referee announced that Winamac had called time-out. There were 7.4 seconds remaining in the game. We did not even discuss kicking a field goal at this point. The boys were extremely focused as they came to the sidelines. As they huddled around Coach Arnold and Coach Tolle, I asked Coach Arnold what he planned to call. Coach Arnold said a quarterback sneak. I agreed, stepped back, and let him and Coach Tolle go to work.

The boys were completely quiet and focused on everything the coaches were saying. Coach Tolle told Darius, our all-state tackle, to move to guard. We would do the sneak on a quick count, and for us that would be on set. We never change our cadence. If we do anything, we usually will go to a long count to draw our opponent off sides or give us time in a particular formation to find a weakness to run a play in a pivotal situation. The boys were excited about going on a quick count, all hands and bodies came together with a common chant: "WIN."

The boys headed back to the field and went straight to the formation on the line of scrimmage. The referee blew his whistle for action to continue. Cody went under center, and you could hear a pin drop as the fans on both sides of the field were on their feet quietly waiting to see what would happen. We would either win the game or be forced into overtime.

Nick hiked the ball to Cody, and Cody's initial move across the goal line was stopped, but he regrouped and got lower, and the push of our offensive line allowed him access to a seam, and the referee signaled touchdown! The Winamac fans immediately sat down as the Tri-Central sidelines and bleachers erupted into total chaos. This was a moment that is impossible to describe in print; it is one that you have to experience. I looked up at the clock, and there was still four seconds left. We missed the extra point, and the score stood at 20–14. Winamac would get one last opportunity to continue their season.

We kicked the ball, and the Winamac receiver went down, immediately stopping the clock with less than two seconds remaining; they were seventy yards from our goal line. Coach Perez frantically called out signals to the boys as Winamac came to the line of scrimmage. The quarterback got back into the pocket, and we dropped our secondary boys back to our own twenty-yard line as he let the ball go. The Winamac receiver caught the ball at about our thirty-yard line.

The game was over. Coach Roth ran across the field and congratulated me, and he was gone. Our team was extremely excited. Their dream would now live on—we would play for a state championship. Everyone on the sidelines was hugging one another, as was everyone in the bleachers and along the fence. As the boys lined up to shake hands, I made sure I personally hugged each and every one of our coaches. They did a tremendous job coaching these boys, who executed passionately.

This was a remarkable victory that for so many seemed impossible. It may have seemed impossible in a mathematical sense, but to these thirty-nine boys and their ten coaches it was possible, and we all had known that it could happen. After the team shook hands with Winamac, they gathered at the center of the field for the award ceremony. The team was recognized as semi-state champions. They then headed to the track to sing our school song to the parents and fans, who were eagerly awaiting them. Everyone stood proud and participated in the singing of the school song. I stood off by myself just so I could absorb everything that was happening. The looks of pride and respect and forty-three years of struggle were all evident on the faces in front of me. When the song was over, the boys headed to the north end zone for their team prayer. Darius led the team in thanking God for this wonderful opportunity and then praised his coaches and teammates for a job well done. It was time for the boys to head off the field, where hundreds of people were waiting to personally thank the boys for their incredible achievement.

As the team headed off to embrace our school community, I went up to the press box to talk with media. I really would have liked to be a part of what was happening with our team, but I needed to represent these young men and coaches for all those who could not be there. I talked with the media for about ten minutes and then I went to the team locker room area. Parents and community were still gathered, and players started to trickle to the locker room. I told the boys to get to the showers. The boys got their last hugs and high fives and went in.

I was approached by a couple of our mothers, both crying, who hugged me and asked if we could have a pep session when we returned. I said yes, and they were excited. They then added, "What about next week?" I said yes again, remembering my promise to the parents that they could put on a pep session if we made it to the state championship. It was still hard to believe that we now were one game away from winning a state championship. I had waited my whole career for this moment, thinking that it would never occur, and now here it was. This group of young men truly believed in the program and most of all, they believed in themselves.

I got to the locker room door, and word came to me that we would be playing Eastern Hancock for the Indiana state championship in class 1A at noon seven days from now. How ironic! We would again be playing the team we opened the season with who gave us our only defeat, but this time it would be in the state championship game.

My phone started to vibrate continuously. People were texting me with congratulations from the coaching community, the Tri-Central community, my family, and yes, the Clinton Central community. I am not very good with texting, so I decided I would look at them when I got home and send a message to each person who had sent me one. Once we hit Howard County on our journey home, we were escorted by police with lights and sirens. We would pick up a whole host of police and fire vehicles escorting us back to

Tri-Central, along with parents and fans as part of the procession. When we arrived back at the parking lot, the lot was almost full with people talking, horns blowing, and excitement everywhere. We took the boys directly to the school for the pep session, where they were given an opportunity to share their emotions with a huge crowd of people cheering nonstop. The pep session went on, allowing the coaches and administrators an opportunity to talk. Then I thanked everyone and they left.

I parked the bus and got equipment back to our field house. When all the chores were completed, I walked into the office where the staff was sitting, appearing exhausted but content. We talked about the game for another hour or so and about where we were when we started and where we were now. None of us could believe that we would now need to prepare to win a state championship.

An unbelievable series of events had now cast us into the limelight and this Team of One would have the opportunity to establish a legacy that will stand the test of time in Indiana high-school football history.

All the coaches left for home, but I sat in my chair in the office, just trying to absorb everything. The whole episode felt like a dream. I have coached for thirty-five years, and each year I have had the goal of making it to a state championship game, and each year up to now my teams have been denied. *Why now?*

The reasoning seemed easy to understand. The coaching staff got along, and they were all skilled, and respectful to fellow coaches, players, and the community. We had twenty varsity players with extraordinary character, and they had taken their talent and developed skill, not as individuals, but rather as a team. Nineteen other boys accepted their role as support players and worked diligently each week on scout teams to prepare those twenty starters to win. We had a parent group that demonstrated incredible character on and off the field, and fans who were quietly hoping for this moment and were embracing the success that they had waited so long to see. If I were to come up with one word to describe this journey with this community it would be "character." When strong character is present, people come together, and great achievements become attainable.

It was now time to go home, read the text messages on my phone, and relax for a couple of hours before starting to prepare for Eastern Hancock. Eastern Hancock would enter this game as the top offensive team in the state of Indiana, covering all classes in high-school football. They were bringing into this game an undefeated season record of 14–0. Their offensive production was over fifty-two points a game, and they scored forty-seven on us the first game of the season.

Well, for a couple of hours I plan to enjoy this milestone, and then I will face the reality of preparation for a state championship!

CHAPTER 13

2013—State Championship

When I arrived home, I talked with my wife for a little while, and then she said she was going to go to bed. I told her I wanted to unwind a little, and she said good night. I decided to get on the computer, check my e-mails, and then go to the high-school football sites to see what was said about our game. As the computer was starting up, I scrolled through the text messages. I read every one of them and sent each sender a message back thanking them for the congratulations. As soon as my computer was on, I checked my e-mail. The head coach from Eastern Hancock was requesting a video exchange via the computer. Coaches Kennedy and Hatcher had already copied the games on hudl.com, so I sent the coach our last three games, and he sent his. I read some of the posts from people about our game, but I was exhausted, and it was 2:00 a.m., so I shut down the computer and went to bed.

Saturday, November 23, 2013
Six days before the game

I wake up at 6:30 a.m., take a shower, and leave without my wife even realizing. My wife, Judy, knows that life is very irregular during football season, and I have been truly blessed by her sincere support through the years during the good times, as well as the bad times.

I want to see what the media has written about the game, and I also want to read about the game statistics of the Eastern Hancock game. The papers are more than kind. We work primarily with the Kokomo *Tribune* and locally through the Tipton *Tribune*. There are only two high schools in Tipton County, and for the first time in Tipton County history, both schools are going to play for a state championship.

The articles and pictures are incredible. For years our football team has had an area sports journalist cover all of our football games. Gene is eighty-five years old and still gets out and backs our Trojan football program. For years, Gene has had to work hard to find something positive to write about, because the Tri-Central football team has only had ten winning seasons out of forty-four years playing varsity football. This marks the first time in school history that a Tri-Central football team has put together three consecutive winning seasons, and Gene has done an incredible job writing humbling stories about our program turnaround. The articles are memorable and after reading them, I am focused on the task at hand. I will meet with the team and coaches as we watch video and start the preparation process for the state championship game.

When I arrive at Tri-Central, the entire team and coaching staff is there waiting on me. It is obvious that the boys are excited about our present opportunity, but it is also obvious that they are very tired. We watch film, and I tell the boys to go home, relax for the rest of the day, and enjoy the win. I told them that they need to begin watching Eastern Hancock tomorrow during their leisure time. I suggest that they only watch our first meeting with Eastern Hancock and allow the coaching staff to direct them on Monday to what we want them to view from Eastern Hancock's tournament games.

The boys leave, and all the coaches sit quietly. It's easy to see that they also are exhausted. At this point in the season, after being together for the past four years, I do not need to tell them what needs to be done. It is clear we all have responsibilities, and we all need to take care of business so we will have a starter-game plan ready when we get together on Monday. I tell Coach Perez that I will diagram Eastern Hancock's last two games. He says that he wants to spend a great deal of time on our first game, and I agree. Coach Arnold says that he will watch for defensive tendencies, and Coach Tolle states he will watch line play to work out blocking schemes. Coaches Hatcher and Kennedy say that they will go to work on special teams and that they would have options available for me to consider by Monday. Coach Hunter tells me that he will evaluate Eastern Hancock's offensive line to prepare our defensive line for them. I tell our offensive coaches and special-teams coaches that I would also take notes on Eastern Hancock's defense and special-teams play. Our plan is set, and after talking with the coordinators, we decide we would meet on Sunday afternoon to start the organization of the game plan.

We do not normally do this but we do not want to miss anything that might be to our advantage. We all say our good-byes, and we are off. I head home to see my wife and relax for a couple of hours before I go to work.

When I get home, Judy and I sit down to discuss the game and all the excitement. We also discuss the fact that Thanksgiving is on Thursday, and she wants to know what to tell our family about our traditional meal on Thanksgiving. I tell her that we will have the meal, but I will need to leave that afternoon after the meal for a scheduled practice. I tell her I have not thought much yet about timing, but as soon as I prepare the weekly schedule we would get together. She agrees and after I eat a light lunch, it's time to go to work. I am Roman Catholic, and my wife and I usually go to church on Saturday night, so I tell her that I'll work up to that point and then we'll attend church, go out to eat, and relax a bit before I return for a long night of work.

The process of diagramming plays is taxing. It usually takes me two to three hours to watch all the offensive plays of an opponent's game to accomplish the task. I cut the game film frame by frame today, as I did when I first started. This is boring, exhausting work, but necessary. When I am done cutting an opponent's game films, I know what they do, and I can prepare for the unexpected come game night.

Football is a game in which all eleven players must know their assignments and execute those assignments for success to be enjoyed. Any team that experiences success has a specific go-to list of plays that they perform well and that will not change throughout the season. If a coach often changes what he is trying to do, his team will usually play confused, and they ultimately won't be successful.

When I return to the computer after church and dinner, it's around 9:00 p.m., and I'm very tired. I decide to get away from cutting film for a while and work on the weekly schedule. One of the most important responsibilities of a head coach is the weekly practice schedule. This week will be filled with interruptions from our normal schedule due to practicing on Wednesday in Lucas Oil Stadium and Thanksgiving on Thursday. The other main distraction is the fact that our game is scheduled in Lucas Oil for a noon start. We played night games all season outside, and now we are scheduled to play an afternoon game inside. At this point going into this championship week, I know that we will not be able to teach anything new, only review what we do well, and win or lose by our season-long preparation come game day.

Sunday, November 24, 2013
Five days before the game

The congratulatory messages keep coming in via e-mail and text messages. It truly is wonderful how thoughtful everyone has been about our newfound success. I get up and finish diagramming the games and start watching special-team play. I watch special-team play for around an hour. Eastern Hancock has an incredible kicker (same skill level as the Winamac kicker), and I realize that if the game is close, they will have the edge in the kicking game. The major concern is the fact that they never punt. They have only punted twice during the season, and one of the two times that they punted was during our first game against them in week one. This makes them very dangerous. This reveals that they believe they can always get a first down with their offense anywhere on the field. This single point will be our primary objective when we play. We must make them punt. I also notice they have strong tendencies with what they do on fourth-down plays, and this also will be important for us to continue to research. I then watch offense so I can listen to Coach Arnold's plan of attack and have ideas on how to respond. It is now time for me to get ready to head to Tri-Central for our coaches' meeting.

When I arrive at Tri-Central, I first visit the high school to run copies of materials I created along with the practice plan to be discussed. The coaches are already out at the field house, working. When I complete my task of running off materials, I head out to the field house. The mood when I arrive at the field house is focused. The coaches are in the office, discussing what they have seen on tape. I hand out materials and tell the three coordinators to first review the practice plan and let me know what changes need to be made.

Coach Hatcher is the first to ask if he can have the same amount of time that he has had the last several weeks for special teams. During the season he got fifteen minutes a day but during the tournament we have been giving him thirty minutes a day because field position is vital in big games. Special teams are a small part of the game, but a mistake can change the momentum, affect field position, or even cost a team a victory. I have always believed that special-team play is the same as officials in a game. If you do not notice them, then they did a great job. Coach Perez and Coach Arnold want to switch time segments around, as does Coach Tolle. I never write a practice plan and make my coaches fit the schedule. I set up a plan, listen to them, and then write up a final plan for distribution on Monday. We work out our details, and now it's time to work on our game plan.

Eastern Hancock has an outstanding offensive team. They are ranked number one in the state (all 322 schools) in scoring. They average fifty-seven points per game for the season. Their running back has over twenty-seven hundred yards running the ball. All of their receivers and backs are fast and very athletic. The focus of our attention is their line. We believe our defensive line is better than their offensive line. Coach Perez and I agree that they will spotlight their all-state running back no matter what. Our objective defensively will be to slow him down and not allow them to have quick scores. Coach Perez says everything will depend on our team pursuit this week and that he needs extra time to drill the boys during the week. I agree with everything he says. Both of us sit down and decide on ten plays that we must work to stop. These are the plays that we will work on the most during the week of preparation.

Defensively, Eastern Hancock is good, but their defense is not comparable to their offense. Coach Arnold starts through all the things he and Coach Tolle want to focus on during the week. I agree with their plan. I feel our offensive line is better than their defensive line. We all agree but also realize they have outstanding linebackers and defensive backs. We decide that our plan must be centered on running right at them to neutralize their speed and getting great fakes on our play-action passing game for us to move the ball successfully. If we are able to run straight at them, it will allow us to hit the outside and exercise our option game.

We work for a couple of hours, and it is time for us to go. We usually do not waste time when we work, as everyone but me has young children and other responsibilities to attend to. That night, I'm in constant communication with all my coordinators as we watch film at home. It seems as if the weekend did not happen, but I have the physical tiredness to assure me that it did.

Monday, November 24, 2013
Four days before the game
On the Monday before the state championship, the IHSAA holds a meeting and press conference for teams playing in the state championship at the Lucas Oil Stadium (home of the Colts) in Indianapolis. Coach Arnold and I meet our principal (Dave Driggs) and our athletic director (Gary Rhew), who are going to accompany us as we tour the facilities and gain important information to guide us on Friday when

we arrive for our state championship game. When we arrive, the conference room is buzzing with coaches talking and media setting up.

The IHSAA does an outstanding job of organizing events, and when we arrive we are given an agenda for our day. We are offered drinks and pastry before the meeting. The atmosphere is one I have never been a part of. Everyone is excited about being at this meeting, and every school represented is hopeful that by week's end, they will take a state championship back to their community. All of the men gathered are very cordial. Coaches are introducing themselves to each other, and those who do know each other are locked in conversation. At 9:00 a.m. the meeting is called to order, and the IHSAA, after introductions, starts through the schedule. At one point, the commissioner introduces the officials and each class of coaches come to the front for the toss of the coin to see who would be home team. We win the right to choose home or away, and I select for our team to be home. After the meeting, we're given a tour of the facility by Lucas Oil staff, and then we're off to talk to the media. There are two schools in the state championship games for the first time, Brebeuf and us. I talk about our amazing journey over and over for a solid hour before things start to wind down. Newspaper sports journalists from all across the state seem eager to talk with me about our Cinderella season and just how we were able to get to this point. I talk about administrators, coaches, and community, but mostly about the wonderful young men who are the reason we have a chance to play in the state championship game.

After talking to the press, the area television sports people request interviews, and I am proud to get the opportunity to share with them information about Tri-Central and this special group of people who have made all of this possible. I tell all the media that we really do not have a superstar "go-to guy" on the team; this is a collective effort by twenty boys and a coaching staff of ten. I share how the community has bought into the program and how so much of the credit for this inspirational season is the vision of our administration giving opportunity and the means for success to develop a successful program. It is a great outing, and we stop to eat and relax on the way home. When we return, I head to Clinton Central to do some schoolwork and look forward to getting back to Tri-Central for practice.

When I arrive at practice, Coach Arnold is just finishing up our Monday conditioning session with the team. Monday is the only day of the week that we condition the boys, and the conditioning session is tough so the boys can work off their weekend and get a good sweat going. The boys finish and then came into the field house for our Monday evening meeting. It is a brisk fall afternoon with a strong southwest wind that makes it feel colder than it really is.

I first congratulate the boys on the incredible season and the success that has provided us with an opportunity to prepare for a state championship game. The boys are very excited, and I ask them if there is anything any of them wish to say. Darius spoke up. "Let's just do this." His sentiment is echoed by the team, and then Seth says, "We all have worked very hard to get to this point, and this is our opportunity to make history at our school and quiet all our critics for good." The boys cheer.

I decide it's time to get focused on our plan at hand. I give each boy a schedule of the week's activities for them to share with their parents. I tell them that we will need to get them out of school for our practice session on Wednesday in Lucas Oil Stadium. The boys are excited about everything, including the pep session that we are going to have Wednesday evening. There are many things happening that concern a coach as potential distractions, but I know Eastern Hancock will be faced with the same issues. I explain the scouting report on Eastern Hancock. I tell the boys that we are still considered the underdog, and this is a billing we have embraced all season. I go over the specifics of what we need to do this week in preparation and tell the boys that we just need to go to work.

The meeting is over, and the team heads out into the cold to practice. Practice goes well as coaches go over our preliminary game plan. Everyone is focused on outworking our opponent.

When I get home, it is time for a quick meal and back to watching film on Eastern Hancock. During the course of the evening, I hear from all the coordinators, including our line coach, to discuss strategy. I tell all the coaches that we will work on strategy until Wednesday. Then it will be time to lock in our game plan. All of us will either win or lose with it. They all agree.

It's a short night with little sleep, but I remind myself I will have all winter to sleep, because this moment we are preparing for is an opportunity that does not present itself very often.

Tuesday, November 25, 2013
Three days before the game

I arrive at practice on Tuesday at my normal time of 3:45 p.m. Coach Hatcher is already working the team through special-team adjustments. As I enter the field house I am met by our athletic director, Mr. Rhew. He wants to discuss and finalize our Wednesday practice at Lucas Oil Stadium. We are faced with having to get the boys out of classes to go down and get acclimated to the stadium. This will be a practice run-through in preparation for our Friday game. The practice on the turf is not a major concern for us, because we played in Lucas Oil the last game of the previous season. Mr. Rhew allowed us to play our final regular-season game in 2012 at this venue against Sheridan with a conference championship at stake. We lost a closely contested game, but the experience is now paying off as we play for a state championship trophy. When we finish talking, it is off to practice.

When I get out to the field, our boys are already engaged in going through our normal routine of individual drills. The boys are focused and working hard, as they have done all season long. Coach Perez had asked on Sunday to be excused during offense to work on defense inside, because he wanted to watch more film and finalize the plays he wanted us to work against on Wednesday.

After drills I dismiss him, and we go to work on offense. Coach Arnold, Coach Tolle, and the rest of the offensive coaches go to work in a segment we call "perfect play." During this time, the team starts slowly and works up to full speed, practicing blocking schemes versus the defense we will see in the game. After they finish with perfect play, they go into a controlled scrimmage and work for about an hour. The offense and the adjustments that the coaches work on seem to be working well, and the boys have confidence in what is being taught. We take a short break, and then Coach Perez comes out and gives the boys a defensive overview before finishing practice with pursuit drills.

At this point, I bring the boys into the field house to go over the agenda for Wednesday and send them home. The coaches stay around for a while and discuss scouting reports and tendencies found by coaches while watching game footage. At around 7:00 p.m., we say our good-byes.

When I arrive home, I talk to my wife for a brief period, and then it is off to watch more of Eastern Hancock on film. I tell my wife that this will be the last night I watch film. I have long made it my rule to not watch any more video of an opponent after the plan for the game is in place. I usually follow this rule, but as in all things, there are exceptions. I do not wish to break this rule for this game, because I do not want any second-guessing during my first opportunity to play in a state championship. Coach Arnold and I talk on the phone off and on all evening long until about 12:30 a.m., and then I go to bed. Wednesday is going to be a long day. The good news is that school is out at Clinton Central for the Thanksgiving holiday, but I know it will be a full day. We will travel to Lucas Oil and practice, come home and practice outside for a couple of hours, and finish the evening with a community pep session.

Wednesday, November 26, 2013
Two days before the game

I get to school at 8:30 a.m. to get a bus ready for our team adventure of practicing in Lucas Oil Stadium. We are expected to arrive around 10:30 a.m. and then take the field for a one-hour practice from 11:00 a.m. to noon. Our administrators have the boys out of class and ready by the time I get the bus up to school. We are taking two buses.

Mr. Rhew is driving the other. The boys board the buses and we are off. The excitement of everything that is happening is very difficult to digest. Our team has been ranked all season long from honorable mention to our current ranking of seventh in the state. We have been constantly reminded that our schedule is weak and that we are really not a championship team. Even after defeating an undefeated Winamac team last week, the common opinion in the football social media circles is that Eastern Hancock defeated us in our first meeting without their quarterback and five other players, and this time it will not even be a game.

Eastern Hancock has scored an amazing fifty-seven points per game throughout the season, with their star running back accumulating over two thousand yards rushing. Eastern Hancock did play a tougher schedule all season long, and their road to the championship was much more difficult, although they breezed through it. During the tournament they have scored fifty-two points per game, which seems impossible, considering the teams they have played. Even the computer analysis shows that they deserved to be in the championship game while we have less than a 3 percent chance of being there. The computer breakdown of the championship game shows that we will lose the game by at least three touchdowns. I don't think our players read much of the hype about us not belonging in this game. As we journey toward Lucas, I look back and see a group of boys who truly believe that we not only deserve to be in this game but that it is our duty to win the game.

The first thing that had to happen when this program was introduced at Tri-Central five years earlier was that the boys needed to believe that it would work. The first year we went 0–10, and there were few who believed at all. The program would not change, but there needed to be a buy-in from the boys, parents, and community for success to begin. I think, looking back, the coaches who were hired in the second year helped to develop the light at the end of the tunnel. Setting small goals that were achievable was another important step. We had to hit rock-bottom in all facets of the program before we could ever start moving in a positive direction.

Then, when a young group of sophomores (who are now seniors) began to believe—and expected others to believe—the program took off and has exceeded all expectations. The chemistry that has developed over the past three years between players, parents, and coaches has been the positive energy that has created this Team of One mentality. The development of the We Believe philosophy must be real and not cosmetic. Everyone must buy in and understand that it is not a motivational tool, but rather something very personal that should be lived; all must believe in order for true success to be achieved.

As I drive the bus down the tunnel to the parking garage at Lucas Oil, it is obvious that this game is more than just a game, it is the culmination for a group of coaches and boys on a mission to not just experience, but rather to achieve something that only they believe is truly possible.

The only boys not familiar with Lucas Oil are our freshmen and new players to the program. Our veteran players are excited to be at Lucas, but they have already played there once, and their focus is not on the hype of the facility, but rather on preparation for a game.

We start by stretching in the hallway so there will be no wasted time on the field. At 10:55 a.m., we are in the tunnel awaiting our opportunity to take the field. They do not have all the lights on, and I remind our veteran players that it will be illuminated differently on game day. The illumination at Lucas is awe-inspiring when you wait in the chute to take the field. It can be somewhat intimidating. We take the field and practice special teams first. When we are done, we go to defense. Coach Perez wants the boys to practice pursuit first to get them used to the turf. Coach Arnold finishes up the hour with offense, and he runs through key plays that he needs to work on. When we are done, we shower and head for home. We have planned to eat something and then go out into the cold and practice defense for another two and a half hours at our place.

The boys eat a snack on the trip back, and when we return, the boys proceed into the locker room to prepare to go outside in the frigid weather to practice defense and finalize our defensive game plan. There are no complaints about the cold from either the players or the coaches. Everyone works hard, and our focus is strong. When practice ends, the boys need to shower and get ready for the pep session. By now, the boys are starving. I had not made arrangements for food—this is the only serious mistake I have made in organizing the week. Our parents are led by Seth's mom, Julie. Our parents' group is truly amazing. I have never worked with a better group during my career. They are incredibly busy, selling hundreds of T-shirts to a community eager to wear our blue, gold, and white shirts. Each week we won a championship, the moms' club sold T-shirts as a reminder of what we have accomplished. The parents are busy preparing the pep session and selling T-shirts, so I ask Jeremy (receiver coach) to order a hundred sandwiches at McDonald's. I give him the money, and he is off. Jeremy returns with the sandwiches, and the boys devour them before the pep session begins.

When we arrive at the high-school gym, the parents want the boys to stay in the hallway so they can be introduced together to our community. I am amazed at how many people are in attendance. Our fan base fills half of the gym. The boys are introduced to an incredible welcome, and the pep session is off and running. Our parents took complete control of all the preparations for this pep session and did a great job in their production. It is an incredible experience for the coaches as well as the players. The parents even put on skits to amuse the community and players. The coaches and players are given an opportunity to share their emotions with the community, and the community does not seem to tire listening to everyone who grabs the microphone. The pep session lasts about an hour.

When the pep session concludes, it is time to head for home, get some rest, spend some time with family, enjoy a Thanksgiving meal, and then return to Tri-Central for our final practice on Thursday evening. When I get home, my wife is very busy preparing things for our Thanksgiving meal along with the help of our daughter. I usually help Judy cook big meals, but I cannot this year. I relax for a while with my daughter, her boyfriend, and my wife. I do not watch any film.

Thursday, November 27, 2013
Thanksgiving
One day before the game

Players and coaches spend the morning and afternoon with their families. Our practice is scheduled for 5:00 to 7:00 p.m. I talked to the boys and advised them not to overeat on Thanksgiving Day. My wife and daughter did an outstanding job in preparing the meal, and our family is able to sit for a short period of time and talk before it is time for me to leave for Tri-Central.

I arrive at the field house around 4:00 p.m. Coaches are already beginning to make their appearances. At 5:00 p.m., we are ready to go to the game field for our last practice of the year. It is extremely cold for this time of year with a driving north wind. Our practice is basically a walk-through and an opportunity to give each coordinator time to go over each segment of the game plan one final time. We did not plan any special new plays, because we decided we would focus all of our attention on playing within our system, which requires discipline and fundamentals in all phases of play. We go to work immediately on our special-team play, and when the boys have finished, I send them in to warm up some before we go over defense. On my way to the field house, Julie (president of our team moms' organization) stops me and wants to know if there is going to be a team meeting at the conclusion of practice. She asks if the parents can present a short video to the boys before they leave. I tell her that will be fine. Julie is excited and thanks me for allowing them to present their video. Julie is a remarkable woman who has done a fantastic job leading our moms' club and providing meals, gifts, etc. for the boys every week. All of our moms have been very involved, and Julie has been able to get everybody to work toward their sons' interest.

We take one more break between defense and offense, because Coach Arnold usually takes the most time with our offense. It is normal in football for offense to need the most time in practice, because it only works well when all eleven players know exactly what they are expected to do.

When we get to the locker room, the boys take off their pads, grab their chairs, and gather for our team meeting.

I start the meeting going over our keys for success in the championship game. I tell the boys that

> We have been the underdog all season long. No one has given us anything. We have earned our way one game at a time throughout the season. We could have easily lost focus after allowing Eastern Hancock to score forty-seven points on us in week one. We did not. Instead we moved players to positions we felt were necessary for us to be better. We moved Seth, Dillon, Cody, and Cody. Each of you believed in what we asked of you, and you, along with the other seven players on defense, have done a remarkable job all season long, allowing our defense to become a top-ten defense, not just in class 1A, but in all the state of Indiana. The football forums are still, for the most part, saying that we cannot win this championship. They have all been wrong so far, so we need to stay focused and prove them wrong just one more time. Our offensive and defensive lines have played together all season long, and each of you young men playing on our line of scrimmage has defined our unified identity. Cody has led us at quarterback along with all of our backs, and they all have done a great job. Garrett, I did not even know until right before the season if you would play right halfback. You have been a solid defensive player the last two years, but who would have believed that you could amass so many yards at running back and set a new school record for yards during a season? Jade, you were involved in a serious injury at the conclusion of the 2012 season, but you came back, and you have had an all-state year, catching the ball on the drive to

set up our winning touchdown in the semi-state. Josh and Ryan missed much of the season due to injury, and when you both came back, you raised the level of play for the entire team. Darius, you have been an outstanding lineman your entire career as well as a critical leader on this team. Darius has taken his level of play and raised it each week. Seth, you have been our emotional leader on and off the field. Seth, you have done so much for this team that there is no way I can share how much you have given to our program. You have an amazing passion (that sometimes gets you in trouble), and that passion has become contagious. Nick and Brandan, you and Seth have been the constants in this program, attending all weight-room workouts, being at all seven-on-seven workouts, and always being accountable for the direction of this program. Colton, Dillon, and Cody, you sophomores have played like seniors on a mission all season long. Each of you has been totally committed and quick to lead by example. Bryce, I remember when you would get down on yourself so easily and lose focus. Now you are a solid performer on both sides of the ball, and yes, you also have become a leader on this team. Keith, you have had such a tough role. You don't get on the field much and have specialized as our returner on special teams all season without one negative thing said. As a senior, it would have been easy for you to be unhappy and cause problems, but instead you have embraced your role, and you have been a solid performer all season long. Lake and Riley, each of you has played outstanding all season long. Both of you have caused havoc along the defensive line, and I have yet to see anyone who can block you consistently. Tanner and Wyatt, both of you played early, and when Ryan and Josh were able to come back, you both accepted the circumstances and gave up your starting role to these seniors. This has been a team of commitment, dedication, role acceptance, and a passion to win that is amazing. No one on the outside believes we can beat Eastern Hancock and win a state championship, but I know this—there is not one breathing person in this room, right now, who thinks we can't.

Tomorrow I will not have time for motivational speeches. Talk at that point is needless. Let me remind you right now of our mission for success. We must start early. We must come out and play the first quarter as if it were the last. We must take care of the ball. We must make minimal mistakes. We will make mistakes. It is how we react to those mistakes that will determine the outcome. We must win the battle of field position. We cannot allow them quick touchdowns. This is the best offense in Indiana, regardless of class, that we will be facing tomorrow. If they are to score, it must be due to long sustained drives that they are not used to. We need to frustrate them. I hope they have been reading all the press articles and believing them. If we can create doubt, they may lose focus. The team that alters its game plan will lose this game. We do not want to create our own problems. We need to play strong, fundamental football within our boundaries of execution and not have penalties. Penalties were the difference for us winning the semi-state, and we must keep our penalties minimal. Remember! Bad things happen during the course of a football game. Don't allow those bad things to become personal. Forget them and think to yourself, "What do I need to do now?" We are on a mission! No matter the outcome tomorrow, your coaches, parents, and community are extremely proud of you and all you have achieved.

I don't know if we will ever have a better opportunity than now to create a standard, a legacy that will define this team forever. Good luck tomorrow. I am extremely proud of where we are, considering where we have been.

I then allow our players and coaches to share their thoughts about the game and the season. Everyone who wants to share has their opportunity to talk to the team. Parents have gathered in the room, and some of them also share their feelings about the season and the championship game. The general theme from all those speaking is the lack of respect Tri-Central football has had over the past forty-four years. This is our opportunity to gain respect and due to being one of Indiana's worst high-school football programs, write a happy ending to this amazing Cinderella story.

When everyone is finished sharing their thoughts, the parents present the boys with a video. I am not overly excited about the video because the meeting has gone well, and everyone needs to get home for some rest before returning early on Friday morning. The parents have been incredible to work with all season long, and it is out of respect that I now give them this opportunity to present this video to the boys.

The video ends up being one of the magical moments in my coaching career. I cannot express how incredible this video is. The parents must have started preparing this video early in the tournament, hoping that we would be in the position we currently are in. I am not a strong technology guy, but this is one of those incredible tools that was not possible years ago. The parents received video from alumni across the country wanting to wish our team well and give some insight on how they feel about us and how we are just one win away from a state championship. The messages are heartwarming, sincere, funny, to the point, and moving to every person in the room. You could cut the air with a knife as past players—from when football began at Tri-Central to more contemporary alumni—wish the boys luck and offer a personal message to share with the boys on this eve of the big game. When it is over, there is a silence among all sixty-plus people in our field house. There are tears flowing from parents and the most determined faces that I have ever seen as a coach. I really don't know when everyone left. There would be no finality to the meeting, just a quiet one-by-one leaving until the room is empty. This singular moment will always be one of the most moving in my entire coaching career. Again, this moment was created by an incredible group of parents who totally believe in their sons and the adults guiding them. I cannot get that video out of my head all the way home.

When I return home, I sit and talk to my family for a while about the video and our mission on the following day. It is now time to get some final rest before the greatest event in my long coaching career.

Friday, November 28, 2013
GAME DAY
CLASS-1A STATE CHAMPIONSHIP

The alarm goes off at 6:00 a.m., and I am off to take a shower. I fix breakfast. Judy joins me, and we converse about the day. Judy asks if I am nervous, and I tell her that I feel good about our chances. It may be hard to believe, but I am not nervous at all. We finish breakfast, she gives me my good-luck kiss (as she has done for the past thirty-four years), and I head to Tri-Central. On my journey to the school, I feel content and eager to see what will happen over the course of the day. Eastern Hancock is the number one team in the state, and they have earned this opportunity to play in the state championship. We are ranked number seven in the state, and we also have earned the right to challenge for a state championship. Eastern Hancock has only made one appearance at the state championship, and that was in 1985. They won. Ironically, Eastern Hancock's quarterback who led them to a state championship was the man who orchestrated the nonrenewal of my coaching contract at Clinton Central. This man was the high-school principal who felt that I needed to be replaced because I was no longer developing the program at Clinton Central in the direction that he, the athletic director, and the board felt the school needed to compete at a state level. That was six years ago, and now, as I get close to school, I smile and feel so thankful that Tri-Central school officials, led by Gary Rhew (athletic director) and Dave Driggs (principal), gave this old coach one last opportunity at a job he has cherished his entire life. It is so amazing that this series of events has taken place, and I feel so fortunate to have the opportunity to end my career on my terms. As I drive back to the bus garage to pick up my bus, I have this incredibly content feeling inside for all that has happened at Tri-Central and this wonderful opportunity facing all of us today.

I drive the bus back to the field house for the boys to load equipment and uniforms. The field house is buzzing. The boys are doing their traditional pregame shaving and packing their gear. The coaches are all very busy loading equipment and addressing the needs of the boys. Everyone seems to be in great moods, and I cannot detect anxiety from any of the players or coaches. The two buses are loaded, and the boys have assembled in the locker room for their last pregame meeting with me. I go over our agenda for the day one more time with everyone. I then tell the boys that this will be our last meeting before the championship, because things will get a little complicated right before the game. I tell them we will come together and pray and then head to the chute and prepare to take the field right before the game. I again tell them how proud they have all made the coaches. I tell the coaches how proud I am of them. I go over our keys to win one more time, and we are off.

As we leave the locker room to load the buses, there is a large crowd of parents and fans taking pictures and wishing us good luck. As we board the buses, the parents run to their cars and take off. I think to myself that we are probably the only school in state history having a team bused to a state championship with the head coach driving one bus and the athletic director driving the other. When we reach the highway, something quite unique occurs that I will never forget. All along our journey to Indianapolis, parents, fans, and students are parked by the road with signs, honking horns as we pass. It is easy to see that this really moves the boys, and this alone becomes an additional motivation toward our hopes of winning a state championship. They honk, display their signs, then rush to the cars and fly past us to set up farther down the road. The community continues this gauntlet of cheering all the way to Indianapolis from Tipton County. I have never seen anything like it before and probably will never see anything like it again.

We finally arrive at Lucas Oil Stadium and unload the bus. Stadium staff is everywhere, and they direct us and answer questions. The boys set up in the locker room and head out to the stadium for a brief walk-around before getting dressed. We are so busy that we have no time to consider what really is happening. Since we played here the year before, the players don't appear to be overwhelmed by the venue. It is now 10:15 a.m., and I advise the coaches to get the boys to the locker room to get dressed for the game. Nerves are now becoming noticeable among some of the staff. The coaches get quiet and mill around by themselves. I decide to leave them alone and let them sort through what is about to take place. It is finally time for us to take the field for pregame. The coaches immediately go into routine, and the stress seems to subside. We are already going through pregame when Lucas Oil allows the fans into the stadium. It is rather chaotic at first as fans from both schools run to get the best seats. On one side of the stadium all you can see is a sea of blue, representing Eastern Hancock. On the other side, a sea of yellow begins to coat the bleachers as Tri-Central fans make their way to their seats. I stand at midfield as I always do, watching the team we are about to play warm-up as our boys warm up. I am impressed as I watch this undefeated Easter Hancock team go through drills. I am interrupted by local Kokomo radio personalities wishing to do an interview before the game. The two men who interview me, Chris and Denny, do a great job gathering information from me to use during the broadcast of the game. When that interview concludes, I have other Indianapolis media wanting interviews. My watching pregame is basically over, and my reliance that things will go well falls on the shoulders of my incredible staff, who continue to take care of business. Time is winding down. It is about thirty minutes before game time, so I have the coordinators finish up, and we march into the locker room.

It is very quiet in the locker room. The coaches assemble outside the locker room to allow the boys some time to relax and talk among themselves. It seems as if time has stopped; every second seems a minute long as we wait. Coach Hatcher, Coach Perez, and Coach Arnold all give final instructions to the team, and I wait outside until it is time for me to rally them to take the field. When I come into the locker room, there is dead silence. I ask them if they are ready, and they quietly respond yes. I again tell them that I am proud of each and every one of them, and no matter the outcome of today's performance, that will never change. I tell the seniors we have had a long journey together, and I tell all of them that it is time for us to seize the moment. We have played as a Team of One all season long, and win or lose, we will always remain a Team of One. We say the Our Father and head down the long corridor to the chute to be introduced. We are home and will be introduced second, so as we stand in the chute, we watch as Eastern Hancock is introduced. The boys are extremely excited and emotionally ready to play this undefeated team considered to have the best offense in the state for 2013.

I cannot believe, as we stand in the chute waiting to be introduced, how many people are in attendance for a class-1A state championship. In front of us across the field is a sea of gold. We look out at our crowd, who demonstrates the confidence this community has developed as they've watched this team of boys become skilled athletes competing for a state championship. The building is jumping between both schools' fan bases, and now it is time for us to make our entrance. As the boys run by me to take the field, it is one of those special moments in life that is unforgettable, especially after waiting and persevering for thirty-four years to get to the state championship game. All the hype is now over. It is time to play a game on the state's greatest stage for a high-school athlete. It is now up to the boys to perform. It is game time!

Class-1A State Championship
Easter Hancock Royals (14-0) v. Tri-Central Trojans (13-1)

The Game

Our four captains (Seth, Garrett, Darius, and Brandan) all lock hands and walk to meet the Eastern Hancock captains at midfield. After introductions, the referee tosses the coin. Eastern Hancock wins the toss. Usually in big games, teams choose to defer until the second half, but Eastern Hancock selects the ball. Their high-powered offense will be first on the field. It is only fitting that Eastern Hancock chooses offense, because their offense has been the best in the state of Indiana throughout the 2013 season, and our defense is considered one of the best in the state all season long. Coach Arnold comes up to me with his traditional handshake as our kickoff team makes its way to the field. He wishes me good luck, and I do the same to him. It is time for all of us to go to work.

Caleb kicks the ball off, and the game is on. Ryan makes a great tackle around the thirty-yard line, where the Royals begin their first series. We instructed the boys all week that we must force them into long drives, and we must play fundamentally and focused from the beginning to the end. Eastern Hancock immediately gives the ball to their great running back the first play, and we stop him for a four-yard gain. On second down, we hold them to two yards, and on third down, we hold them to three yards, bringing up a fourth-down-and-one play. The ball is at their thirty-nine-yard line, and they decide not to punt. They have only punted twice all season, and one of those two times was in game one against us. The new philosophy in coaching these days is to go for it on fourth down no matter what, and the Royals have been successful all season long with their coach's philosophy. Their running back gets the one yard and a new set of downs. On the next set of downs, they have a fumble and a penalty, creating a fourth-down situation once again around our forty-five-yard line. Again they go for it, attempting a pass. Darius gets to the quarterback, who fumbles the ball, allowing our defense to hold. Coach Perez's defensive preparation is working, and we take over on downs for our first offensive series. On first down, Coach Arnold runs a veer dive and wins about three yards. On second down, we run a counter and gain another three yards, and now we are facing a third-down-and-four situation. Coach Arnold calls for a play-action pass to our big left end, Jade, and Cody delivers the ball to Jade as he breaks loose and runs the ball down to the five-yard line. Eastern Hancock now is faced with us at the goal line. They play great defense, and we have a fourth down and one yard to score. Coach Arnold calls for a veer dive right, with Garrett getting the ball. Our offensive line responds, and we score the first touchdown of the game. We miss the extra point, but we are leading 6–0.

On the ensuing kickoff, Eastern Hancock is able to get to the thirty-five-yard line to begin their second series. Our defense is swarming. Our defensive line, along with our linebackers and defensive backs, are playing hard, and Eastern Hancock is faced with another fourth-down situation. They decide to go for it again and try a reverse pass, and they catch us with this trick play. We do not defend the receiver downfield, but the throw is out of his reach, and we take over on downs. Cody begins to orchestrate a ground-control drive, and then we attempt to throw the ball to Jade again deep, but Eastern Hancock intercepts the ball in the end zone.

Our defense—led by Riley, Dillon, Cody, Seth, and Colten—puts on another great display for Coach Perez, and Eastern Hancock is faced with a fourth down. This time they are on their own twenty-eight-yard line and decide to punt. The punt is shanked and goes out of bounds only eight yards downfield. On our third offensive series, we are in a third-down situation, and Coach Arnold calls for a short flat pass to Colten that again is intercepted. Coach Arnold is furious, as is Coach Perez, that our offense has been stopped twice now with back-to-back interceptions. Cody runs over to the sidelines. Coach Arnold is trying to talk to him, but Cody is not listening at this point. Cody tells Coach Arnold it is his fault, and it will not happen again. Coach Arnold is a seasoned coach and an incredible mentor to our young men. He looks at Cody and says OK, and that's that. At the end of the quarter, we are leading 6–0 with Eastern Hancock in possession the ball.

Eastern Hancock begins to drive the ball. For the first time, they are getting large chunks of yardage with each carry. Coach Perez comes up to me and says, "Coach, I need a time-out." I advise the side judge that we want a time-out. During the time-out, Coach Perez first calms the players in the huddle and tells them what they need to do to stop this drive. Coach Perez is an outstanding coach on the field, and the boys have a great deal of confidence in his leadership. He never shows any panic, and he does not yell at them. The boys are focused as Coach Tolle talks with the linebackers about what they need to do to stop this drive. Coach Perez and Coach Tolle are great friends, and the boys easily sense their understanding of our defense and their ability to get the boys to fix problems on the field as they occur. The time-out ends, and we are able to again stop Eastern Hancock on downs. It is now Coach Arnold's turn (along with his line coach, Coach Tolle) to take over. The boys begin to move the ball, and again we are stopped around our thirty-yard line, facing a fourth-down situation.

I tell Coach Hatcher that we need to punt, and Dillon goes back to punt. The Royals apparently do not believe we are going to punt, because they do not put anyone back to receive the punt. Dillon gets off a great punt (his best of the season), and it rolls all the way down to the fifteen-yard line. Eastern Hancock again starts to drive the ball before they are faced with another fourth-down situation around our forty-yard line. Again, Coach Perez and his defense stops them, and it is our ball. Every boy is contributing defensively as Seth, Colten, Dillon, and Cody are making great plays, thanks to the efforts of Bryce, Lake, Ryan, Darius, and Riley. The half is winding down, and there are only two and a half minutes remaining in the quarter. On first down, Garrett is able to have a great run that gives us the ball around midfield. On the next play, they stop Garrett for a two-yard loss. On second down, we only are able to get back to the original line of scrimmage, creating a third down and ten. Coach Arnold calls a play-action pass, and Cody is under pressure immediately. Cody runs first to his left; seeing the defender, he reverses his direction to the right and sees a wall of blockers allowing him to escape outside, where he finds Bryce fifteen yards downfield. Cody throws the ball across his body for a perfect strike to Bryce. The clock now shows a minute and a half left in the first half. Coach Arnold sends the play to the field. I come up and tell him and Coach Tolle that their backside safety is sneaking up to the line, setting up our counter-trey pass. I am rather passionate about what I see, but Coach Arnold only nods at me that he heard me. I usually leave my coordinators alone unless they are struggling on the field. I do give suggestions, and the rule of thumb for all of them is to basically acknowledge me and my requests. I haven't needed to help these guys all season, and I am not going to do it now. Their decision-making skills—and the boys' performances—have gotten us this far, and I am not about to change anything. I have complete confidence and faith in this coaching staff.

I walk down to where Coach Perez is standing and tell him that the counter-trey pass is wide open. He asks me if I said something to Coach Arnold, and I tell him I did. Cody brings the team to the line, and the ball is snapped. The play the boys are going to attempt is the same play I have just requested. Cody takes the ball and fakes it to the running back. A defender comes at Cody, but Cody is able to roll around the defender to the left. Downfield, Seth has gotten behind the safety, and Cody throws a perfect ball to Seth. It is a touchdown. We attempt a two-point conversion but do not have success, so we are now up 12–0 with thirty seconds left in the first half. Our fans are screaming and waving yellow towels. The excitement is palpable.

Eastern Hancock takes the following kickoff and begins passing the ball. They are able to move the ball down the field to the twenty-five-yard line, showing some of the skill that has allowed them to make it into this game. There is one second left on the clock as their kicker kicks a thirty-seven-yard field goal.

It is half time, and we are up 12–3 in the state championship. A team that has scored an average of fifty-seven points per game has been held in check to just three points by this small rural team from northern Tipton County. We have made our presence known by playing great fundamental football, and now we're only twenty-four minutes from claiming the greatest prize in high-school athletics: a state championship.

After doing the television interview, I walk into the locker room to meet with coaches and players. When I arrive, Coach Hatcher is already going over the special team's play. Coach Hatcher does an incredible job in preparation, and I do not need to concern myself with his preparation; he has proved time and again his value to our program and to the school community. Coach Hatcher is the only Tri-Central teacher on our coaching staff, and he has been a valuable ally since he joined the staff three years ago. While Coach Hatcher talks with the team, I go to Coach Perez first, because he will be the next coach to talk to the team. I ask Coach Perez what he is thinking. He feels that our plan against the run has been very effective, but we need to fix some things versus their pass. He then tells me what his plan is, and I do not need to add anything. To be quite honest, the only help I can give Coach Perez is what I see as issues on the field. He then usually will make adjustments as he sees fit, since he is our defensive specialist. When you are a head coach, it is important to surround yourself with smart quality people and then allow them to exercise their talent. On my staff, every coach has outstanding character and skill in teaching our athletes. I then go to Coach Arnold and Coach Tolle to discuss offense. Coach Tolle talks about adjusting some of the blocking schemes in the second half to keep Eastern Hancock off balance. Coach Arnold discusses how well our game plan is working and the importance for our offense to not necessarily win the game, because that is the job of the defense, but rather not lose the game by making errors and turning the ball over.

We discuss how well Cody has done since the back-to-back interceptions he threw. Most young men (especially underclassmen) would not have recovered after throwing two interceptions, but this young man is truly special. He not only kept his poise, he became more committed during the rest of the first half, and that commitment led to a higher level of play. The second quarter of this game was one of the best quarters this young man has played all season.

It is time for Coach Arnold and Coach Tolle to talk with our offense, and I step back and let them go to work. When they are done, Coach Arnold has some inspirational comments to motivate the boys, and with that, I congratulate the boys and say, "Now let's go out and win this championship!" When the boys first arrived in the locker room they seemed tired after playing such a physical first half, but now they seem to have recovered and are ready to go to war against an angry, undefeated team. Eastern Hancock has been behind at half time twice during the course of the playoffs before coming back in the second half and pounding their opponents. We all know they are very athletic, well coached, and in excellent physical condition. Therefore, we know that they are going to give us their best during the second half, and it is up to us to continue to be aggressive, to continue to keep them off balance by our aggressive pursuit to the ball, and to continue the mental advantage of playing ahead.

When we return to the field, our crowd continues to be loud and supportive. They have to be tired, too, and they needed the half-time break to catch their wind. The team goes through our routine of stretching. The half time seems to continue longer due to the television coverage. The good news is that we will get the ball first and hopefully have some success, either by scoring or at least moving the ball into their territory. We need to continue to win the field position game.

Eastern Hancock finally kicks off to start the second half, and Keith runs the ball back to the twenty-two-yard line. Keith has done a great job all season. He is reliable, which is important for the special team's receivers. Coach Arnold calls a flanker reverse to start the second half, and Seth runs for nine yards. Coach Arnold is on his way to perhaps calling one of his best offensive games in his coaching career, although it will never compare to the drive at the end of the Winamac semi-state that allowed us to win the game and advance to the state championship.

Our offense is able to get a couple of first downs, and then Eastern Hancock forces us into a fourth down around the forty-five-yard line. I decide we need to punt. Dillon gets off another great punt, but this time they have a receiver back to receive it. The officials never notice that the receiver put his knee down as he caught the ball, which in high-school football downs the ball. The receiver then puts together an outstanding return to around midfield. I choose not to say anything to the officials at the time because they are doing an incredible job officiating, and I certainly do not want my nitpicking to make them mad. Eastern Hancock seems to be really excited and ready to make their presence known during this drive.

Eastern Hancock begins moving the ball. They are able to get a first down to start their first drive of the second half. The ball is now at our forty-five-yard line, and on first down, the Royals' star running back rambles through the middle of our defense for five yards. On second down, they run off tackle for three yards, bringing up a third down and short. On the third down, they run a read option, with the quarterback keeping the ball and running right. Dillon (our sophomore outside linebacker) had stopped this play in the first quarter. This time he reads the play again and grabs a leg of the quarterback as Seth comes in to clean up the tackle. Eastern Hancock now faces a fourth down and long. On fourth down, the quarterback hands the ball off to the running back running right, and Davee (our cornerback) tackles him before he can get a first down, turning the ball back over to us at the thirty-eight-yard line. It seems that when we stop them during this series, it is emotionally draining for them. Dillon's tackle on third down and Davee's tackle on fourth down have stopped what momentum they have developed.

This will now be our second possession of the second half, and Cody goes to work. Garrett gains five yards on first down, and Dillon gains four yards on second down. We are faced with a third and one at our forty-five-yard line. Cody hands the ball off to Cody, and he is stopped short of the first down. I tell Coach Arnold to set a formation and go with a long count to see if they jump off sides. If they do not jump off sides, then our quarterback will call time-out, and we can decide what to do from there. They do not jump, and Cody calls time-out. I ask Coach Arnold what he is thinking as the boys come to the sidelines to get drinks. He says, "Coach, I want to throw the post to Jade off play action."

I said, "Really? Really! Are you sure we want to do this here and now?"

Coach Arnold replies, "Yes! The safeties are drawn up to stop the run, and this could be a big play."

"OK! Let's go for it!" I immediately walk over to our defensive coordinator, Coach Perez, and tell him that we are going to throw the ball deep and get ready to play defense. He says, "Great!" I now walk down to the thirty-yard line and decide to allow Coach Arnold this time. It is the right call, but we have a two-possession lead, and this could change the game, either putting us in a position of control or causing a shift in momentum, allowing Eastern Hancock back into the game.

As the boys head back to the field, I remind myself of a statement I made when going over game planning with the coaching staff. I told them that we needed to treat this game like any other game and not be afraid of being aggressive either on defense or offense.

Cody takes the team to the line of scrimmage. Nick hikes the ball to Cody. Cody fakes a dive to Garrett and drops back to throw. Jade has cleared the safety, and Cody throws a perfect ball that Jade catches in stride, and he is tackled at the thirteen-yard line. What an incredible call! I walk by Coach Arnold as he is preparing to send in the next play and say only, "WOW!"

Coach Arnold calls in the next play, and we have a short gain. On second down, Eastern Hancock stops us, bringing up a third-down situation. At this point, I am away from Coach Arnold and Coach Tolle, who are scheming their next move. I want them to completely focus on what they are doing instead of anything I may think. Coach

Arnold calls a dive to Dillon, Dillon picks up the first down, and the ball rests at the three-yard line. Coach Arnold calls in his next play as the clock continues to count down. Cody takes the snap and runs a quarterback sneak, literally running over their linebackers as he falls into the end zone. Touchdown! The score is now 18–3 with our point after coming. I show Coach Arnold two fingers, which means we are going for the two-point conversion, and he calls in a play. Cody drops straight back. Jade and Seth are on the left side of the field and run in patterns while Dillon slowly runs an out pattern. There is no one around Dillon when Cody passes him the ball for the two-point conversion. With thirty seconds left in the third quarter, we are up on Eastern Hancock 20–3. As we wait for the television time-out to be over, we tell the boys that this team is explosive and to remember what happened against Winamac the week before in the fourth quarter that almost cost us this opportunity to play in the state championship. They agree and seem focused, but tired.

Eastern Hancock receives the ball and begins to march down the field. They are getting large chunks of yardage faced with the urgent need to score points. Our boys appear less aggressive. I can't decide if they are fatigued or believe they are in control of the game. Eastern Hancock continues to move the ball all the way down inside the ten-yard line with a first down and goal. This will be the defining moment for both teams. We stop them on first down with a short gain. On second down, they receive a penalty for illegal procedure, pushing them back to around the twelve-yard line. On third down, they are unable to get to the end zone and now are faced with a fourth down and goal. On fourth down, they run left as our entire defense is chasing them. Bryce slows down their running back as Garrett forces the running back to continue toward the sidelines. Cody (our linebacker) comes in and performs a terrific open-field tackle that stops Eastern Hancock's running back short. It now is Tri-Central's ball; eight minutes and thirty seconds remain in the game. This goal-line stand proves how outstanding our defense has become—from the boys playing on the field to Coach Perez, who orchestrates the scheme. All of my staff has had a huge impact on what we have done all season long, and now each of them has the opportunity to showcase their talents to the entire football community in the state of Indiana.

We go back on offense, and clearly Eastern Hancock is beginning to realize their dream is starting to fade. We move the ball up to around midfield and are facing a third down and long. Coach Arnold calls a play-action pass to Bryce, and Bryce catches the long ball, but then a Royal defensive back forces him to fumble. The defender picks the ball off the turf and is off to the races, running forty yards before we are able to catch him. Eastern Hancock puts together their best drive of the day, and with 5:40 remaining on the clock, they score their first touchdown of the game. The extra point is good, and now our lead is down to 20–10.

I immediately get involved in conversation with Coach Hatcher. He and I both believe that they might try an onside kick, but we are uncertain if we want to put our hands team in the game to receive the kick. We decide that we will go with our regular return team, because most of them are very athletic, and they are all mentally prepared for the possibility. Some of the boys who are on the hands team have not been in the game all day, and I do not wish to put them in a situation that could change the course of the game. As the team gathers on the field, my attention quickly shifts to Coach Arnold, who is deep in conversation with Coach Tolle. I approach them and say to them, "We need three first downs to win this game." They agree and continue their conversation. I walk down and see Coach Perez speaking with Coach Hunter about defense. I tell him that if they get the ball back, we need to create a rush and be ready for the pass. He also agrees. Now my job is to wait and see if I need to make any critical decisions. The wheels in the mind of a head coach are constantly turning with what-if scenarios, and my head feels like it is going to explode.

They decide to kick the ball long and attempt to stop us and get the ball back. It is now our offense's job to stay on the field and eat up this last 5:40 of the clock. Coach Arnold meets with the offense before they take the field and confides in them that it is now up to them to make a statement offensively. A constant criticism over the years about the double-tight-end veer offense is that it is too simple and predictable. Football coaches believe it is easy to defend an offense that is considered "old school." This is an opportunity for us to show that our offensive philosophy works on our state's greatest stage. Coach Arnold reminds the boys that we need three first downs to seal our victory and our school's first state championship.

The boys are excited as they rush to the field. Coach Arnold and Coach Tolle go to work, calling in plays to the left side of our offense behind Darius and Ryan. We begin to move the ball in large chunks as our backs work to stay inbounds, and the clock continues to tick down the seconds. The Eastern Hancock boys are realizing that they are running out of time ten points and two possessions down. Cody begins moving the team down the field as Eastern Hancock uses two of their time-outs. Eastern Hancock puts us in a fourth down and one at the thirteen-yard line before calling their last time-out with one minute left in the game.

As the boys come to the sidelines, all the coaches share that we need this yard to secure the victory and not allow Eastern Hancock any more opportunities to put their high-powered offense on the field. Coach Arnold calls a play-action pass that we have used three times during the game. We have completed it twice thus far. Cody fakes the ball to Garrett. He then drops back and finds Jade for the first down at the three-yard line. Now it is a matter of one more snap to end the game. I tell Coach Arnold, and he agrees to send the boys to victory formation and allow Cody to go to a knee with the ball to end the game. At this point, it would not be right for us to try and score, because we have already won the game. The sidelines are chaotic. Coaches and players start shaking hands and hugging. Our crowd is ecstatic and screaming. Cody takes the ball from Nick, our center, and goes to a knee.

It is over! We are State Champions! I raise both fists into the air as our boys come together on the field in relief, in pride, in respect for our school community, our parents, our coaches, and most of all, our players. We finished this adventure as we began it, a Team of One!

CHAPTER 14

In Retrospect

Tri-Central high school is a small rural school with an enrollment of 305 students, of whom 120 are boys. Football has been a part of the extracurricular sports offered at Tri-Central since 1970. A full schedule was first made available in 1972, and Tri-Central has played a full varsity schedule since. Between 1972 and 2010, the Trojan football program was only able to win eighty-four of 389 games and secure just five winning seasons over the years. There was a time in the eighties when the program went three years straight without winning a game. From 1995 until 2010, Tri-Central went through a period again when winning became very difficult, amassing a record of twenty-three wins and 135 losses. Overall, during the past forty-four years Tri-Central has won 27 percent of their games, including the three consecutive winning seasons in 2011, 2012, and 2013 (three-year record of 30–7). It is easy to see how the high-school sports community found it difficult to consider Tri-Central to be much of a threat as a competitor against the state's top programs.

Timing and fate can come together at the most extraordinary times. I had just been fired as a football coach at a school where I had been head coach for twenty years by a principal and an athletic director who would not stay past a couple of years. The principal who fired me was the quarterback for Eastern Hancock—the team we would face in the state championship—when they won their only state crown back in 1985. Since I left as the football coach at the school where I still teach, they have gone through three coaches in six years. My first year at Tri-Central we did not win a game, but a group of eighth graders would see what was happening, and they planned to make a statement when they entered the high-school program. In a matter of three years, this struggling high-school football program would systematically become, in 2013, a state championship team.

It all started with an aging football coach who felt wronged by a school community to which he had given so much. A Clinton Central community became frustrated with a program that consistently was considered one of the top programs in its class but was unable to advance through the tournament as they thought they should.

The Tri-Central community, constantly embarrassed by their football program and on the verge of considering whether or not the school could continue to field a team, needed hope. It became an issue for that old coach to make peace with what was happening to him and find one last chance to finish his life's work with dignity. It became an opportunity for Clinton Central to see if new leadership could take the established program to another level of achievement.

All of these events led to Tri-Central attempting one last time to offer young men in their school district an opportunity to play football. Sports programs are an important part of young people's lives but should never overshadow the true purpose of high school: to earn a diploma. So often today, sports have become more important than an education. This must be remedied, because the true focus must always be on academic development. I present to my football team at the first meeting with them each year a model that I define as my perspective of order for teenagers and that is: first, God (if they believe, their relationship with him is always first); second, family (I emphasize family is always before all else except their religious convictions); third, school (they must take care of their school responsibilities before anything else except the previous two facets). I put all other things under miscellaneous (sports, girlfriends, etc.). It is important for coaches to mentor young people toward those things that are most important in life and aid them in creating their own order of priorities to live by.

This wonderful story began with an e-mail from a coach reaching for straws to an athletic director going through a rough time at a small school in Indiana. The athletic director then proceeded to show faith in the coach and gave him an opportunity to interview for a job that no one seemed excited about. It took vision from a school board to give this coach one more chance to develop one more program before he faded into obscurity. It took the confidence of a principal to believe that this old coach might offer a glimmer of hope to a dying program. It took a community that had to watch their football team getting beaten unmercifully for years to exercise patience and give this coach a chance. It took a group of coaches' willpower to endure another new system with another new coach. It took a coach who was coming from a program that he developed from the ground up and now must start over from scratch.

Throughout my thirty-four-year career, I never had a season quite like 2009 when the team I coached lost every game. We were only able to average 8.9 points per game while our opponents that year averaged 48.7 points per game. We had nothing to draw from for the future, because over half the team was seniors. If there is one constant through the years at Tri-Central, it is perseverance. I had developed two programs prior to taking on this challenge, and I knew that it would take time, because this situation lacked that flicker of light at the end of the tunnel.

I decided to first start by fixing the coaching staff problems. As coaches left the program, I selected men who had a vested interest in wanting to see success and the passion to pursue it. I continued to offer opportunity for boys to lift weights and play seven-on-seven as I looked for leaders. I needed leaders who would commit to regular attendance, who would follow a set of rules that would not change, and who would challenge each young man's comfort zone. As the athletes began to join the program, I started to gradually raise the expectations. Young men are really looking for discipline, expectations, and attainable goals. The struggle all of us encounter daily requires a reason.

The administration at Tri-Central was as important as any part of this success story. The board of education received some criticism when they hired me. I came from a rival school, and many people in the community did not like my brand of football. They felt that the smash mouth approach to football would not work at Tri-Central. The principal (Dave Driggs) allowed me the room to develop the program. Mr. Driggs never has said a negative thing to me throughout my tenure as Tri-Central's football coach. He not once has complained when we lost games, and he is the first to praise when success is achieved. Probably the most important boss I have is the athletic director, Gary Rhew. Mr. Rhew has been one of two athletic directors in my coaching career who I have felt are outstanding. I worked with an athletic director at Clinton Central for years by the name of Linda Barnett. Mrs. Barnett always had impeccable character, and she demonstrated passion toward student-athletes every day. When she retired from Clinton Central, it was a sad day for every person affiliated with Clinton Central athletics. When I started working with Mr. Rhew, it did not take long for me to realize that he had the same impeccable character. Mr. Rhew has never denied me anything I needed, and he has supported everything we have done at Tri-Central. Every time I have been faced with situations that I needed to act on, he has been right there supporting not only me, but the entire Tri-Central sports community.

Our community, although not overly excited, was for the most part willing to give me a chance as head coach. Even during the worst seasons possible, the stands have always been close to full. Our community really wanted to have a football program. As we started to win more, the community remembered those tough years. I remember how they would cheer passionately when we would get a first down, knowing that might be the only time they got to cheer the entire game.

The opportunity to create success for the Tri-Central community has been enjoyable. I believe the community response and support became truly apparent this season during the playoffs and the championship game. Most of northern Tipton County appeared to be present at games, supporting the program with their blue and gold attire on.

Our parents have been very active throughout the development of the program. The mothers work together to provide everything from meals for the boys to treats with creative themes each week during the season. The mothers take care of every little detail possible to show their support for their sons and everyone else's sons on the team. There have been concerns over the years from the parents. They attempted to understand the direction I sought for the team. I have always respected the opinions of parents, and I feel it is important for a head coach to give parents insight behind his motives. It has been a welcome task, because our parents usually do not mince words, and their questions have always been direct, seeking a direct answer in return. I have worked hard to provide reasoning for the process I have worked so hard to implement at Tri-Central, and the parents have allowed me the room necessary to achieve that direction. We do not always need to agree on all subjects, but it is necessary that open communication and mutual respect be maintained. I have been truly blessed, because our parents support everything from my expectations in the weight room to the importance of punctual and consistent attendance at all meetings and practices. Our parents went way above all expectations this season and were a part of everything their sons achieved through the course of the championship run. This created memories not only for the boys, but for the parents, who will cherish their memories forever.

A high-school football program is only as successful as the leadership presented. There has been a history of good men willing to give up their time and energy to make sure Tri-Central football would survive. It is much easier to coach when success is taking place. It is quite difficult to coach when success is not possible. Every coach must have a passion to teach young men to play a game they all love. This program has struggled since its inception, but these men continued to embrace the hope of turning the program around. We live in a society that only embraces success, and that is who we are. It takes a great deal of inner strength to deal with the time commitment of coaching when very little seems to be accomplished. Several men on the current staff have weathered the storm and now have been able to feel vindicated for their efforts. I have been truly blessed with all ten men in the high-school program. Each man brings skills and personalities that have helped us bond as a unique and special coaching staff.

This process at Tri-Central really began to take shape when a group of dads started a youth program. A man by the name of Jerry Reeves took the leadership role and surrounded himself with quality men who have changed the direction of Tri-Central football. The first group these men graduated was in the class of 2012 when the high-school program won ten games. This was the second group they have graduated, and these boys won fourteen games and a state championship. Without their volunteering to make a difference, it is possible all of this might not have happened. I have talked about the coaches individually, and I will add that I have never worked with a greater, more passionate group of men in my entire coaching career. I really do not think this story would have happened without their character and leadership.

The true heroes of this story are the players. Everybody involved had a role, but it was the players who believed in the program. They decided for themselves that they were going to go beyond dreaming of success and instead live it. The team commitment was something I have never experienced before. I would love to be able to duplicate it, but each year the chemistry is different as new boys come in as freshmen and the seniors leave. This group of boys has had to deal with the rhetoric that our program is traditionally bad, we don't play a competitive schedule, and we do not defeat teams soundly enough to be considered a great team. This group came into camp focused and prepared to prove something. They never cared, all season long, about what outsiders were saying. They wanted to prove to themselves that they could beat the odds and create a new tradition at our school that would leave a legacy that all football programs around the state could attempt to duplicate. It is easy, when there are great numbers of fast athletic players, to win consistently. Here at Tri-Central, our players made their own way by proving themselves each and every week during the season. The all-in tournament series in Indiana began in 1973, and up to now there have been twenty-five teams of sixty-four currently in class A that have won the Indiana class-1A state championship. These boys became the twenty-fifth class-1A team to win a state championship since the tournament began. In 2009, Tri-Central was ranked at the bottom of class-1A teams, and just four years later they proved themselves worthy to call themselves champions.

Football has been a major part of my life. I cannot thank the school board and administration at Tri-Central enough for giving me a chance to develop one more program. Coaching is like riding a roller coaster. The true test is weathering the storm. The average length of time anywhere in America that a man is a head high-school football coach is three years. I have been truly blessed to have had the opportunity to be a head coach for thirty-two years. I have been blessed with great children who all, at one time or another, worked in the program. I also have been blessed with an understanding wife who has been by my side for thirty-seven years, living through the tough times and cherishing the good times. Nothing in life that is of value comes easily. If good things came easily, then the value would be diminished. When we have a vested interest, when we give everything we have, then and only then are those good times valuable.

In 2013, Tri-Central High School achieved a season that usually only happens in books and dreams. It has not been a journey without pitfalls along the way. I have tried to share what made this a true Cinderella story—how we started with nothing and ultimately won everything. I hope the message has been delivered clearly that when coaches receive accolades and accomplishments for the successes of their teams, there are many more factors that contribute to the achievement of team goals. That is why at Tri-Central High School, we consider ourselves—school board, administration, student body, community, parents, coaches, and players—a TEAM OF ONE!